I'LL LOVE YOU FOREVER

I'LL LOVE YOU FOR- EVER

Notes from a K-Pop Fan

GIAAE KWON

Henry Holt and Company
New York

Henry Holt and Company
Publishers since 1866
120 Broadway
New York, New York 10271
www.henryholt.com

Henry Holt® and ® are registered trademarks of Macmillan Publishing Group, LLC.

Copyright © 2025 by Giaae Kwon
All rights reserved.
Distributed in Canada by Raincoast Book Distribution Limited

Portions of these essays were originally published in the author's *Catapult* column, From a K-pop Fan, With Love, under the following titles: "Dear H.O.T., I'll Love You Forever" (2021); "Dear IU, Our Bodies Are Fine" (2021); "Dear Irene, I'm Still Learning How to Be a Feminist Too" (2021); "Dear TVXQ, Shipping Showed Me a Way Out of the Church" (2021); "Dear Taeyeon, It's Okay Not to Be Okay" (2021); "Dear Shinhwa, I Found My Joy in K-Pop Fandom" (2022).

Library of Congress Cataloging-in-Publication Data

Names: Kwon, Giaae, author.
Title: I'll love you forever : notes from a K-pop fan / Giaae Kwon.
Description: First edition. | New York : Henry Holt and Company, 2025. | Includes bibliographical references.
Identifiers: LCCN 2024039936 | ISBN 9781250886231 (hardcover) | ISBN 9781250886255 (ebook)
Subjects: LCSH: Kwon, Giaae. | Popular music fans—Biography. | Popular music—Korea (South)—History and criticism. | LCGFT: Autobiographies.
Classification: LCC ML429.K96 A3 2025 | DDC 782.4216/3095195 [B]—dc23/eng/20240830
LC record available at https://lccn.loc.gov/2024039936

Our books may be purchased in bulk for promotional, educational, or business use. Please contact your local bookseller or the Macmillan Corporate and Premium Sales Department at (800) 221-7945, extension 5442, or by email at MacmillanSpecialMarkets@macmillan.com.

First Edition 2025

Designed by Gabriel Guma

Printed in the United States of America

1 3 5 7 9 10 8 6 4 2

to my fellow bbasooni out there—

네가 세상에 없다면
우리도 없겠지
H.O.T., "너와나"

if you weren't in the world,
we wouldn't be here either
H.O.T., "YOU AND I"

CONTENTS

－ － － － －

I'LL LOVE YOU FOREVER

TONY

The only boys I have ever loved have been K-pop idols.

They've been different kinds of loves, each entering my life at some kind of juncture and marking a turning point. I don't know that we, as humans, are necessarily wise in retrospect or if it's human nature to want to make sense of things, but, as I look back on the last twenty-some years of being a bbasooni, I can chart my growth by my K-pop obsessions.

And it all started because of an idol named Tony.

K-POP

Hey, Baby, Welcome to My World
aespa, "Welcome to My World"
MY WORLD, 2023

The rules of K-pop fandom are pretty simple: be loyal. Your boy band must be number one. Be faithful, steady, and true. No one had to teach me the rules for me to know them. I was born and raised in the United States and grew up with K-pop from a distance, the internet at the time a fledgling technological wonder that required a phone line and constant arguments with your parents because they needed the phone, they were waiting for a call, but you also needed the line—you needed to log onto Soompi, the primary Korean American forum at the time, to get more news about H.O.T., the K-pop boy band that established the formula for idol groups that still exists today.

H.O.T. was made up of five members: 문희준 (Moon Heejun, the leader), 강타 (Kangta, birth name 안칠현 [Ahn Chilhyun], the main vocalist), 장우혁 (Jang Woohyuk, the main dancer), 토니안 (Tony An, Korean name 안승호 [An Seungho], the One From America and my bias), and 이재원 (Lee Jaewon, the maknae). H.O.T. debuted in 1996 from SM Entertainment, and they sang and rapped catchy pop songs while performing what became known as 칼군무 (knife, or razor-sharp, choreography). Their fan club name was Club H.O.T., their fan color white, their primary rival SechsKies, a six-member boy band from DSP Entertainment, which meant that SechsKies was dead to me, as were any of my friends who listened to them, because H.O.T. was *my* boy band, *mine*, and I had to be loyal to them, not only I myself but also the people I kept in my life.

I joke that fandom is built into Koreans because we do nothing in moderation—we feel deeply, drink to excess, glom onto trends, whether it's the American Brand of the Moment (Gap, Tommy Hilfiger, The North Face) or protesting American meat en masse. Korean Koreans like to have the same eyebrows (straight and fluffy, not arched), and we like our intense skin care routines and no-makeup makeup. We yell a lot and talk about our bowel movements during meals, and we tend to throw our bodies around when we laugh, alternating between covering our mouths and clapping—why we clap or whom we're applauding, I have yet to figure out in my thirty-some years of being alive, but I know that was written into my body, too, just like my obsessive fandom.

Many Koreans and Korean Americans like to attribute this intensity to the concept of han, which, to put it reductively, means this simultaneous melancholy and fire within us that comes from a centuries-long history of conquest and war. We like to argue that, as a people, we feel too much because of han, this way of being that is impossible to translate adequately in a pithy manner. Koreans and Korean Americans both like to call upon han to explain away rage and depression and any extreme emotion with a negative connotation, really, never mind that han has its roots in colonialism, as the Japanese came up with this idea of Korean melancholy as a way of Othering their inferior Korean subjects.

When Japan formally annexed Korea in 1910 after having occupied the country since the late 1800s, its intent was to fold Korea into itself as a way of legitimizing its move into the Korean peninsula, from which imperial Japan would conquer the rest of Asia. Japan claimed that there were ties between Korea and Japan that made the annexation valid, an act of bringing Koreans back into the empire, so to speak. However, Japanese imperialism couldn't actually put Koreanness and Japaneseness on equal footing—to this day, ethnic Koreans who were taken to Japan and have remained there are unable to have Japanese citizenship, even though there are now multiple generations of Zainichi Koreans born and living in Japan. Attributing han, this innate melancholy, to Koreans was a way for the Japanese to delineate between the two, even claiming that this melancholy made Koreans physically distinguishable.

Not that I grew up with much awareness of this history, though—I was born in the mideighties in Flushing, Queens, to 1.5-generation immigrant parents, 1.5 because they both immigrated to the US at younger ages, my mother when she was ten, my father after graduating from college. My younger brother and I were both born in New York City and are considered second-generation Korean Americans, and I was fortunate to grow up in a Korean community in suburban Los Angeles, a statement that makes me pause because growing up within a Korean community is also what caused me the most harm. My first year of high school, I started being intentionally body-shamed by my Korean community because my overweight body didn't conform to Korean beauty standards. This would go on for over a decade, complete with name-calling, insults, and mockery, and I was told that I would never date, have friends, or even be gainfully employed until I could bring my body in line. That would lead to a total fracturing of my sense of self, and, after body-shaming took ten years from me, it would take another ten years for me to heal and find myself again—and, in turn, connect with my Koreanness.

It was my Korean family and community that broke me down, but, despite that, I am and have always been fiercely proud to be Korean. Growing up in suburban Los Angeles in a primarily Korean, and entirely Asian, community, I didn't have the experience other diasporic Asians had of being shamed for my food or my culture. My friend group was entirely Asian, hailing from Korea, Vietnam, India, and Thailand, and we were immigrant children who understood implicitly where we came from. The church my family attended was all Korean, so, while K-pop was generally deeply uncool when I was an adolescent, I was still surrounded by people who were familiar with it, who listened to it and learned the choreography and knew all the big groups, even if no one was a bbasooni like I was. We made each other mixtapes (recorded on cassette tapes!) and shared VHS recordings of music shows and flipped through the glossy pages of Korean magazines when they arrived in the US months after being published in Korea.

Not all my friends watched Korean dramas themselves, but their parents did, borrowing episodes from the video store during weekly trips to the Korean market. I went to a high school that was diverse, but Asian kids made up the majority in honors and AP classes. Not being aware of or feeling ashamed of my Korean-ness wasn't a struggle for me growing up—instead, my shame came from not feeling Korean enough, for not having the right body to belong among Koreans. I was bilingual and bicultural, and I spoke Korean without the telltale American accent, but one look at me and it was clear—I wasn't Korean Korean but an Other in my own community.

K-pop, therefore, occupied a strange corner of my life, my access point into a culture with which I have a weird, fractured relationship. My parents are immigrants from Korea, and I lived with my paternal grandparents through middle school. My first language was Korean. I entered an American preschool without knowing any English.

I grew up watching mostly Korean dramas, eating the food, and speaking the language, but I didn't have much awareness of Korean culture or traditions because we didn't observe many of them throughout my childhood and youth. My paternal grand-father was the eldest son in his family, which had meant some-thing when he lived in Korea, but, in the US, he no longer had the responsibilities that came with that position—and, because of an injury, he avoided large gatherings, even familial ones.

That meant that I learned that Chuseok was a major Korean holiday via Korean dramas and that Seollal was celebrated by Koreans because K-pop idols would release photos of themselves wearing hanbok and sharing New Year's greetings during the lunar new year. I got a glimpse of annual gimjangs through TV shows and learned about Korean social hierarchies and titles by watching how hoobaes acted around and responded to their sun-baes backstage at music shows and concerts.

I also internalized the misogyny running through K-pop, the way girl groups were treated differently by their companies, the public, even their fandoms. Watching groups like 소녀시대 (Girls' Generation) frozen in their cutesy, faux-innocent personas even as they grew into young women reinforced the purity culture I was being taught in my conservative Korean church. I learned about distorted, manipulative, at times violent love as K-pop fandom created spaces for toxic desire and possessive feelings to fester and flourish, as the romance depicted in dramas and music videos involved a lot of wrist-grabbing and angry confessions of love.

Even with its more toxic elements, fandom can be a beautiful thing, and I'm not one to write it off. I am here, still alive, largely because of it. There's a tendency to look down on pop culture, to reduce fangirls to immature girls prone to extreme behavior, high-pitched screams, and vapidity, as if being a fangirl is something to be ashamed of. For a time, I wanted to flee from the label myself, to rebrand myself essentially as someone more "serious-minded" and "mature," and one of the reasons I wanted to leave Los Angeles so badly in my late teens and early twenties was to leave my bbasooni self behind. Everyone I knew in Los Angeles knew I was a fangirl and had been there to witness my crazed obsessive self through my adolescence, and I wanted badly to go somewhere new and start over.

I did take a bit of a break from fandom between roughly 2015 and 2022, following the industry from a distance but refusing to go near another boy band. My favorite member, 재중 (Jaejoong), of 동방신기 (TVXQ), had left the second-generation boy band with two other members around 2010, and I had a brief dalliance with Big Bang before I could no longer stand their toxic masculinity and constant blatant cultural appropriation. By 2015, I had been in K-pop for almost twenty years and was tired. Being a bbasooni is all-encompassing; it occupies so much of your waking thoughts and requires so much time to keep updated daily about your bias and participate in online fan communities and collect and organize photos, videos, interviews. It also costs a fair amount of money to buy CDs, magazines, and other fan collectibles. I was broke and emotionally exhausted, my heart already broken twice by H.O.T.'s abrupt breakup in 1999 and TVXQ's dramatic split in 2010.

Then, in late 2022, after avoiding them for nine years because I knew myself, who I was as a bbasooni, I got into 방탄소년단 (BTS or Bangtan), my timing impeccable as they were on hiatus as a group before going to fulfill their mandatory military service, each of the seven members releasing their own solo projects in the countdown to enlistment. It happened exactly as I expected: I immediately fell for one member and became obsessed. It helped that 슈가 (Suga), my bias, was in his late twenties then and shedding his baby face, so it felt less icky to stan him even though he is my junior. We have eight years between us. He will likely be my last idol, as the age gap between me and the idols debuting and active today is in the double digits.

That feels a little bittersweet because my life has been shaped by the ways I was a good fan. I started with H.O.T., and, to this day, I would still consider myself loyal to H.O.T. Because of this group, I have stayed with SM over the decades, which means that, of the Big Four dominating the K-pop industry, SM is the company I know best, JYP the one I know least (JYP debuted g.o.d.— Groove Overdose—also one of H.O.T.'s rivals). YG is the company I despise for its most blatant misogyny and mishandling of its groups. HYBE, formerly known as Big Hit Entertainment, the newest company of the four, mostly amuses me, but the fact that it didn't debut a girl group until 2022 (Le Sserafim) puts me off it.

(To be fair, Big Hit collaborated with Source Music to debut a girl group, GLAM, in 2012, but the group disbanded in 2014. Source Music was acquired by HYBE in 2019.)

I don't think I'll ever leave K-pop behind, though, even if I don't have a bias like I have in the past. Over the last almost thirty years, this industry has woven itself inextricably into my life, and it has, in many ways, taught me how to exist in the world, how to think critically about culture and history and gender, and how to not take things so seriously. It has taught me to value life and to be willing to share what makes me vulnerable, even (or maybe most importantly) when it comes to my broken brain. Being a bbasooni has helped me lean into my niche obsessions even when they are deeply uncool because there will be someone out there who also shares this interest and might throw up a metaphorical bat signal that yells out, *Hey, you too?! Me too!*

And, most of all, K-pop has protected my connection to my Koreanness even through a decade-plus of body-shaming that destroyed who I was, and, over the last ten years, as I have finally started healing from that trauma and piecing myself back together, K-pop has helped me settle into a happy place in this liminal space that is being Korean American.

■ ■ ■

As a history primer—서태지 (Seo Taiji) is considered the father of K-pop, the revolutionary leader of 서태지와 아이들 (Seo Taiji and Boys), a trio that openly embraced the West, turning Korean gayo, which had been heavily focused on trot (an older genre of music that started during the Japanese occupation and features a distinct rhythm and style of singing) and folk, on its head, as they rapped and sang and danced. It wasn't that Korea hadn't been exposed to Western music or pop previously, but this music had mostly filtered in via Japan and had still come through more "traditional" genres like trot, folk, and ballads. In the postwar period, Western music arrived full force with the US military. As American bases were established around the lower half of the Korean peninsula, they facilitated the introduction of nightclubs where Korean musicians were hired to perform Western-style band music and dance clubs—specifically in Itaewon in Seoul—where Koreans gained exposure to American hip-hop and dance. Seo Taiji and Boys introduced this music to the general Korean public and led a fandom largely made up of young girls who showed up in droves to performances and purchased records, even as the media industry shunned the group, helping the trio build an image as leaders of some kind of youth rebellion, standing against the "Institution." The trio made the Korean mainstream so uncomfortable that, in 1994, with the release of their third studio album, *Seo Taiji and Boys III*, media claimed that if you played "교실 이데아" (Classroom Idea) backward, you would hear a demonic message.

It's worth noting that Seo debuted into a still fairly nascent democracy, Korea having emerged in the late 1980s from decades of military dictatorships, punctuated by demonstrations held by students and factory workers. Korea hosted the Summer Olympics in 1988, and, in the 1990s, it was trying to move toward wealth and democracy, holding fair elections for the first time, allowing its elite and wealthy (the chaebols) to lead development and industry, and heavily investing in its export economy. By the 1990s, after decades of postwar poverty and political instability, South Korea had been introduced on the world stage and was eager to become a more influential player—just in time for the Asian Financial Crisis to strike. In 1997, South Korea declared bankruptcy, and the International Monetary Fund provided the country with a bailout package worth roughly $60 billion.

Seo abruptly retired from Seo Taiji and Boys in 1996, setting the fandom ablaze in panic, but, in 1998, he staged a surprise comeback as a solo rock musician, releasing an album every few years. He also started signing other bands to his Seo Taiji Company label, most notably (for me) four-member band Nell, one of the rare indie rock bands in Korea to break out of the indie scene and reach mainstream success.

Seo has kept a relatively low profile over the last twenty years, though he has staged the occasional comeback, raising a fervor among Koreans. He maybe best embodies the concept of 신비주의, a philosophy of not revealing the personal to keep an air of mystery, as little is known about him—we know he didn't go to college and didn't serve mandatory military service, but is still considered the "President of Culture." He was married once to actress Lee Ji Ah, whom he met in 1993, when Seo Taiji and Boys were still active. He was twenty-one, and she was a fifteen-year-old living in the Los Angeles area. They married in 1997, and he moved her to Atlanta, where she lived hidden away as he traveled between Korea and the United States, until they finally divorced in 2006. She moved back to LA and went to ArtCenter College of Design, then eventually became an actress in Korea. All of this, however, was a secret until she filed a lawsuit in January 2011 at the Seoul Family Court for alimony and division of assets, at which point this secret life and relationship became very public and completely blew up Korean entertainment news. The suit was settled out of court in July 2011.

In 2013, when he was forty-one, Seo married again, this time to actress Lee Eun-sung, sixteen years his junior. They have one daughter, born in 2014. Lee has basically disappeared from the public eye since, but, according to interviews she did before they even met, she had only gone into acting to support her family.

Is this gossip, though, or is it pertinent to culture? Seo's second marriage isn't noteworthy for any reason other than Seo's fame and their significant age gap, but it's also not out of the ordinary for there to be significant age gaps between men and women. Korean entertainment is riddled with these relationships, and there isn't something inherently sinister at play—or is there, when there's power involved? The founder and head of YG Entertainment, Yang Hyunsuk, a former member of Seo Taiji and Boys, is married to a woman twenty years his junior, whom he met when she was a middle school student, accepted to YG when she was sixteen to be a member of girl group Swi.T, then officially started dating five years later after the group disbanded. He confessed his entire love story on an episode of SBS's talk show *Healing Camp* in 2012, even admitting that, had he invested more professionally into Swi.T, they likely would have been more successful, but that popularity would have made it hard to date her. In 2019, Yang became embroiled in the so-called Burning Sun scandal, which involved another of his artists, Seungri of Big Bang, and included claims of prostitution and blackmail. Yang temporarily stepped down from YG.

Then there are all the allegations of exploitation and financial abuse—in 2009, three members of TVXQ sued SM Entertainment and focused a spotlight on what we've come to call "slave contracts," yearslong agreements that lock idols into unfavorable terms and abysmal pay, justified by companies as the only way to offset the costs of training, debuting, and managing their stars. In Korea, entertainment companies control everything—they audition and scout potential idols, they train and house them, they debut them and manage everything from their music schedules to TV appearances to CF (commercial film) modeling contracts and brand ambassadorships. It costs a reported $1.5 million to train and produce one idol group, and companies are unsurprisingly eager to recoup their costs as quickly as they can and profit as much as they can, all off the bodies, talent, and labor of their often-teenage stars.

From the late 1990s to mid-2010s, the Big Three sat at the top of K-pop: SM Entertainment, the company that launched the first K-pop idol boy band, H.O.T., in 1996 and the first girl group, S.E.S., in 1997, and laid down the formula for idol groups that lives on today; YG Entertainment, the more hip-hop-focused company founded by Yang; and JYP Entertainment, founded by pop star Park Jin-Young. In the mid-2010s, these became the Big Four with the addition of HYBE, the parent company of Big Hit Entertainment, founded by "Hitman" Bang Sihyuk, a producer and songwriter who had cut his teeth at JYP, producing and writing hit songs for top singers like Park Jiyoon, Rain, and Wonder Girls, among others. Bang would famously debut and manage BTS—or, as the Korean in me prefers to call them, Bangtan.

In 2024, we are currently in the fourth generation of K-pop (though some argue that we have already crossed into the fifth), and the industry has gone truly global in the last ten-ish years, with more people around the world familiar with the bigger names in idoldom, like Bangtan and BLACKPINK (YG). It's so popular that the question of whether it should be called K-pop or simply pop comes up often—has K-pop become big enough, reached high enough heights, that the *K* should be dropped? Is it racist or Othering to distinguish K-pop from pop? What makes something K-pop, anyway? Is it the language, the ethnicity of idols, anything that clearly points to Koreanness?

I personally take no issue with K-pop being called K-pop and maybe find pride in it, so I'm loath to release the *K*. For one, I don't understand Korea's love for the West, this placing of Americanness, specifically, on a pedestal that dates back to the postwar period and has become so woven into contemporary Korean culture that I don't believe it would be possible to decolonize Americanness from Korea. For another, K-pop functions at a speed and an organizational intensity that feels unique, from the way companies control their artists to how each group essentially has a tiny cult built around it.

There is a rite of passage to idoldom—before you debut, your company releases photos and profile information about you and your group, including teaser images, promotional video clips, and music previews. After you debut, your fan club gets an official name, and you ideally get a unique light stick for your fans to wave at concerts, music show tapings, et cetera, as well as an official color. Like, for girl group Girls' Generation, their fandom name is SONE (소원), their color is pink, and their light stick is heart-shaped: two Gs, one reversed, forming a geometric shape. When Girls' Generation members refer to their fans, they call them SONEs. The fancy light sticks, which can be synced via Bluetooth during concerts, didn't really take full hold until third-generation K-pop; before, there were glow sticks, and, before that, for the real OGs, like H.O.T. (fan club: Club H.O.T., color: white) or Shinhwa (신화창조 [Shinhwa Changjo], orange) or BoA (Jumping Boa, yellow), there were balloons.

Fandoms are organized with memberships, and fan clubs used to have leadership, though I admit I'm unsure how it currently works in Korea, as the fan club systems seem to have become more corporate and automated. Each idol, whether soloist or group, has their own Naver (the Korean equivalent to Google, as Google largely failed in Korea) cafés—and anti-cafés, for those who would rather express their obsession of a particular idol with hatred and vitriol instead of adoration—and now they also have accounts on social media sites like Weverse or Bubble that provide ways for idols to interact more personally with fans via posts or live streams (called lives). Accounts on YouTube, Instagram, and Twitter (now X) are a given at this point, though it can take a while before an idol is settled enough to get their own account—the Bangtan members didn't set up personal Instagram accounts until 2021.

K-pop is also maybe unique in that it is an industry that has, from the beginning, thrived on parasocial relationships, and I would argue that the real work of an idol isn't performing or singing but nurturing these connections with the public. Of course, parasocial relationships in and of themselves aren't unique to K-pop and have generally become par for the course with any kind of celebrity, but there's an intentionality to the way they have been built into K-pop fandom—idols play into shipping (fans' imaginary pairing of group members into same-sex couples) and readily make themselves available via lives and signing events (fansigns) and social media. Parasocial relationships in K-pop aren't a byproduct of fame but a foundation upon which that fame is intentionally built. The cynical part of me wants to call them faux connections because how real can they be, these one-sided love affairs where neither side is actually, genuinely knowable to the other? To idols, we are the faceless mass of The Public. The idols we fawn over, love, declare devotion to are public personas.

And, yet, this line gets blurred constantly, and Korean extremity also pops up in fandom in the form of sasaeng fans, fans who are *so* extreme that they violate their idols' privacy in horrifying ways. Jaejoong has spoken repeatedly of sasaengs who would break into his apartment and steal his underwear. In 2006, members of Super Junior, a second-generation boy band from SM, were driving home when they were chased by a group of sasaeng fans in a taxi, which caused them to get into an accident so bad that Heechul's femur was shattered. Bangtan's maknae, Jungkook, has pleaded with fans on Weverse lives to please stop showing up at his gym and sending food delivery to his home.

However, that is the darker end of things, and not all fans behave badly. There is a sweet earnestness to fandom that I have experienced, both in the way that I have loved my K-pop idols and in how I have been able to build friendships through fandom, so I'm loath to give in fully to cynicism because, to a fan, what an idol makes you feel is very real. The connection you feel, the hope, the joy—that all means something, and it has tangible effects on our lives.

In the mid-2000s, at the height of the angst around TVXQ, a member of Club H.O.T. wrote a long letter to Cassiopeia, TVXQ's fan club. There was a lot in it, but the part that has stuck with me is this:

As you grow older, even if you find a boyfriend
don't ever forget that you are DBSK fans.

At first it may just be a fantasy for you
but as time passes and as you grow older
you will realize that they mean a lot more to you than
you know[1]

▬ ▬ ▬

t would take me a few years to realize: the fan who wrote that letter was *so* right.

Fandom, at first, felt like a fantasy, an escape, a glimpse into another world I could never really belong to, but, as I've gotten older and gained both more distance from and more knowledge of K-pop, my fandom has acted in major pivots in my life. The idols I loved and admired have influenced me more than I ever expected, and I no longer feel shame about being a bbasooni. Looking back, I'm grateful for my fandom years, as intense, obsessive, and, yes, often irrational as they were. They include behavior I might not repeat—but also, who knows, maybe I would.

With H.O.T., I was so young, trying to figure out who I was as a preadolescent, then, with Shinhwa, BoA, and Fly to the Sky, I needed solace during those early years of trauma. With TVXQ, fandom became my deepest comfort during my loneliest years, when I was isolating myself from people because of fear—they provided a safe space in which I could figure out who I was as a writer. With IU and Taeyeon, I learned to try to love and accept myself as a woman in my body, with my broken brain, though this was

---

1 "A Message from a H.O.T. Fan to Cassiopeia," translation, https://candysky.tumblr.com/post/216122993/a-message-from-a-hot-fan-to-cassiopeia. DBSK is an unofficial name for TVXQ, commonly used by the fandom, that reflects how the name is pronounced in Korean: Dong Bang Shin Ki.

less an accomplishment than a daily effort to show up for myself. With Suga, I came to recognize and acknowledge how much I had changed over a decade—and to reckon with the anger and resentment I feel toward writing.

K-pop itself has changed massively since the days of H.O.T. We've gone from cassette tapes to CDs to MP3s to streaming, from Cyworld to Twitter to Instagram to V App to Weverse, from balloons in fan club colors to glow sticks to intricate light sticks that flash in synchronized colors during concerts. We've gone from dial-up to DSL to high-speed internet, and we've gone from K-pop being a very niche thing in the West, deeply uncool even among the Korean diaspora, to K-pop idols selling out stadiums around the globe.

So much has changed but so much hasn't. Male idols are still not allowed to interact with females, sasaeng fans still find their idols' phone numbers and home addresses, and I've become an old fogey who constantly sighs that she misses old-school K-pop. Things were simpler then—fandom was simpler then—or maybe it's that I was younger, not so saddled with life and adulting, or maybe still locked in trauma during the late nineties and early aughts. K-pop was a refuge for me, even though I lacked the awareness or ability to put it into so many words.

And, so, here I am. I am a bbasooni. I am a fangirl. I have loved intensely, and I have grown up with this industry, literally *with* the industry, and, as K-pop has stretched and grown and changed, so have I.

H.O.T.

늘 함께있어 *We Were Always Together,*

소중한 걸 몰랐던 거죠 *So We Didn't Know How Precious This Was*

H.O.T., "빛 (Hope)"

Resurrection, 1998

The first time I hear H.O.T., I'm in the sixth grade, and I think theirs is the music of the Devil. I'm in a car with my Sunday school classmates, and we're driving to Disneyland when one of them slides a CD into the car's stereo, filling the space with the catchy pop beat of "Candy" from H.O.T.'s debut album, *We Hate All Kinds of Violence* (1996). Stuck in the middle of the back seat, I'm horrified as my classmates start loudly singing along, writhing their bodies in dancing movements.

In a year, I'll be wading deep into an obsession with H.O.T. that will influence the rest of my life, but, in that hour-long car ride, I'm terrified for my classmates' souls. I'm certain they're bound for hell.

— — —

n 2012, the drama 응답하라 1997 (*Reply 1997*) airs on tvN, a cable channel in Korea. Set in Busan, a port city on the south-eastern tip of the peninsula, the drama centers a high school student named Sung Shiwon, the only child of a baseball coach father and a stay-at-home mother who makes comedically excessive amounts of food.

After I watch the first episode, I immediately text my parents. *You should watch this. It's about us.*

A few hours later, my dad texts back, *What do you mean? Should we be insulted?*

I laugh. The Sung household is loud: the parents bicker with each other, they bicker with Shiwon, and Shiwon freely bickers back, showing no regard for the polite hierarchy that structures Korean society. Children are meant to use honorifics with their parents, to defer to elders, but Shiwon does none of that. Moreover, she's a bbasooni, a fangirl. She's obsessed with H.O.T., and her favorite member is Tony An (or An Seungho), so her nickname is 안승부인, An-seung's wife. When Shiwon's dad wants to rile her up, he mockingly calls Tony "that monkey boy" because Tony's ears stick out.

When *Reply 1997* airs, I'm living in Brooklyn, across the country from where I grew up in suburban Los Angeles. My parents still live in the same house, and we chat occasionally as we watch the drama, having pirated the episodes. It's been fifteen years since my own 1997, which marked the beginning of my own fangirl days. In the show, Shiwon is a few years older, in her last year of high school, while I was just starting junior high, but we shared an intense love for H.O.T. that would dominate our whole lives.

Today, my parents and I laugh about how we used to fight because of my obsession with H.O.T., as if my preadolescent years weren't filled with heated conflicts, verbal fights, and broken CDs. I still wonder what it was about H.O.T. that stirred up this devotion in me, but my fangirling was much like Shiwon's—it simply was. I could try to spin a narrative in retrospect, something about how H.O.T. represented a new world to me, one that existed outside of my conservative Christian bubble, but I don't think I really thought that profoundly then. I just loved H.O.T. with a love so deep, it eradicated any self-awareness, any consideration of my behavior and how it may have been perceived. We don't talk of the shame my parents must have felt because everyone in our small Korean community knew I was a bbasooni, my love limited only by physical distance from Korea—in a communal culture like Korea's, where the social unit overrides the individual, a child's shame becomes the parents'.

We laugh because there's safety in the passage of time, in assuming that my fandom years are past me—but are they? My love for H.O.T. may have cooled after they abruptly disbanded in 2001, but I still carry around a playlist of their songs on my iPhone. Whenever I hear "빛 (Hope)," the title track of their third album, *Resurrection* (1998), my heart starts beating faster and I immediately start bopping my head and singing along because I haven't forgotten any of the lyrics.

Almost three decades later, H.O.T. is still a part of my life.

- - -

onsidered the first idol boy band in K-pop, H.O.T. marks a turning point in Korean musical history, the moment when it shifted from more traditional trot- and folk-heavy music to mainstream pop with more Western leanings and stylings. Of course, though, they didn't come from nowhere; H.O.T.'s predecessors, Seo Taiji and Boys, had already shaken up the music scene with their hip-hop-influenced music and rap in 1992. H.O.T., however, was the first idol boy band, the first pop group. SM, the company that created, trained, and essentially owned H.O.T., would go on to replicate this formula over and over again, making tweaks and adaptations with each generation of idols. H.O.T. was followed by Shinhwa, a six-member boy band, the longest-running boy band in K-pop history, and then TVXQ (debuting in 2003), then SHINee (debuting in 2008), and so on, each idol group with its own style and look but fundamentally coming out of the same machine for the same purpose: to charm legions of dedicated fans and make as much money for the company as possible before aging out.

And then there are things SM wouldn't replicate. By H.O.T.'s third album, the members were writing and producing their music, composing songs that took a leaf from Seo Taiji and tackled social issues—from political corruption ("늑대와 양" [Wolf and Sheep], *Wolf and Sheep*, 1997) to a fire that led to the deaths of children

("아이야!" [I Yah!], *I Yah!*, 1999). Heejun and Woohyuk were choreographing their dances, and they experimented constantly with their sound, getting darker and less pop, less mainstream, as their albums progressed.

SM would never give its idol bands this much control over their music ever again.

■ ■ ■

Generally, the K-pop machine is run by entertainment companies, the top three of which are still SM, YG, and JYP, with HYBE its newest fourth.

These companies host auditions for aspiring idols. They sign trainees to their labels and put them through grueling preparation—singing, dancing, language learning, acting, media training. Often, trainees move into "dorms," which are company-owned apartments, and they are closely monitored and controlled, weighed and measured, their phone access limited.

To form a group, the company selects from its pool of trainees—who will be the leader? The lead vocalist? The Visual? What kind of personality will each potential idol cultivate? How will this set of trainees look together, feel together? Will each potential idol be able to play her or his part well, embody the role of Idol, follow the rules?

The group members then move into their own dorm to start acting out the story that they're like family. Their image, sound, and narrative are drafted for them. Everything about them is micromanaged to help them play their parts flawlessly. They need to perfect their choreography, learn how to dance in precarious high heels and skirts that barely cover their pubic bone if they're girls, chisel out their abs to flash midmove if they're boys. They need to learn their vocals, do interviews, go to photoshoots, nail their introductions and greetings, learn to function on little sleep and dangerous diets.

After they release new music, idols do their rounds on television music programs and variety shows. They appear on radio shows and do more interviews and photo shoots, and they're constantly on the road with teams that are just as exhausted as they are. They interact with fans who line up to attend the music programs, buy the merchandise and products idols advertise, come to fan meetings and signings.

Idols are never allowed to turn off, but, if they're lucky, their hard work and sacrifice are paid back in fame, success, and fan loyalty.

— — —

Fandom is a standard rite of passage for many young people, so maybe my descent into obsession was nothing remarkable. It was the suddenness of it, though, this obsessive part of me that came out of nowhere—one year, I was worrying about my classmates' souls for listening to H.O.T., and the next I was going through AA batteries like they cost nothing because I couldn't stop listening to H.O.T. on my Discman, persevering through the pain inflicted by terribly designed, uncomfortable headphones. I still don't know what it was that flipped the switch in my brain, that broke through the distorted Christian teachings that had brainwashed me through elementary school. That first summer on the drive to Disneyland, I truly *did* believe that H.O.T.'s music was of the Devil. That thinking was fully in line with what I'd been taught at my private Christian school, via our regular chapels, scheduled hours when we would fill our school's auditorium en masse to pray and receive our teaching.

I distinctly remember one chapel about music in the third or fourth grade. We sat in the quiet, air-conditioned hall and watched a video, in which the speaker played a line from a classical composer, either Beethoven or Handel. The narrator praised the music and talked about how it glorified God, then played a remixed version of the same line, with bass running underneath it, a beat through it. The narrator paused for dramatic effect when the music stopped, letting his point sink in—this God-glorifying music had been corrupted. This music was no longer in worship of God but had been made sinister and evil by the Devil.

This seems ridiculous to me now, but I was a child, and this faith-based point of view was the foundation of the world I was growing up in. My parents didn't subscribe to such extreme thinking, but they disapproved of contemporary pop, I suspect because they thought it corrupting, a negative influence that could fill my head with secular thoughts and ideas. Hymns and worship songs were safe, even if they had bass lines; they reinforced our Christian beliefs via easily digestible music and ensured that every part of our lives existed within our religious bubble. Classical music was acceptable and encouraged because many of the European greats, like Bach and Handel, wrote music with God at the center, and the grandiosity of many of these symphonies would invoke feelings of our glorious Lord. There were elitist elements woven into this, too—classical music was seen as intellectual and was thus preferred, an attitude that extended to literature. I only read the "classics" when I was young, books written by dead white people, almost always dead white men, and I didn't read a single piece of contemporary literature written by a living author of color until I was twenty years old. Kazuo Ishiguro's *Never Let Me Go* continues to be my favorite book, a novel I've read at least a dozen times and return to constantly when I need inspiration.

My family went to church every Sunday, and, on the occasional weeknight, I would follow my parents to Bible studies at the houses of other church members, where my brother and I would sit around, waiting for the solemn sounds of the adults' study to give way to bursts of laughter and slices of cake. I was a good Christian child, quiet and docile. I didn't get into trouble at school, other than some snafus with grades in subjects I hated, and I could rattle off Bible passages from memory and correct adults on biblical facts. My faith wasn't shallow; my extreme commitment to it would prepare me well for fandom.

When I fell into H.O.T. in middle school, it wasn't only my world I was flipping upside down. It was my parents' as well. My parents believe it had to do with my switching schools for middle school when I started carpooling with another Korean American girl, one who *was* interested in pop music and wanted to have fun instead of studying and going to church. Almost overnight, I went from being a sweet, friendly, awkward child to a preadolescent who wanted to dance, wear wide-legged white jeans, and do anything but study. I still faithfully attended all my church youth group's social functions, but I had other motives in going now—to share in my all-consuming passion for H.O.T. All this change, my parents rightfully thought, was because I had moved on from a good, Christian best friend who was going to be a doctor to a new friend who danced, drank Starbucks frappuccinos, and went to church on Sundays only out of obligation.

And I was obsessed with H.O.T. I couldn't talk about, or think about, anything else.

Like Shiwon in *Reply 1997*, I existed in constant tension with
my parents. H.O.T.'s music wasn't cute bubbly pop; they sang and
rapped about social injustice, young rebellion, and seeking hope
in bleak times. Their rap sections were littered with mild curse
words and "oh my god"s, causing my mother to lose her temper
when I played their music in the car. *How can you listen to heathens
who take the Lord's name in vain?* she asked. I would sneak VHS
tapes to oppas at church, begging them to record H.O.T.'s performances on music shows for me, and, as I was now old enough
to be left at home when my parents went to Bible study, I would
watch my bootlegged videos over and over again, quickly shutting
the TV off, ejecting the tape, and running to my room to hide my
treasure when I heard the sound of the garage door opening.

Whenever I was careless about hiding my stash of CDs and
magazines, my parents would take them, break the discs, and cut
up the glossy pages featuring my H.O.T. oppas' faces. Then they
would scold me, and I would cry in the wreckage. None of us
knew how to handle my obsession, though looking back, I understand why my parents were concerned. I'd changed in a matter
of months, and my love for H.O.T. was taking over every single
part of my life. It must have seemed like an all-consuming *thing*
that was unhealthy and destructive. I had become a daughter who
snuck around, printing out fan fiction and disguising it as notes
in a three-ring binder so I could read it in class, sneaking batteries
from the study to keep my Discman powered, and spending my
allowance on magazines to stare at my oppas' faces. To this day,
people who knew me then remember me for my fandom, even if
we weren't very close. I was a bbasooni who couldn't be stopped,
not by my parents' anger or by the public's opinion of me, and
now it was my soul my parents worried about.

▬ ▬ ▬

Reply 1997 was a resounding success when it aired in Korea, so much so that it kicked off what would be a trilogy of dramas, each set in a year nostalgic to Koreans—1997, 1994, 1988. Each drama highlights different happenings in contemporary history, from the collapse of the Sampoong Department Store in 1995 to the 1997 financial crisis to Korea's rise in the 2002 World Cup.

What the dramas do so well is tap into nostalgia, conjuring familiarity and warmth even if you didn't have the same experience as the characters in the dramas. Reply 1997, however, stood out to me because it was the first time a drama really felt like a reflection of me, my adolescence, my family, not only in Shiwon's love for Tony, but also in her relationship with her parents. They fight constantly, and Shiwon never shows much obvious respect for her parents, but they love and cherish each other deeply.

Much like Shiwon as she grows into adulthood, I'm not inclined to look back on my bbasooni days with shame. I was a teenager, and my love for H.O.T. took me down a different path, one that ultimately led me away from the church and the heteronormative life expected of me, with law school and a conventional career. Even though I didn't grow up in Busan, watching Reply 1997 feels like coming full circle, revisiting those intense, tumultuous years and realizing how much has changed—but also how little. I still feel too much. I still grapple with feeling like I exist on the outside, like I am forever that girl standing out in the cold, staring through a window at a room that exudes warmth, filled with the people I want to be with, the people I want to be. I still love H.O.T.

— — —

've joked that, had I been raised in Korea, my father would have cut my hair multiple times in punishment because my obsession with H.O.T. was so all-encompassing

In *Reply 1997*, Shiwon ditches school to get on a bus to Seoul to camp out in front of Tony's house just to get a glimpse of him. She even goes so far as to jump the wall onto his property to ring the bell—like, *this* is the kind of fangirl Shiwon is. She's the kind of fangirl who'll ditch after-school study sessions to take a bus to another city to attend H.O.T.'s performance, spend her allowance sending Tony personalized gifts, get into fights with her classmates who are fans of H.O.T.'s rival boy band, SechsKies. She'll wake up at 5 a.m. to stand in line to purchase H.O.T.'s second album, which she's already preordered, just so she can have it immediately. She'll camp out in front of the bank overnight to buy concert tickets. She'll memorize all kinds of minute details about H.O.T. to win a T-shirt drenched in Tony's sweat. She'll even write a confession of love with blood pricked from her fingertip for a chance to join the leadership of the Busan chapter of H.O.T.'s official fan club, Club H.O.T.

So, when her dad cuts her hair after her little trip to Seoul, Shiwon is marked. All her classmates know she's 안승부인, so everyone knows what her haircut means—she's done something even more extreme than her usual fangirl shit. She's gotten caught.

I wished I could have my hair shorn. I got into trouble for my obsession, yes, but I felt I couldn't *really* give my obsession free rein, not while I was living in Los Angeles. I couldn't *really* be a H.O.T. fan because I wasn't in Korea. I didn't have a Korean registration number because I wasn't a Korean citizen, so I couldn't apply to be a member of Club H.O.T., which meant I couldn't get the merch or access to fan sites with insider knowledge or anything that would give me "official" acknowledgment of my fandom.

To be an international fan is to exist on the fringe, and I didn't get to experience Shiwon's kind of fandom—"real" fandom—for much of my adolescence. My rebellions seemed so sad and pathetic. Sure, I could hide the wire of my earphone in my sleeve and listen to music during class, but I couldn't send Tony a personalized teddy bear. I couldn't sneak out to another city to attend a live performance; all I could do was sneak blank videotapes to an oppa at my church. CD releases and music show performances arrived in Los Angeles late, magazines a few months behind, and, living as I did in the suburbs of LA, I had to wait until my parents went grocery shopping at our Korean market to sneak over to ArtBox, buy a CD or magazine, and hide it in my messenger bag, nervously hoping I wouldn't get caught, so I could still participate in that world at least in this small way.

What idols sell is fantasy. One such fantasy is that these groups are like family; they've trained together for years, and they live together, forming close, loving bonds. Idols sell the impression of a close camaraderie that is unique and special, and this fantasy extends to the fans. By loving idols, fans enter into a parasocial relationship that is predicated upon unspoken rules—you are to be loyal and faithful to your idol group, you are to protect their image, you are to devote yourself to them.

K-pop fans don't simply attend performances and tapings and buy merchandise. They bestow upon their idols extravagant gifts (including cars and, once, a forest), send catering trucks to idols' film sets, and prepare gifts for their birthdays. Fans also donate to their idols' favorite charities and do community service in their idols' names. This is the sweet and positive side of it, but the unspoken contract between idols and fans runs deeper and is much more possessive. In return for their devotion, fans expect idols' faithfulness. As the most obvious example, idols aren't allowed to date. If they were to date, they would disrupt the fantasy between themselves and their fans, and fans have sometimes resorted to vicious measures to remind idols of this.

I didn't care much for this fantasy of marrying my oppa. Despite my obsession with him, I didn't feel the need to possess Tony, though I did feel protective of him. I didn't like to think of him being corrupted by some girl, but he had to get married eventually, didn't he? For the most part, though, my feelings seemed like an extension of my love for H.O.T.'s music, which was so different from anything I'd ever heard, so charged with an energy I'd never encountered before. And H.O.T. was *Korean*. They sang and rapped in Korean. That alone gave them an appeal that Western boy bands like the Backstreet Boys or NSYNC could never have—H.O.T. came from a culture that was both mine and not.

I couldn't articulate this at the time, but I wanted so badly to be a part of something. I was a lonely, awkward preadolescent who didn't make friends easily, who didn't know where she belonged— even in the church group she'd grown up in, even if that church group was all she had. Fandom gave me something that was mine and mine alone, and, though I didn't know this at the time, loving H.O.T. was the first active step I took away from the life I knew as a second-generation Korean American daughter of devout Christian immigrant parents. It's not that I'd ever veer wildly off course, though; I still studied hard, didn't get into boys or partying, and was a very straitlaced kid.

It's kind of like this, though: Academically, Shiwon's consistently been the last in her class, which makes her prospects for college very dim. In Korea, in November of their final year of high school, students take the 수능, the nationwide exam that determines where they go to college. The most ambitious look toward SKY, Korea's trio of top universities: Seoul National University, Korea University, and Yonsei University. When asked where she wants to go to college, Shiwon chirps, "Dongguk University," because that's where her beloved Tony oppa is enrolled. Unsurprisingly (and, maybe, a little deservedly), she's laughed at.

Throughout the drama, Shiwon gets plenty of shit from her parents, teachers, and friends who don't understand her behavior and find her commitment extreme. Maybe her behavior *is* extreme and irrational, but I can't help but think it's also kind of fine—she's a teenager. She's discovering who she is.

Her homeroom teacher tells her that, with her grades, she should give up on her dreams of getting into college at all, but then he learns that she writes fan fiction about H.O.T. because a classmate gets caught sharing pages in class. He laughs as he reads the pages chronicling the over-the-top sexual romance between Tony and Woohyuk, but, after he's finished reading, he looks at her and says, "I think we've found a way for you to go to college." Together, they turn her homoerotic fan fiction about Tony and Woohyuk into a sweet heterosexual romance between fictional characters and enter that story into a competition. Winning the competition gets her into her beloved Dongguk University, which then leads to a job writing for television.

Shiwon is a fictional character, but here, too, her life intersects with mine. Being a fangirl brought me into the realm of fantasy, giving my brain space to daydream freely and wildly, and fan fiction took that blossoming imagination and shaped my dreams into stories. Fandom, ultimately, took my childhood interest in words and taught me how to be a writer.

◼ ◼ ◼

I n 2001, H.O.T. disbanded. It was messy and abrupt, following months of rumors the members tried to quell. When their split was made official, it came out that SM had been paying H.O.T. pennies (reportedly $10,000 for every one million records sold, to be divided among the five of them) and wanted to renew only Kangta's and Heejun's contracts. Enraged fans camped out in front of SM's headquarters in protest, graffitiing the building and blocking the roads. From the other side of the ocean, I was trying to get as much news as I could on Soompi, at the time the main online forum for Korean Americans, which I logged onto from my crappy dial-up. Months later, in my AP European History class, I flipped through magazine articles about the disbandment, feeling empty and lost. For four years, I had found my identity in H.O.T., and now they were no more. Where did that leave me?

◼ ◼ ◼

I n the mid-2010s, several of the big idol groups from that first generation of K-pop staged reunions. They held concerts and appeared on variety shows; some even released new music. Groups like g.o.d., S.E.S., and SechsKies came back together to the delight of fans. H.O.T.'s fifteenth anniversary, however, passed without a reunion, as did their twentieth. There were constant rumors that the members were meeting and discussing a reunion, but for years, nothing happened. I didn't think it ever would—H.O.T.'s disbandment had not seemed amicable—but I hoped that I would be able to fly to Seoul to be there when it happened. It never happened, at least not for me.

H.O.T. did reunite in 2018, but I didn't find out about it until a few years later, when I watched the videos on streaming platforms, still across the ocean, feeling a mix of overpowering emotions as the cameras panned over the audience members wearing white jackets, waving white balloons, and screaming in delight. The camera closed in on women's crying faces as they yelled the age-old fan chants in freakishly timed unison—*H.O.T.! H.O.T.! Saranghaeyo, H.O.T.!*

I wish I could have been there, actively participating in the act of being a fangirl in a way that felt more tangible and meaningful than hiding CDs, recorded VHS tapes, and magazines in my closet. I wanted to wear a white raincoat and wave white balloons in the air and scream the fan chants. I wanted to be in the same room (okay, arena) as my beloved oppa-deul, to shout their names and cry and sing and rap along with the lyrics I still remember, so many years later. I wanted them to know that I, too, was a fan, I was a bbasooni, I was still loyal.

I may never have officially been a part of the fandom, but I know that doesn't make me any less of a fangirl. H.O.T. was a part of me for four intense years, insulating me from the painful loneliness that has been my constant companion since youth. Fandom protected me by wrapping me in its consuming obsession during very vulnerable years of my life, so I didn't worry about what other people thought about me, my awkwardness, my lack of social grace. I could lose myself in fandom, and, while I was lost,

I could find new ways of existing, being creative, and thinking outside of Christianity.

And, like I said, I was still loyal—after H.O.T. disbanded, I would go through several fandoms, mostly groups managed by SM, from Shinhwa to Fly to the Sky to TVXQ, with a brief stint with Big Bang and a few J-pop idol groups, but H.O.T. has never left me.

Over the last two decades, I've come back to H.O.T. over and over again. Through technological progressions from battery-powered Discmans to bulky iPods to sleek iPhones, I have carried a playlist of my favorite H.O.T. songs with me. Their music still holds up, and I find comfort in the nostalgia, in sinking into the familiarity of their songs, singing along, and swaying my body in dancing movements, much like my classmates did on that car ride to Disneyland so many years ago. If I could, I'd go back and tell that young girl on the cusp of adolescence that this boy band is going to change her life, it's going to change who she is, and she's going to be better for it—and her soul is going to be just fine.

보아 BOA

It Feels Good to Be a Woman
BoA, "Woman"
Woman, 2018

PART I

BoA, the queen of K-pop, is born in Korea in November 1986, when I'm almost one year old. I was born in Queens, New York, on a cold December dawn in 1985, and I'm growing up in North Jersey, staying with my grandparents while my parents commute into the city, my mother to her job on Wall Street, my father to his doctoral program in Brooklyn. There isn't much I remember about my early childhood, just little hazy scenes—wandering into a darkened bedroom during a visit from my aunt and being startled by her green face pack. My father raking autumn leaves into bright red-orange piles, me dragging my giant teddy bear into the leaves with me. My mother bundling me up for snow.

When I am two or three, my grandfather is in the city for work, and he's crossing a street when he's hit by a bus. Paralyzed from the waist down, he'll never walk or be independent again, forever attached to my grandmother. She'll care for his every need, replace his catheter, push him in his wheelchair from their bedroom to his chair in the living room. She'll never be independent herself, not that she ever was or had a chance to be. My grandmother was born in occupied Korea and married before the war to a first son, with whom she had seven children, six living. She sent every single one of them to university, a major feat in post-war Korea, especially when five of those children were daughters. When my father decided to immigrate to the United States to get his doctorate, she immigrated, too, with her husband and youngest daughter, and, for years, they lived in a tiny, roach-infested apartment in Queens, where she would lose every last shred of independence in a country whose language she didn't know.

If she'd had the opportunity to be educated, my grandmother would have been a force.

- - -

hen BoA is eleven years old, she follows her older brother to an audition at SM Entertainment. She's just tagging along as her brother auditions to be a breakdancer, but it's her the scouts notice, her the company signs.

After two years of training, she debuts at thirteen years old, a small girl with long straight hair, flanked by her all-male dancers.

K-pop is still a fledgling industry in 2000, and, at the time, she's rare not only for her young age but for being a female soloist who doesn't sing ballads but makes R&B-inflected pop music while performing rigorous choreography. She doesn't seem daunted, though, as she dances and lip-synchs to her debut, "ID; Peace B" (*ID; Peace B*).

I'm unimpressed. Her debut song isn't that catchy, not to my ear, and I've already decided that I'm not a fan of this girl who gets to hang out with my H.O.T. oppas because they're labelmates. I try to be snooty about it—her voice is too unpolished, her look boring with her straight, layered hair and plain makeup, her stage presence lacking gravity—and I think she'll fizzle out soon or just go on to have a middling career because what could people see in a girl so young, so slight? What kind of star power could she have? I don't want to be a pop star myself, but I wonder constantly what BoA had that got someone to notice her. Could I have that quality, too?

▬ ▬ ▬

My grandmother's first child is a girl, and my oldest aunt is the reason all her sisters are educated. She's the number-one student in her school in their small city of Nonsan, so her father can't dismiss her for being a girl or make her out to be a burden because of her gender. For middle school, her parents send her away to Seoul, so she can get a better education. In Korea, you have to test into middle school, into high school, and into college, and my oldest aunt makes it all the way to Ewha Women's University, the top women's university in the country.

The second sister follows her unni to Seoul and gets into Seoul

National University, the best university in the country. One after the other, all the siblings—except for the sister with a scar that runs down her face—go to Seoul, and they'll all study hard, test well, go to college. All but one will graduate. Two will go on to earn higher degrees, one a doctorate, the other an MD. They'll marry, have children, and care for their parents in their old age, a success story by all accounts in a tumultuous, hungry, postwar Korea, where education is the rope out of poverty and provinciality.

■ ■ ■

According to a 2007 documentary produced by Arirang TV, when BoA joined SM at eleven years old, one of the first things she focused on was language learning, primarily Japanese. At the time, Japan had the third-largest music industry in the world, while Korea's was far from the global presence it is today. SM's long goal was never simply to be a power player in the small pool of K-pop, but to cross borders and hold soft power. That meant that BoA didn't learn just Japanese—she learned Mandarin and English, while also taking vocal lessons, dance training, and everything else that goes with turning a child into an idol who will stand on the international stage.

A year after BoA debuts in Korea, SM sends her to Japan under the local label Avex Trax, putting her on a mini-hiatus in Korea to focus on Japan, the first of many long breaks she'll take from her home country, earning her criticism from Koreans. Once in Japan, she realizes quickly that her textbook Japanese makes her stand out even more and emphasizes her foreignness. She starts paying attention to how people actually speak, learns to bend her grammar and inflections to colloquial language, and I have to admit she has a natural talent for this, a good accent and poise that extends beyond her years.

Twenty years later, BoA says she'd tell her younger self not to try so hard, not to live so much on the edge of life and death. All her hard work, all that discipline and intensity, would pay huge dividends, but maybe it would have been okay to allow for some softness and youth.

— — —

My second aunt is born several years after the first, and there was a son between the two sisters, a son who didn't live long, who died as an infant from carbon monoxide poisoning, a common occurrence in those days.

In Korea, spaces are heated from the floor, and we call them ondol floors. In modern apartments, the heating is via gas or electricity, but, in older buildings, heating is provided by charcoal briquettes that are lit then placed under the floors. The briquettes keep inside spaces warm, but rooms have to be properly ventilated and the briquettes properly placed, or the people inside can be susceptible to carbon monoxide poisoning.

The younger the body, the more vulnerable: the boy dies, and a girl takes his place. At Seoul National University, she meets a boy who's studying law. They fall in love, but his family doesn't approve of her, wants someone from a more vaunted family for their soon-to-be-a-prosecutor son.

There are other boys after him, but the one she marries loves classical music as much as she does. He has a resonant tenor voice, and he's a student at Sungkyunkwan University, a school with a deep history that's only second tier at the time. They have two girls a year apart, and they immigrate to the States, where he'll try his hand at a variety of businesses, including hat making, before running a small store in suburban Pennsylvania.

Both of her daughters are brilliant. The older forgoes Columbia Law School to marry and have a family, pursuing literary ambitions when her children are of school age. The younger will test in a high percentile for the MCAT but decide to get her doctorate in philosophy at Cambridge instead. I'll wish for years I'd grown up on the East Coast knowing them, instead of out in California, intimidated by the legends I build them up to be in my brain.

■ ■ ■

I n 2009, BoA sets her sights on the United States. She seems to be a good candidate for this—she's been compared to Britney Spears for years because both are soloists, sing pop music, and perform powerful choreography. BoA's dancing sets her apart from other female idols, and, with her agility and adaptability, she could be a professional dancer if she weren't a pop star.

Breaking into the US comes with its own set of challenges. For all the differences between Korea and Japan, East Asia has its commonalities thanks to centuries of influence and entanglement. BoA was able to establish herself in the Japanese market, cementing her place as one of J-pop's solo queens. She holds records in Japan, and she's demonstrated a natural skill for picking up languages, so I think she has a good chance at finding a niche in the US, where no K-pop star has previously been able to establish themselves. As long as her agency handles her debut with care, highlighting her strengths as a performer instead of compromising her art in a misguided effort to appeal to the West, as long as they give her good music that maintains her sound and style, as long as she can get on stages to show off her choreography and charisma, her US presence would be a slow build but maybe— *maybe* she could do it. Or maybe those are too many variables, but she *is* BoA. She didn't reach success in Japan overnight; she built a strong foundation she could vault off once the opportunity came along.

Unfortunately, SM tries to mold BoA to the Western market with songs that sound like Britney or Rihanna rejects, instead of staying true to her own kind of pop. Within a year, she wraps up promotions and returns to East Asia.

— — —

When my third aunt is a child, her maternal grandmother takes her to the temple to pray for a brother for my aunt. On the way back, my aunt stumbles and falls, hitting her face on the stone steps and gaining a permanent scar on her face.

My third aunt doesn't go to Seoul to join her older siblings. She loves literature but drops out of college to marry because her husband-to-be doesn't give up in his pursuit of her until he convinces her and my grandparents that she should marry him immediately. They have two children and immigrate to the US later than the other aunts, and her husband sets up a small mom-and-pop store in rural Pennsylvania, putting in long hours and working on holidays to pay off their house and save up for retirement.

I grow up thinking my third aunt is the prettiest of the five and only learn that she had a scar when I'm in my thirties. As I've been told, she's had it treated over the years, so it has largely faded.

— — —

n the eyes of my mother, I am a disappointment, in my thirties with no husband, no children, and no prospective spouse on the horizon. Unlike my cousins, whose collective CVs read like a guide to the Ivy League, I didn't get into a top university. I was admitted to law school on a full scholarship but dropped out after the first year to pursue a life of writing. I live with major depressive disorder, anxiety, and ADHD, and it wasn't until my early thirties that I became fully financially independent. In their eyes, nothing about me, about my life, has been a success.

But what defines success?

Today, twenty-one years into her career, BoA is considered the queen of K-pop, a trailblazer who has set records and established the standard for what a young female pop star can be, fierce and independent, forging her way forward. I'm sure, in the eyes of some, those successes mean little, as she is now in her midthirties, still unmarried with no children. What have the decades of celebrity brought her? Fame, yes, and wealth, status, prestige, but family? A spouse? Who will she grow old with? What is the point of all the fame if you're still alone in the end?

Is this my mother's voice in my head? I've had no great success like BoA's, so what's my excuse for being unmarried and childless? What do literary dreams or professional accomplishments mean in the face of my solitary life? But, then, even if a woman were to marry and have children, does that mean she has lived a successful life? How much pressure was placed on my paternal grandmother to have a son?

How do you measure a life, and does it matter?

— — —

All that temple praying and bowing are for naught, and when my fourth aunt is born, she's dressed in boy's clothing, her hair cut like a boy's. Koreans have a superstition that cross-dressing will bring about a boy next, and coincidence strikes and reinforces this superstition because child number five is the long-awaited boy. When my father is born, my aunt is finally dressed in girl's clothing, her hair allowed to grow long.

After my dad is born, my grandparents think, *So, we had a boy. Maybe we've turned our luck. Maybe we should try for another boy.*

My grandparents' sixth and final child is my youngest aunt.

PART II

Korea is a tiny peninsula nation that juts off Asia into the East Sea. Nestled between Japan and the rest of Asia, Korea was viewed as a stepping stone onto the continent by the Japanese empire, and, in 1910, Japan formally annexed Korea, after having brought Joseon Korea within its sphere of influence in 1876.

Japan took a unique approach in its occupation of Korea. Unlike in other countries, where the Japanese army simply went in and conquered, committing heinous acts of violence, Japan knew it needed more legitimacy when it came to Korea, to lend credence to its conquest of Asia. To be fair, Japan did a lot to industrialize Korea, investing in infrastructure and supporting Korea's economic development. At the same time, Japan exercised military control over Korea, running its media, law, and government and brutally quelling the Korean independence movement, and, to be honest, everything good that Japan did for Korea, it did for the betterment of Japanese civilians who had moved to the peninsula. Gradually, Japan tried to fold Korea into itself, claiming that Koreans were actually Japanese. The Japanese tried to eradicate Koreanness in phases over decades, forcing Koreans to visit Shinto temples on major holidays, take Japanese names, and speak only Japanese.

The Occupation ended with the end of World War II in 1945, when the US dropped atomic bombs on two Japanese cities. Before Korea could reclaim itself, though, the US and then–Soviet Union fought each other in a proxy war that has divided the peninsula and its people for over fifty years.

As a second-generation Korean American, I'm not far removed from this history. My grandparents were born and raised during the Occupation and spoke and read fluent Japanese. The war is technically still ongoing; all Korean males are required to serve two years' mandatory military service because of it. Meanwhile, the US military maintains bases throughout the southern half of the peninsula, an ongoing act of imperialism that metes out violence and environmental harm—but yet, with all the devastation thrust upon them, Koreans have flourished, investing aggressively in the exports that would bring them wealth and carry them closer to American-like success, power, and influence.

One of the clearest examples of this is Hallyu (or Korean Wave), the term for the popularity of Korean dramas and K-pop that started to surge throughout East Asia, Southeast Asia, and the Middle East in the late 1990s and the early aughts. Over the last thirty years, the Hallyu Wave has continued to spread across the globe as the Korean government has aggressively invested in the export of its pop culture, from music to video games and, more recently, literature.

BoA, as a mere teenager jumping between Korea and Japan, helped create that wave. She was the first Korean artist to achieve major success in Japan and open the doors for other K-pop stars to follow into Japan's lucrative market. To this day, tensions between Korea and Japan remain high, forcing her into a tough balancing act as Koreans both loved to see one of their own succeeding in Japan and criticized her heavily for spending so much time in the country of their former colonizers.

PART III

I am my father's first child, and he is the only son of a first son. In a patrilineal culture such as Korea's, my birth is eagerly awaited—and my family hopes I'll be a boy. When my paternal grandfather finds out I'm a girl, he refuses to name me.

■ ■ ■

I n the early 2000s, LA's Korean newspaper, the *Korea Daily*, starts holding its annual Korean Music Festival at the Hollywood Bowl. The organizers bring in a mix of top idol groups and older talent to perform on a warm spring night that ends with fireworks. The event is festive and joyful as families and friends pack picnics and fill the Bowl, waving Korean flags and wrapping themselves in blankets as night descends.

In 2003, BoA comes to perform as part of that year's lineup,

the first of two times I'll see her live. I remember nothing about
the other performers, but I remember BoA. I can still picture her,
in an olive-green cropped tank top and loose pants with gold
trim, hair straight, layered, and dyed a brownish red. Her makeup
is light. She walks onto the center of the stage, surrounded by her
backup dancers, and takes a deep breath. The Hollywood Bowl
sits nestled in the Hollywood Hills and seats 17,500 people. The
remixed opening to "No. 1" starts to play.

"No. 1" is the first BoA song I love, the title track to her second
Korean studio album, released in 2003. It's an upbeat pop song,
the chorus—*you still my number one!*—easy to belt. It's just one
year after her debut in Japan, where the few singles she released
didn't perform as hoped. *Listen to My Heart*, though, her first Japanese album, released in 2002, did incredibly well, the first in a
string of albums that would hit number one on the Oricon charts
and solidify BoA's position at the top of the top in J-pop. "No. 1"
is her first number one in Korea.

By the time BoA comes to perform at the Hollywood Bowl on
April 26, she's already a phenomenon. When I see her walk out on
the stage, I think, wow, but she's so small, just a girl on the cusp
of young adulthood—and, yet, she fills the entire Bowl.

— — —

Korean names are built on characters, and each character
has its own meaning. Historically, East Asia as a region
(China, Korea, and Japan as we know it today) used
Chinese as a writing system because China was, unsurprisingly, the dominant country. Both the Japanese and Korean

writing systems today still incorporate Chinese characters—in Korean, they're called hanja, and students learn roughly 1,800 characters over the course of their schooling.

Hangul, the Korean alphabet, was created in the year 1443 to represent the vernacular language of Koreans and promote literacy, particularly among commoners who did not have access to education and were unable to read Chinese characters. Hangul, today, is considered one of the easiest alphabets to learn to read, and it gave women access to communication and education that they hadn't before, barred as they were from classical literature because they weren't taught to read Chinese.

Korean names can be created in two ways—built off Chinese characters or taken from pure Korean, words that don't have counterparts in hanja but exist only in hangul.

My father names me 지애 (Giaae)—지 (智) for wisdom, 애 (愛) for love. There's a more common name that sounds similar to mine—지혜 (Jihye)—which means I'll be correcting people my whole life. *Giaae, not Jihye. Aae, not hye.* Even my maternal grandfather continues to get it wrong to this day.

My name is a point of pride for me because it's a name my father gave me. He tells me he was secretly glad my grandfather refused to name me because then the privilege fell to him, and he chose my name with care. It sounds deceptively common, but it's not, and that's the kind of person I'll want to be, someone who seems ordinary but isn't. I want to be brilliant. I'll be constantly disappointed in trying to attain that goal, and I'll never quite learn how to navigate that disappointment.

— — —

The second time I see BoA live, it's 2009, at San Francisco Pride. She's trying to break into the US, and she's just released an album in English, *Eat You Up*. I'm unimpressed by the album, a clumsy effort that, to me, exposes SM's insecurities when approaching the Western market. Where SM sent BoA to Japan with confidence in her ability to adapt to a new market while retaining her identity, for the US, it tries to bend her to some idea of what an American pop star should be, instead of playing up her strengths and uniqueness.

I think people, whether producers, artists, or consumers, place undue emphasis on language when approaching the US market, as if an inability to speak English is the first and major barrier to success. I disagree, though—while language does present a challenge, I think this focus on it betrays a fear, an insecurity, as if K-pop is somehow inferior to its Western counterpart, as if Western audiences are the ultimate arbiters of an idol's value or abilities. In the face of this supposed great hurdle, SM falters, thinks more about mimicking the sound and style of Western pop stars than introducing BoA's style of pop to the US, and, ultimately, botches her American debut.

While her stage presence isn't diminished and she works well with what she's given, BoA quickly wraps up her promotions. I still wonder how far she might have made it in the States had SM invested more thoughtful time and effort into her US debut because BoA has all the elements that could make her stand out as a pop star here—the vocals, the choreography, the presence— but maybe I'm being naive. As it is, 2009 is too soon for the US to be ready for a K-pop star.

— — —

oA and I share the same family name, 권 (權, Kwon), which means descendants, power. As someone who is not a national Korean, I don't necessarily find significance in this, other than being amused that we're from the same line of Kwons. Family lines, however, still matter to Koreans—until 2003, two people from the same family name (which was determined by the Chinese character) weren't allowed to marry for fear of muddling family lines—and, often, when Koreans meet each other, they'll ask what line of which surname from what village they come from.

BoA's origin story doesn't really work its way into my brain until I'm in college and struggling. She didn't go to SM to audition—she was just tagging along—but a scout saw her and noticed something in her, even though, at eleven years old, she was just a child. Someone thought there was star quality in her, something special and unique worth nurturing, but, like I said, when BoA debuted as a thirteen-year-old, I didn't like her, and I didn't *want* to like her. Only later, when I'm grown and able to look back on my life, do I wonder if my dislike didn't come down to something very simple: I wished someone would notice me. I wished I had that special spark that could make someone look. All I wanted growing up was to be like the smart, resilient women I came from, to be liked by the older cousins I so looked up to, but, instead, I felt my whole life like I was falling short. I would never shine. I would always be invisible.

Add to that my body—I wasn't thin, which was unacceptable by Korean beauty standards, and, because I didn't *look* "right," I could never *be* "right." I could never be like BoA, and, so, as an adolescent, I started to pull back and withdraw into myself, to lose myself to shame.

PART IV

For BoA's tenth anniversary, SM releases a documentary. In one scene, we see her learning new choreography. She jokes with her choreographer that she wants a so-called crane dance like the one Girls' Generation does for "Genie," but her choreographer laughs that he would never do something like that for her. She needs something more powerful, more complex.

"Because you're BoA," he says simply.

– – –

My fourth aunt is the only aunt who remains in Korea. She goes to Seoul National University and is hired as a flight attendant for Korean Air, a job that's notoriously difficult to get, requiring all women to have a certain look and speak multiple languages. She doesn't take that job and instead goes to work for Amore Pacific, where she meets her husband. They have two kids and spend a few years in Colombia, so my cousins grow up trilingual, toggling effortlessly from Korean to English to Spanish. We meet only a few times because of the geographic distance, and, even though, of all the cousins, we are the closest in age, I am intimidated by them, this brother-sister pair who seem so cultured, so traveled, so smart.

My fifth aunt wants to study philosophy. She goes to medical school instead, becomes an ophthalmologist, and marries a neurosurgeon. They have four children. I'm closest to their family, my cousins becoming like younger siblings. Our families spend a considerable amount of time together, going on joint vacations, congregating at my aunt's house for family events, and, when my cousins and I are older, traveling internationally together. There's an ease to them that I am grateful for, these younger cousins who laugh from the moment they wake to the moment they sleep, who simply accept me as one of their own.

My cousins and I joke that my fifth aunt and my mom are the same person. During our formative years, they fixate on our weight, meting out the same damage with the same intentions using the same language. They love us fiercely, too fiercely, their love a distorted one that believes that it is okay to hurt if that hurt forces us to change for the better. It is okay to wound, put down, criticize us for our bodies and the parts of our characters that seem at fault, if it will shame us into losing weight because they believe that will mean better lives for us, more opportunities, less external hurt and rejection.

"Because you're BoA," her choreographer says as he teaches her more intricate dances, and I wonder what it might mean for someone to say, *Because you're Giaae*. When I was in my early twenties, I would have said, *Lazy and undisciplined*, my overweight body a visible manifestation of my flawed character. My body was yet another way I fell short compared to all my illustrious older cousins, who were not only smart but also poised, put together, thin. If I couldn't even scrounge up the discipline to bring my body into line, how was I supposed to have the discipline to get a 4.4 GPA and go to an Ivy—or, if not that, at least a prestigious liberal arts college? How was I going to succeed in life? How was I ever going to be someone worth seeing?

— — —

BoA dropped out of school to move to Japan at the age of thirteen, and she had to grow up fast, a child in a world of grown-ups, learning to stand up for herself against adults who wanted to dismiss her and make decisions for her. In an August 2020 interview with *Vogue Korea* to commemorate her twentieth anniversary, she says, "I tried to talk about my complaints in a rational, intelligent manner. I thought that if I didn't logically explain why I felt a certain way, people would think that I was whining. . . . I didn't like it when people treated me like a child just because I was young and then expected me to be perfect onstage. I realized that I needed to speak rationally to adults if I was going to be active as a singer. That's why I've heard people call me an old soul. It made me emotional to have to clash with adults."

I didn't learn to speak to adults rationally or emotionally but retreated further into myself as the body-shaming started to break me down. When I would fight with my parents, I would clam up, my stubbornness greater than theirs. I would sit sullenly at our kitchen table, in my dad's study, on my bed, until they admitted defeat and dismissed me. It's only in the last ten years I've realized how much that worked to my disadvantage. I am in my twenties when I finally start to talk, to yell, actually, to scream about how I am tired of being broken and afraid.

— — —

In my early twenties, my older cousins get married in close succession, one wedding following another. I *despise* weddings; they require me to think about what to wear because I can't hide in my usual uniform of a sweatshirt and baggy jeans. I am also hyper self-conscious because I am often the only girl who shows up in pants, shamed out of wearing skirts or dresses because they show my legs. Finally, for the last wedding, I rebel and go shopping on my own, thinking I'll buy myself a dress, some tights, a pair of heeled shoes. That frustrating outing to the mall ends with an ill-fitting outfit I settle on after hours of trying things on and not finding anything I like—unsurprising, given that I have never learned how to dress myself, only to hide my body in dark colors and baggy clothes. I hide my outfit until I arrive at the venue and have to change in the bathroom. I am uncomfortable, squeezed into a form-fitting gray dress from H&M that doesn't fit me, with red patent heels I don't know how to walk in, but I have no choice but to wear the outfit, writhing inside with shame and discomfort all afternoon.

I've never worn or seen that dress again. I've never seen a single photo from the wedding, and I'll never ask for one. I still cringe when I think back to it, and I feel sorry for my younger self—I just wanted to fit in, for my older cousins to like me. I grew up admiring them so much from a distance, but that admiration paralyzed me. I was just so young and damaged then, so lonely and desperate, with no sense of how to dress or present myself in a body I had been told over and over made me a disgusting monster, and I didn't know who I was—I just wished I could be someone else, someone like my brilliant, beautiful cousins, someone like BoA.

— — —

ecause you're BoA," the choreographer says, and she laughs. I wonder what it's like to be chased by that kind of reputation, one in which you are seen as capable and strong and desirable, in which you are respected and admired for what you are able to do. No one would ever view me in that way—would they?

PART V

Why do K-pop stars want to break into the Japanese market? Sure, the Japanese music industry, at the time, was the third largest in the world, right behind the US and the UK, but the Occupation and the war were not far removed from my generation. Why did SM send a teenage girl to this country that was, not so long ago, the enemy, and where she had to learn to fully integrate herself into that culture? The obvious answer seems to be that it was for money and prestige and cultural power, and the work certainly paid off—BoA set records in Japan that placed her in the ranks of J-pop's queens, Utada Hikaru and Ayumi Hamasaki—but it also came with plenty of criticism from Koreans who didn't like that she spent so many long years in Japan, accusing her of being Japanese even as they held up her success as a source of pride—look what she did, a Korean, look how she infiltrated the Japanese market.

After BoA broke down the doors, it's become standard for K-pop idols to cross over to Japan. Learning Japanese has become part of the training for any aspiring K-pop star because now debuting in Japan is just part of being a K-pop star. Many K-pop idols go for the easy route of releasing their Korean music with Japanese lyrics, simply riding the Hallyu Wave without trying to establish a more unique, creative presence that fits in with J-pop, which is markedly different from K-pop, more bouncy, more cutesy, more nasal. K-pop idols are meant to look perfect and doll-like, while

J-pop stars can be rougher around the edges, less perfect and poised.

BoA didn't completely ascribe to that J-pop-ness, but there was nothing half-assed about her efforts to succeed in Japan. As the first Korean idol to break into the Japanese music industry, she didn't have the option to coast; failure would reflect poorly on Koreans, bring shame upon them. She spent years learning the language and adapting her music and image to meet the tastes of J-pop fans. Later in her career, she would release select Korean tracks in Japanese, but, in the early years, she more often went the other way, releasing her Japanese singles in Korea with Korean lyrics. For the most part, her Korean and Japanese careers have run parallel to each other, infrequently intersecting.

That commitment to learning the market and becoming a version of herself that was loved by the market skyrocketed her to fame in Japan—and earned her criticism in Korea. BoA spent years in Japan, which meant long gaps between her Korean studio releases and fewer appearances on Korean broadcast television. She did arena tours in Japan every year from 2003 to 2008, but she didn't hold solo concerts in Korea until 2013. Japan was where the money was, and Koreans criticized her for it, accusing her of wanting to be Japanese. Koreans are a proud people, and Japan's history of attempted erasure of Koreanness, its brutal, violent suppression of Koreans who fought for their independence, its kidnapping of young Korean women to serve as "comfort women" to be raped by Japanese soldiers as the Japanese military moved across Asia in conquest and war—all of this is only two generations away. Even to this day, Zainichi Koreans are looked down on and refused citizenship by Japan.

Given all this, K-pop's prominence in Japan today has complex historical layers, and BoA is the only K-pop artist whose Japanese releases I consistently enjoy. Her J-pop side feels like a natural extension of her K-pop self. Yes, she adopted the more nasal tones preferred by the Japanese, but she retained the elements that made her BoA: her choreography, independence, and charm. She created a niche for herself in J-pop that was true to her, so her collective Korean and Japanese discography weaves together seamlessly. Her success in Japan shows why her attempt to break into the US market in 2009 fell so flat—her American debut, *Eat You Up*, flopped for a myriad of reasons, but, to me, it was because the album was too blatant an attempt to cater to the West instead of playing to her strengths.

There is a price for all this success, and BoA has spoken of the loneliness of being in Japan. As a soloist, she didn't have group mates to live with or be around. During the early 2000s, as she blew up in Japan, I thought she was starting to feel arrogant and full of herself based on the ways she carried herself in interviews and media appearances, but she was alone in a foreign country, a very public figure who couldn't go anywhere without being noticed, who couldn't be with her family or friends whenever she wanted. Years later, when she first spoke publicly of that loneliness, I finally felt the deep, personal connection that made my interest in her click. Even as I expressed my dislike of her over the years, I couldn't stop following her, listening to all her new releases and watching her music videos, performances, interviews. There were so many other women in K-pop I could follow, so why did I stay with BoA for twenty-two years?

I often ask myself if my enduring love for K-pop is connected to growing up in Los Angeles while my extended family was out east, if I would have fallen so deeply into K-pop had I grown up in

New Jersey with my aunts and cousins in easy reach. Would their influence have kept me in check? Would I have found such solace in, such closeness to K-pop? Would I have needed it so much? Looking back, I'm glad I had K-pop, that I had BoA.

For one, BoA has managed to skirt many of the gendered expectations placed on Korean women, the cutesiness and saccharine sweetness and giggling girlishness expected long past adolescence and deep into womanhood. Her image up until her third Korean studio album, *Atlantis Princess* (2003), was less cutesy than it was juvenile—and then, rather than trying to be simultaneously innocent and sensual, BoA vaulted straight into young womanhood. It helped that her choreography differentiated her from other female idols; BoA knew how to dance, so she danced, performing complex routines that required more than body rolls and arm waves. For her fourth Korean studio album, *My Name* (2004), BoA was more "fierce," her hair pulled back, her abs on full display in crop tops and low-rise pants, her makeup heavier. Her choreography was less cute, more strong, sexual, and empowered, a style that evolved with her fifth studio album, *Girls on Top* (2005), into a more tomboyish look, her hair cut into a mullet as she was styled in bomber jackets and Hammer pants, eyes rimmed with dark eyeliner.

And then there is this—in 2005, during her promotions for *Girls on Top*, BoA performed at the Mnet KM Music Video Festival. She used two stages for her seven-minute performance, which required her to run halfway around the concert floor, on top of performing live with her usual powerful choreography. Once her set was done and she exited backstage, she crumpled. Soon, there were photos of her being carried out on the back of a staff member circulating on the internet.

As the public later learned, BoA had the flu that night. She performed so well, though, that no one suspected anything was off, that she wasn't well, that she had pushed herself past the limits of physical well-being. Online responses largely praised her for her professionalism, for pushing through and showing her strong work ethic, but I couldn't stop thinking of her small figure draped, unconscious, over someone's back, her dark hair cascading over his shoulder as her hands hung limply around his neck—and I hoped she had someone who would care for her and fight for the parts of her that were soft.

PART VI

Here's a moment I thought was profound for ten years before realizing otherwise: on a cold December night in 2013, I'm waiting for the G train at Hoyt-Schermerhorn. It's late in the evening, and, as I stand there on the platform, it suddenly slams into me—no matter what I do, no matter how much I accomplish as a writer, my parents will never truly be proud of me.

I know there is no malice on their end; they just don't know the world I live in, this world of books and writing. They won't understand the significance of the milestones I might accomplish. They will always think of who I could have been—an attorney, a doctor, even a stay-at-home mom—because those are ambitions they know, futures that seem safe and desirable, with prestige and financial stability. Pursuing a life of instability and uncertainty in order to chase literary ambitions is not understandable to them.

That night on the subway platform, I'm overwhelmed with

sadness, but, at the same time, I am resigned. Now, though, eleven years later, I think how narrow my perspective was then. Sure, it would be nice for my parents to understand the literary world, to know the names of magazines, to be able to support me directly, but I recognize now that it is more than enough for people to love and support you, even if they don't "get it." Maybe it means even more.

PART VII

I n my brain, there's me in my life, then there's me in a number of alternative lives, versions of me that *could* have existed had my life somehow been different. In one version, I'm an art school kid. In another, I'm a lawyer with an international career. In yet another, I'm like BoA, a superstar, multilingual, charismatic. In this life, though, there is only me.

— — —

I n late 2021, BoA works with aespa on a remake of S.E.S.'s "Dreams Come True." S.E.S., a three-member girl group from SM Entertainment, was active from 1997 to 2002, one of the top girl groups of that first generation of K-pop. "Dreams Come True" is a K-pop classic, released in 1998 as the title track of S.E.S.'s second album, and SM, in recent years has gotten nostalgic, releasing remastered versions of classic music videos and rerecording a version of H.O.T.'s "빛 (Hope)" during the holidays. aespa is SM's newest girl group, with four members, all of whom were born after "Dreams Come True" first came out. The group debuted in 2020, SM's female representative in fourth-generation K-pop. aespa also makes SM the only major entertainment company in Korea to house four generations of K-pop women.

This is BoA's first time producing someone else's music, though at this point in her twenty-plus-year career, she's produced many of her own songs and albums and concerts. She joined SM shortly before the original "Dreams Come True" was released, and, in the behind-the-scenes video SM releases on YouTube, she talks about her nerves approaching this project.

BoA's a natural, though, as she guides aespa through the recording of the song, shows up to watch them practice the choreography, comes to the music video shoot to give advice and encouragement. The members of aespa are rightly awed to be working with her, surprised at how involved she gets and touched by her support and her mentorship. On my end, as a fan, it's really nice to watch. BoA is part of the first generation of K-pop, aespa its fourth. In her midthirties, BoA might be older and less active as an idol, and she might not chart as well or have as much visible popularity, but she is highly respected and regarded.

She is still the queen of K-pop. So much of what we take for granted in K-pop and Korea's soft power today was made possible because of her, because she excelled in a local industry and took it international, giving K-pop exposure in Asia at a scale it hadn't had before. BoA normalized K-pop idols debuting in Japan and achieving a certain degree of fame and financial stability (Bangtan, according to their lore, was largely supported by their Japanese fanbase in their early years), and, from there, K-pop got a stepping stone into the rest of the world as it could think beyond its borders. Because of BoA.

Everything I learned about strength I learned from the women in my life, from my grandmother, my mother, my aunts, and my cousins—and from BoA. It meant something to be young, watching someone my age grow into a leading figure who would—thanks to her choreography, stage presence, and discipline—set the standards for an entire industry.

I needed to have that strength and courage modeled for me when I was young and lonely and afraid. Once I'd moved past my envy, I found pride in BoA's existence, in her accomplishments and success. Her existence comforted me, and, finally, as I grew older and learned to let go of the fear and shame I'd held on to for so long, I began to find more encouragement in BoA as she began to represent infinite possibilities. If I worked hard, kept myself open to the world, and maybe regarded myself with more kindness instead of trying to meet arbitrary standards, maybe I, too, could be who I wanted to be, whoever that was, without losing the heart of what I was.

Because BoA never lost sight of who she was, down to her Koreanness. During one of her performances, her stylist dresses her in a bomber jacket. The original design features a Japanese flag patch attached to the arm, but BoA asks her stylist to sew on a patch of the Korean flag to cover it. She is Korean, and she knows who she is. She's BoA, and she doesn't have anything to prove.

ㅁㄴ
타블로 TABLO
- - - - - - - - -

나를 보고 꿈꾸는 너의 그 꿈은 *The Dream You Dream as You Look at Me*

깨고 보니 악몽이 아니길 *That I Hope Doesn't Turn Out a Nightmare*

Epik High, "개화 (開花)" (Lost One [feat. Kim Jongwan])

WE'VE DONE SOMETHING WONDERFUL, 2017

've told two big lies in my life. They're really the same lie, told twice, that I had to sustain for several years, and they go like this—I dropped out of school twice, the first time from undergrad, the second from law school, but both times I pretended that I was still in school.

Korean culture is renowned for being obsessive about schooling, which I'd call a stereotype if it weren't so true. In Korea, students face tremendous pressure to get into a good university, the prime target being SKY, an acronym for the top three universities in the country: Seoul National University, Korea University, and Yonsei University. A young person's life is dedicated to this goal from childhood—students want to get into a competitive grade school to test into the ranked middle school that will help them test into the ranked high school that will bolster their chances to get into SKY. To better their chances, they spend hours at school then, if they can afford it, hours late into the night at hagwons, after-school cram schools, to test well on the 수능, the national university exam that's held once a year in November.

This hyperfocus on schooling didn't come out of nowhere; it stemmed from the postwar period, when Korea was a war-torn country with nothing. Education became the ladder out of poverty, an opportunity for even those without wealth in tiny villages to get to Seoul and eventually bring their families into an upwardly mobile life with better possibilities. Today, Korea's obsession with academics feels more cynical, ultimately a run for prestige and great wealth—to attend one of the SKY universities is to have a better chance of landing a job at, say, Samsung, which is to attain a certain kind of status, especially if you don't have a parachute to ride. Korea has modernized so rapidly that there is only a single-generational gap between postwar Korea and the glitzy economy we know today.

This attitude carries over into the diaspora, at least into my generation. Second-generation Korean Americans like me were expected to study hard and attend the Ivies or their storied equivalents, and we were expected to become high-earning professionals in competitive fields like medicine, law, or engineering. It makes sense that our immigrant parents would carry over their belief in education above anything else as they crossed oceans and borders in hopes of a better life for their children, many forgoing their higher degrees in Korea for blue-collar, labor-intensive jobs in the West. For these opportunities given to us, we were expected to study hard, excel, and succeed.

I'm going to follow that by saying that my parents didn't put a lot of pressure on me about school. They wanted me to do well, of course, but I wasn't expected to go to Harvard or another Ivy League. My father had grown up with that pressure, had gone through it himself, getting into Seoul National University and graduating with a degree in electrical engineering. He understood the stress involved in getting into a status school, as well as the bullshit of these institutions, and he didn't find much value in them and didn't want to pass that expectation on to his children. There is its own privilege attached to that (Koreans might say he's 재수없어), but my father's priority wasn't rankings or numbers but simply that my brother and I try our best to excel.

He didn't have to, though. I put that pressure on myself.

I am my father's first child, and, even though I am a girl, I felt the burden of being the only son's first child. How could I not excel when my older cousins' collective CVs read like a guide to the top universities in the US: Yale, Princeton, Columbia, Stanford, Berkeley? How shameful would it be for me not to join their vaunted ranks?

Against these high standards, I felt like I fell very short—University of California, Irvine—and so, after two years of struggling with depression and adapting poorly to university, when I failed a core class, lost my scholarship, and left school, I didn't tell anyone, especially my parents.

— — —

Tablo is a member of Epik High, a hip-hop group of two rappers (Tablo and Mithra Jin) and a DJ (Tukutz). Epik High is one of the few hip-hop groups to break into the mainstream in Korea, debuting in 2003 and spending years in the indie scene before striking a hit with their third album, *Swan Songs*, in 2005, thanks to their lead single, "Fly."

I don't actually remember how I was introduced to Epik High, given that (1) I was into mainstream K-pop, à la SM, and (2) I was in the US and didn't have much access to Korea's indie music scene, which is a term I use very loosely (and probably inappropriately) to capture any genre that isn't mainstream K-pop. If I remember correctly, I got into Epik High after they released their fourth album, *Remapping the Human Soul* (2007), which is when I feel like they really burst onto the mainstream scene, thanks to tracks like "Fan" and "Love Love Love." "Fan" certainly left an impression on me; it's a song about a bbasooni expressing her possessive love for her idol; and the music video is haunting, a fangirl kidnapping her idol because she loves him and he is hers, only hers.

Remapping the Human Soul was probably one of the first rap/hip-hop albums I'd ever listened to, and I was astounded by Epik High's wordplay, rhythm, and sociopolitical rage. This was 2007, when I was supposed to be graduating from college, but I wasn't, and only my best friend at the time knew. Tablo was kind of everywhere, appearing on variety shows and garnering the admiration of the broad Korean public. As a hip-hop group and not an idol boy band, Epik High wrote and produced their own music, and, as a writer, Tablo displayed a unique thoughtfulness and depth in his lyrics. All of this made it particularly easy for Korea to place him on a pedestal, an Artist who could also serve as inspiration for young people.

I listened to Epik High's music, but, even as a longtime K-pop fan, I was never (and still am not) the type of fan who watches every variety show or performance or interview. I don't read every magazine article, and I don't need to know every single thing my favorite K-pop idols do. When Tablo was appearing on all the big variety shows in the late 2000s, from *X-Man* to *Love Letter*, it was also hard to access them and find subtitles—my Korean might be fluent on a conversational level, but it isn't advanced enough for me to understand the slang and quick wit of variety shows.

I had learned enough about Tablo, though, to know that he was born in Korea and raised in Canada, that he had gone to Stanford and was fluent in English and wasn't an idol but an Artist. Idoldom, then, was already known for being manufactured, so indie musicians in the hip-hop or rock scene got more credit. They wrote their own music, and they weren't polished and dolled up, and they had that grit and tenacity that seem to follow indie musicians around. On top of that, Tablo had his fancy American education, and he was a writer, publishing a collection of stories, *Pieces of You* (2008), that he had written during his time at Stanford. Then, in 2009, he married actress Kang Hyejung.

In short, Tablo seemed to have it all.

■ ■ ■

In 2018, the drama *SKY Castle* aired on the cable channel JTBC. The title refers to a fictional gated community where wealthy families live in Western-style mansions, the husbands working prestigious jobs while the wives are stay-at-home moms dedicated to their children's educations. They all have the same goal—to get their children into SKY, whatever the cost—and when their children succeed academically, the neighborhood gathers to celebrate and congratulate the mothers because all the children's successes are, after all, due to their mothers' devotion.

There are four main families in *SKY Castle*: the Kangs, at the top of the pecking order, with two daughters, the elder of whom (Yeseo) is obsessed with becoming a third-generation Seoul National University med student; the Woos, a more easygoing couple who chase the heels of the Kangs; and the Hwangs, the newest family to the neighborhood, who move in after a tragic accident removes another family. The family most pertinent to me, though, are the Chas, who are led by a husband who was once a prosecutor with presidential dreams. He and his wife, a stay-at-home mom like the other women in SKY Castle, have three children—twin sons who are both rising seniors in Yeseo's class, one of whom is expected to accomplish his father's dreams of the Blue House. They also have a daughter, Seri, who is a first-year student at Harvard—or, as we find out, is *supposed* to be a first-year student at Harvard. She's actually been faking it all semester.

— — —

There is a desperation to wanting something so badly but not being able to achieve it that feels so basic but is so real. My father is the second youngest, so most of my cousins are older than I am. After he finished his doctorate in Brooklyn, he got a job in Los Angeles, so our family left Jersey and moved out west, away from my paternal extended family. While we did often travel over holidays to see my grandparents, aunts, and uncles, my cousins were older than I was, with their own lives, ambitions, and, eventually, families, so they became these larger-than-life figures in my mind, paper tigers that I constructed, giving them long shadows I could never escape.

I wanted to go to Columbia. Columbia is an Ivy. I wanted the prestige, to join the ranks of my illustrious cousins, but Columbia was also in New York City, and, for years, I had longed to move back to the city where I had been born, across the country from Los Angeles and away from all the sun and my past. I wanted to go to college somewhere I didn't know anyone, though I didn't think much beyond that—I didn't think about how difficult an adjustment that might be, how sheltered I had been growing up, how I expected to stand on my own two feet when I was so crippled by my own inferiority complex and the body-shaming that had started my freshman year of high school.

These were questions I didn't really have to answer because I didn't get into Columbia. I also didn't get into Berkeley, UCLA, or Wellesley. I did get into Occidental, UC San Diego, and UC Irvine, and the choice, ultimately, came down to San Diego or Irvine. I had friends from church who would be attending both, so I would also be able to plug into a local church, and I would be within driving distance from my parents in the Valley—three hours to San Diego, one-and-a-half to Irvine, without traffic.

In the end, Irvine won because they gave me a full scholarship and admitted me into their honors program. In September 2003, my parents drove me down to my dorm in the Shire in Middle Earth (one of two housing communities for undergraduates), and I was away from home for the first time in my life.

I had no idea what to do with myself. I felt like I had failed, and I didn't know how to talk to my roommate or my housemates. I didn't know how to structure my life on my own, how to hold my day-to-day together without an external source applying pressure on me, how to be a social human being. I had no way of realizing how depressed I was or what to do with that; I hadn't grown up in a family, in a community, where mental health was ever acknowledged. I just knew that I was supposed to be in college and that I had to do well because I couldn't lose my scholarship; I couldn't bring further shame to my family by not being able to do well at *Irvine*. This wasn't an Ivy or some fancy private liberal arts school—surely, I couldn't fail here.

At the end of my first year, I was put on academic probation.

In the first quarter of my second year, I failed a core honors class.

I never started my third year because there was no scholarship, so there was no tuition.

I held up my first lie for almost four years. I pretended to stay in school for the first two; because I'd been going to school on a full scholarship, I could pretend I'd registered for classes and was attending. After my freshman year, I had moved off campus to share a one-bedroom apartment with a friend, so there were no school fees to pay, just rent, books, and living expenses. My flatmate was a chemistry major, so she was gone for many hours most school days, so I didn't have to go out of my way to pretend I was going to class. When I told her the truth years later—that I had not been going to school for two of the three years we were roommates—she was completely surprised and caught off guard. If there is someone outside my family I'm sorry about telling this lie to, it's this friend.

In June 2007, I pretended I'd graduated but didn't want to go to graduation—I hadn't gone to my high school graduation, after all—then I moved back to my parents' and tried to get a job without a BA, while pretending to apply to grad school. Looking back, my parents were so kind and gracious with me, allowing me to live at home without putting a lot of pressure on me to find a job and move out. I'm sure they were deeply concerned, and maybe they voiced those concerns, but I don't remember much from those years, just that they were supportive as I told them I was going to apply to grad programs in English. I didn't have a plan for how I would handle this in the long term: I obviously wasn't getting into grad school, and I was struggling to find the kind of job I thought I should have been able to get with an undergrad degree.

Around the time grad school decisions were supposed to be coming in, I finally reached the end of my rope. I still didn't have a job, and I hated lying. It felt like I was spitting in my parents' faces, especially as they both continued to work full-time to support my grandparents (my paternal grandmother mostly lived with us, and my maternal grandmother was dying of lung cancer), and they had enough to worry about without also having to worry about me, their grown child who was allegedly applying to grad programs and searching for legal assistant and publishing jobs but finding nothing. The economy was in a recession, so maybe that, too, worked to my advantage.

When the lying became untenable, I left home, packing two bags and heading up to Sacramento to visit a friend I had grown up with at church. She had gone to Cal for undergrad and was now in Sacramento for law school, and I had no idea what I'd do once I got there, thinking I'd try to find my way out east—me, a spoiled, sheltered kid who had no real-life experience and whose parents had met all her needs. I was naive and stupid and scared, so I left my parents a note when they were at church and flew out of town, crying nonstop because I felt so guilty, so sorry, so terrified. My friend was gentle with me as she picked me up from the airport and took me to her place, helped me set up the air mattress, and listened to the truth tumble out of me. She asked me what I wanted to do, said I was welcome to stay as long as I needed.

My mother started calling me that night, calls I ignored. The calls became texts telling me to come home, it was all right, we could work past this. Eventually, I got on the phone with my parents, and, a few days later, I flew home.

To my parents' credit, they didn't give me a lot of shit when I got back to Los Angeles. Their worry and concern for me overrode their anger—or, at least, their ability to express that anger—and, instead, they just took things in stride. I worked full-time in a boutique law firm for over a year, and I wrote to my university to see if I could be readmitted. Luckily, I could, so, in 2010, I went back to school. I had no scholarship then, and my parents paid for my tuition and living expenses. I graduated in 2012 and went straight into law school, again on a full scholarship that also covered the cost of my books.

I went into Brooklyn Law School figuring one of two things would happen—either I'd find the study and practice of law tolerable enough that I could pursue it professionally, or I'd hate it. I didn't necessarily know what would be on the other side of me hating law school, just that, I supposed, I'd be looking at a lifetime of unhappiness. Hopefully, I'd land a job that would pay enough to make the emotional sacrifice worth it, but I never thought I'd drop out of law school—and certainly not as dramatically as I did.

By the end of my first semester, I was depressed and suicidal. I spent almost every day of my second semester thinking about dying—if I could get out on the roof of my building and jump, if I could somehow manage to jump off a bridge between boroughs. I couldn't fathom this being the rest of my life, and, finally, in June

2013, terrified that I would actually hurt myself, I quietly withdrew from law school.

And, again, I kept this secret.

■ ■ ■

Celebrity brings out some ugly behavior in people. For as long as there has been K-pop fandom, there has been K-pop antifandom, and the internet has made it too easy for netizens to spew all kinds of vitriol anonymously. I'm actually a little surprised by it—at one point, it was hard to sign up for any Korean website without a Korean registration number. Even today, to be able to make a reservation at a restaurant in Korea, you have to have a Korean phone number. To use Kakao Taxi and enter your credit card, you have to input your registration number. Anonymity, theoretically, seems difficult in Korea.

And yet, netizens hide behind their screens all the time. Influencers, politicians, and public figures can buy services that skew what appears to be public opinion; they can pay people to sign up for accounts, leave comments on websites and message boards and social media, and, probably, harass people. It's not like this service really *needs* to exist, though—Korea is impressively wired, and people are online and have no qualms about expressing their thoughts and venting their real-life stresses by taking them out on people in the public eye.

Tablo, unfortunately, became a key example of this.

In 2010, a group called Tajinyo surfaced on the internet. Short for 타블로에게 진실을 요구합니다 (We Demand the Truth from Tablo), the group alleged that Tablo had lied about his academic background because, they claimed, he couldn't have graduated with his bachelor's and master's in three-and-a-half years. The group didn't simply spread these lies and misinformation on the internet; it escalated to threats against his life and family.

Tablo withdrew from music and tried to do what he could to prove that he had indeed graduated when he did, releasing his transcripts and degrees. He filmed a documentary at Stanford, reminiscing about his student life. Stanford itself released a statement backing him up, and his former professor, the American writer Tobias Carroll, did an interview to speak about Tablo as a student. It didn't matter what Tablo or Stanford did, though; Tajinyo dismissed everything as a lie.

How do you fight someone who refuses to see facts in order to believe the lie?

■ ■ ■

In *SKY Castle*, the patriarch of the Cha family, Cha Min-hyuk, is a law school professor who worked previously as a prosecutor. He had presidential ambitions that were dashed with the fall of his wife's father, a two-term congressman who was supposed to be Cha's step to the Blue House. Cha never lets his wife, No Seung-hye, forget this, bringing it up at every opportunity, and has since shifted his high ambitions to his sons, expecting one of them to pick up his crushed dreams as he sits them in a soundproofed study to run through math questions and holds up a statue of a pyramid as a visual—they must climb the pyramid to that lofty top. The only problem is that only one person can sit at that peak, so his sons, both warm, social teenagers who aren't the most academically oriented, are to think of their friends, of each other even, as competitors.

Cha is inflexible and tries to run his home with an iron fist, and his daughter, Seri, is the apple of his eye. We don't meet her until halfway into the drama, when she comes home for the winter holidays, but her joyous arrival is chased a few days later by a phone call from Seung-hye's sister, who has been looking after Seri in the US for years. Harvard is pressing charges against Seri and demanding tens of thousands of dollars in damages. For the past semester, Seri has been impersonating being a Harvard student, somehow living in the dorms, sneaking into lectures, and presenting a false front on social media.

Her mother initially keeps this from her father, waiting until Seri comes clean herself, but, as it happens when lies start to leak out, the news quickly spreads within the small community, until it seems like everyone except her father knows. In a panic, Seri takes off to Jejudo, and I have to laugh to myself because I recognize this impulse to run.

When her father finally finds out, he gently calls Seri home, then calls his sister-in-law to tell her he'll wire her the money demanded by Harvard. Initially, when Seri crawls home, he doesn't get angry but goes automatically into problem-solving mode, which sets Seri off—she's sorry and feels guilty, but she doesn't need her father to start charting out the rest of her life again. She knows what she wants to do: work while saving up with her friends to own and manage a club together. Her father finds this laughable. What can she possibly do without a college degree? What will she amount to?

As they scream at each other in the foyer, I can understand why her father is upset and agitated, but I empathize deeply with Seri, who tries to explain. When she started high school in the US, she couldn't keep up. Her grades were falling, and, eventually, in a fit of desperation, she plagiarized an essay, which went on her academic record and basically made Harvard an impossibility for her. When college admission news was coming out, it felt like the better option to say that she had been accepted to Harvard because her father had wanted it so badly. She couldn't disappoint him. She couldn't be that failure. She would make it up to her parents later, but, for now, it was better to lie, to let them be happy and proud.

It would be okay, she reasoned. She would make it okay.

In the same way, I had also believed—I would be okay. I, too, would make it okay.

— — —

What did I *do* in those years I was supposed to be in school but wasn't?

I wrote.

The first time around, during university, I wrote a lot of fan fiction. My best friend at the time and I were in love with TVXQ, specifically three of the members (Jaejoong, Changmin, Yoochun), so we made them into characters, gave them new names, and spent hours on G-chat putting them into imaginary stories. Of course, we were characters, too, and our cast went on adventures—in one world, they were pirates; in another, students at uni; in another, owners of a bakery. In all these worlds, they were friends. I would write short stories about our cast, generating hundreds of pages about these worlds we built together.

When I was supposed to be in law school, I was taking writing more "seriously," working on a novel-in-stories that I planned to pitch to agents. I started a book blog and developed a nonfiction voice. I read a lot, shared a lot on Instagram, developed friendships and relationships with other readers and other writers.

And, maybe, that's the main defense I have for myself: that with my lies, I bought myself time, and, with that time, I honed my craft. At the same time, that has also become my source of deepest self-loathing. After I withdrew from law school and started focusing on getting published and Being A Writer, I was so confident that I could accept the struggles that would come of pursuing a creative life. I would be okay with never making much money, with not having a dependable paycheck, with not having a steady Career, at least in the way that society at large defined it. It would all be worth it if I could just write, if I could pursue my passion.

Ten years in, I both miss and despise my naivete. It isn't that I secretly thought I would have some kind of luck and not struggle so much; I've never had much in terms of luck, and I sincerely knew that trying to be a working writer would be hard. I just didn't have a real sense of how that difficulty would translate into actual life, into loneliness and discouragement and resentment. It didn't help that I've been single through all of it, that I've had to figure out how to support myself financially and get myself health insurance (or go without insurance for years) and take care of all the other miscellaneous necessities that make up being a human in the world without a partner to help carry these burdens.

Sometimes, when I think about idols, I ask myself if I want what they have. I don't want to be famous because I think fame is a terrible cage, but I admit I would love their success, money, and clout. On my ugliest days, I *envy* them their success, and I think I can understand what might drive a group like Tajinyo, that I can recognize that twisty gurgling in your stomach when you see someone who seems to have everything you want. I console myself by saying that I would at least not try to make lies of the truth to help myself feel better. It may be human to feel envious and inferior, but what you do with those feelings is what counts, isn't it?

When I finally got into Bangtan in October 2022, I had a lot to catch up on. One of the key moments in Bangtan lore is when Jin let slip during their acceptance speech at an awards show that Bangtan had seriously considered disbanding earlier that year. They had been going through a hard time, both as a group and individually, and, when I first learned of this, I thought this had happened earlier in their career, when Bangtan was a middling group from a small company struggling to find success. I was highly sympathetic because I know firsthand how hard it is to be a creative person in the world, trying to succeed and be financially solvent. I can't imagine how much harder it would be to be an idol, trying to make it in *that* world.

As I learned, though, this actually happened in December 2018, *after* Bangtan was already on their meteoric international rise.

Once I learned this, I found my sympathy shrinking. I wouldn't go so far as to say that they sounded ungrateful, but there was something about Bangtan talking about their challenges after they'd hit unimaginable success that was hard to listen to. As someone who struggled so much to be a writer, who didn't get a byline until 2019, seven years after I started trying to write for publication, who still works a day job and is trying to establish a capital-C Career in another field entirely because writing is so untenable—Bangtan talking about how they were overwhelmed by their accomplishments seemed tactless. Whether that was a fair judgment or not, the truth is that most creatives don't succeed. Most of us burn out. Most of us don't find success.

Even today, when I think about the success I aspire to, I think that what I want is not so much money or even critical acclaim but simply some kind of assurance that all the terrible decisions I've made—lying about school twice, withdrawing from law school, choosing not to pursue a professional career to focus on writing—have somehow paid off. Ten years into this, even though I've sold a book and published food and culture writing, as I exhaust myself working a full-time job and pitching and writing in the time left in between work and life, I wish I had chosen differently. I wish I had a professional career with all the usual corporate milestones to show as progress. I wish I had invested more in myself personally so I could date and find a partner instead of so singularly prioritizing writing. I wish I had the money to take my parents on trips and buy my mom a luxury handbag and pay back my brother for all the times he showed up for me, helping me move apartments, buying me a laptop, being the peacemaker between me and my parents when I dropped the bomb of withdrawing from law school. I wish I could believe that I haven't wasted my youth.

— — —

SKY Castle, in my opinion, generally has a far too optimistic, neatly bow-tied ending. The interpersonal tensions in the drama escalate with the death of Yeseo's classmate and main academic rival, who turns out to be Yeseo's half sister, born of an affair her father had. Yeseo isn't directly responsible for the death, but she has been unwittingly tangled up in it and holds the key to the truth—her private academic coordinator, hired to help her get into Seoul National University, has been stealing the exams from Yeseo's high school and using them during her tutoring sessions to ensure that Yeseo gets top grades.

Even though Yeseo hadn't consented to this or been aware of it, she would still have to come clean about it and risk expulsion.

I don't believe it is the role of dramas to moralize, but I do believe art is in a unique position to critique, to reflect society back at us. We've seen an influx of dramas that take on unreasonable academic expectations and pressures, bullying, and now sexual assault and gender violence, but, often, these issues that have very real ramifications for young people in real life are utilized merely as plot points, issues to provide tension and "realistic" drama because they happen to be our current talking points.

The ending of SKY Castle is a little too feel-good and nice, given that a girl has been murdered, a boy falsely accused of her murder and nearly sent to jail, with everything hanging upon the confession of one girl, for whom confessing is an agonizing prospect because it means she would lose her opportunity to go to Seoul National University's medical school and become a third-generation doctor in the family.

When written down, it sounds absurd and irrational—and it is. The idea that adolescents should have enough presence of mind to have these ambitions or that these ridiculous pressures to "succeed" should be placed on them by their parents, by society, by dramas that highlight and elevate these lifestyles—it's a lot. Maybe one could argue that SKY Castle is making a critical argument against it because Yeseo does confess and gives up her path to SNU, the Woos accept that their son doesn't need to aspire to such heights, the Chas prioritize their family relationships over their children's academic "achievements," and the Hwangs find peace, but it's all so happy, so unbothered and easy—too easy, when I consider the cost. These families can all reach enlightenment because they didn't pay the price; they weren't pushed off a veranda to their deaths, all so one teenager could proceed on her mad path of ambition.

In an interview with *Rolling Stone* in February 2023, Tablo says, "People are like, 'Oh, you overcame [Tajinyo]!' But what did I overcome?" He mentions the death of his father, which he attributes in part to the stress of the false accusations. "I lost my dad and two or three years of my life that I will never get back. I have barely any recognition of [my daughter] Haru's early childhood. I was physically there because I couldn't leave the house, but mentally I was absent. And they say I overcame it? They say I won? What did I win exactly?"

There is a cost to everything, but who pays the price?

Young people in Korea call it Hell Joseon. Korea has one of the highest rates of suicide in the developed world, at one point vying with Japan for the number-one spot. It's hard to get an apartment in Korea, with rentals requiring anywhere from the equivalent of ten thousand to forty thousand dollars as a *deposit*, and the competition to get a job is steep. If you are able to find a corporate job, you're working frankly insane hours, unable to go home until your sunbaes do because Korea is a hierarchical society.

It's easy to fixate on these dark statistics, though, to make a spectacle of the toxic aspects of Korean culture. We see plenty of writing in the West that still does this, and, as a Korean American, even one who has grown up with the dark sides of Korean culture, I get annoyed by how reductive and racist this oohing and aahing is.

In an interview with a Spanish magazine in March 2023, RM, Bangtan's leader, loses his patience with the interviewer, explaining point-blank that Korea is a country that, just a few decades ago, had nothing. If there is an extremity to K-pop, to Korea's pursuit of academics, it's because it came out of extremity, having just recently been a poverty-stricken country that had been colonized, torn in two by external forces, then decimated by war. The history doesn't excuse the extreme nature of Korean society that is literally killing young people, but it does explain it. Nothing comes from nothing, after all.

Idols debut young, in their late teens or maybe early twenties, and I find it mind-blowing that anyone at that age is supposed to know what they want, to pursue it with such diligence and discipline. It's incredible that they survive the K-pop system to the point of being able to debut. The idols we see onstage are those who have been selected—from however many aspiring adolescents at auditions, then from the pool of trainees fostered at entertainment companies—to win a position in an idol group, be assigned a role (essentially), and debut.

It's just so much to place on young people's shoulders.

━ ━ ━

Halfway into *SKY Castle*, tired of Cha's obsessing over the pyramid, his family leaves him, Seri to friends, Seung-hye and the twins to her secret hideout. Left alone in the giant house with his pyramid, Cha Min-hyuk first tries to cling to his beliefs and ambitions, to his stubborn insistence that his children must study hard and be ruthless and succeed, but the silence starts to eat away at him. He starts drinking heavily, and, finally, one night, after many bottles of soju, he calls his wife, who shows up the next morning. Hungover but relieved to see her, he wants her and his children back, but she has her conditions—the pyramid must go, for one. And he must respect his kids and her, or she'll leave again and go back to her hideout.

It's not easy for Cha to accept, and I appreciate the way the drama handles his reluctant growth. Change is never easy, even when we want it, and Cha continues to slip into his old habits and statements, to let his worldview narrow again, but his wife is a steady rock, leaning in to whisper *hideout* into his ear when he looks like he might start up on the kids again. Ultimately, Cha realizes that having his family in his life, having actual relationships with them, is more important than his long-dead ambitions for the Blue House, and it's really cute to see him spending time with his daughter, donning a frilly apron and dancing as they prepare dinner together.

As someone who clung so tightly to her literary ambitions and refused to entertain any other way to live my life, I recognize that it's really hard to let go of your worldview and of your ideas of success, especially when those ideas have been ground into you your whole life. When Cha first finds out that Seri lied about school, I felt for him, even when he is being an asshole and saying shit he shouldn't. I don't condone violence, but I even felt for him when he slaps Seri out of the sheer shock of her lie. It might sound inconsequential to any rational person, but I understand the extreme pressure Korean culture places on education—I don't agree with it, but I understand it, so the total shock of losing that makes sense. As someone who has told a very similar lie, who has done to her parents what Seri did to hers, I very much felt for them, and, as someone who grew up with faith, then lost it in her early thirties, I know how disorienting it is to lose a foundational belief in your life.

W hen Tablo asks what it means for him to have won, I wonder that, too. Yes, he's alive and well now, and he's still making music, and he's touring and doing cool collabs with other artists and sharing his story with the world. He's still successful. His kid is now a teenager, and his wife has published a book of essays. He is a hugely respected musician in the Korean music industry.

What was the price, though? And when does the price become too high? Those lost early years when Haru was a baby, years parents understand are precious and so fleeting? The blow to his mental health for years and the uncertainty of not knowing whether he would have a career again? The loss of his father, whose health was impacted by these people online who thought they could say whatever they wanted, who *were* able to say whatever they wanted without consequence?

And this isn't just a question relegated to fame—why do so many parents place so much pressure on their young children instead of just loving and supporting them? Why do we strive so much for these goals and ambitions?

We hear stories from creative young Asians of unsupportive parents all the time, making jokes of the stereotypes that we are expected to become doctors or lawyers and that's it, those are the only options we were given by our parents. We mock it constantly (because what low-hanging fruit it is!), but, for my generation, I think it's understandable. My parents' generation was born and grew up in poverty-stricken Korea under military dictatorships. My father spent more time going to demonstrations during university than in class. My mother didn't have a toilet that flushed until she immigrated to the United States when she was ten; before then, she had to walk out to the outhouse with newspaper in her hand to use as toilet paper. The only reason my father's sisters were educated and sent to Seoul was that my oldest aunt was the smartest student in her village. Korea didn't have much when my parents' generation was young, and education was their sole way out of a difficult life, farming land or working in a factory. The stability of a white-collar, highly educated profession like a doctor or a lawyer: that wasn't something to dismiss or look down on.

The easy thing is to lean into the stereotype of Asian immigrant parents as obsessed with education and being harsh and unloving, but I'm tired of that narrative. It isn't that I subscribe to the sentimentalized fantasy of parents only wanting their kids to be happy—I don't really think it's about *happiness*, per se—but I do believe that what parents generally want is to know that their kids are going to be all right. Their kids aren't going to struggle like they did. Their kids aren't going to have to spend long hours doing manual work in the hopes of giving their families a better life. Their kids aren't going to have to flee their home countries for more stable dreams.

Even when it comes to Cha placing his Blue House ambitions on his sons, when you come from a world where that kind of ambition on its own was not allowed to you because you were born into the wrong family, it makes sense. It's misguided and wrong, but it is explainable.

And maybe that's the other thing about *SKY Castle*—I understand that we all live in a world where so much is beyond our control. Korea, unfortunately, is a society where academics matter and can very much shape the trajectory of your life. When you believe that your children's place in life is absolutely dependent upon attending a specific school, you believe that loving your children means putting them through hell, even if they're unhappy and stressed and have no sense of self or identity outside of studying. You're a good parent because you're thinking of your child's future.

Woo expresses as much to her husband. Their son is in middle school and doesn't care about studying, but she knows she should be pushing him, enrolling him in hagwons, and drilling into him the need to study and get good grades and go to medical school. He hates all the pressure, though, to the point that he runs away from home, which finally softens his mother. She understands she needs to push him if he doesn't want to be left behind in cutthroat Korean society, but, by the end of the drama, she's fully caved, acknowledging that he doesn't have to go to a specialized high school so he can go to med school—it's okay for him to live life in the middle.

She still frets, though. High school is going to be competitive and stressful, and part of her still can't let go of those academic pressures, but she concedes, saying, "I heard from somewhere that, even in that stressful environment, kids who are loved and supported by their parents are okay."

She hugs her son and tells him she loves him. I'm relieved that she comes to this realization when he is still young, before he's been fully traumatized and abused, and I think that this is what I wish the viewers of *SKY Castle* would take away from it—that parents should be soft spaces of comfort and safety. The world puts enough pressure on us; it doesn't need to come from the people who love us, too; and, oh, how lucky I have been to have the parents I have.

재중 JAEJOONG

Jaejoong is the idol I carry with me.

My online ID on most platforms is 쫑이 (jjoongie), which comes from 재중이 (jaejoongie), as it becomes 중이 (joongie), then 쫑이 (jjoongie). When TVXQ debuted from SM Entertainment in 2003 with "Hug," I was immediately drawn to Jaejoong in the music video because he's just so *pretty*, with his long, tousled hair, giant eyes, and pouty lips. I didn't even really take in how ridiculous and creepy the lyrics are—하루만 니방의 침대가 되고싶어 (*for one day, I want to become the bed in your room*)—because he sounds so good with that light husk in his voice and I'm just so enchanted.

Jaejoong is the flower boy of TVXQ, and, for several years, he sports a shaggy cut, circle lenses, and moody pouts. I find him the most alluring during TVXQ's *Rising Sun* (2005) days, when he is his prettiest with his mullet, lean musculature, and most feminine appearance. He bulks up more in subsequent albums, shows off his washboard abs more often, and, eventually, the circle lenses become too much for me, as Jaejoong starts to look a little like an alien.

In 2009, Jaejoong, along with fellow members Junsu and Yoochun, sues SM to terminate their contract, shedding light on what would come to be known as slave contracts. Their contract length reportedly was thirteen years, and the boys had had no say in their intense, exhausting schedules and received dismal pay (allegedly, roughly $150,000 per member in a year). The lawsuit is settled in 2012, the three members released from their contracts and going on to form their own trio, JYJ, before each going their own way, Junsu into musical theater, Yoochun into acting, Jaejoong into a mix of acting and singing.

I stop following Jaejoong as he embarks on a solo career, though I do think about him occasionally because I can't *not*—I've taken my online ID from him, so I think of him every time I share my Tumblr or Instagram or Twitter with someone, sign up for whatever new social media platform is coming into vogue even though I know I'll never actually use it (hello, Snapchat and TikTok), and have to answer the number-one question I'm asked, *What should I call you? Nana? Giaae? Jjoongie?*

In 2023, he launches a new YouTube show (because, in 2023, everyone has a YouTube show) called 재친구 (*JaeChinGoo*), and I'm reminded of how much I missed him, with his wacky humor and his general lack of seriousness that belied his charismatic, sultry stage persona. I missed TVXQ more than I cared to admit when

they split up; Yunho and Changmin stayed with SM and continued the band as a two-member unit, though I never listened to
them again. TVXQ had sold the concept that they were a family,
a tight group with an unbreakable bond, and I know I wasn't the
only fan who bought into it. The five members had great chemistry, and their vocals fit together beautifully, especially in a K-pop
landscape where big voices weren't the focus, and they were hilarious on variety shows, each having his own personality.

Jaejoong, in particular, was so 4D in character, weird and spacey
as if he existed in the fourth dimension instead of the third like
all other "normal" people, and he had a difficult time keeping a
straight face, often collapsing in laughter, his hand covering his
mouth as he crumpled because he laughed with his whole body. All
this nostalgia comes flooding over me as I watch him on *JaeChin-
Goo*, still so all over the place and chaotic as he cooks a meal
to share with his guest, whose identity he actually doesn't know
because guests are invited by the staff. He's not a very good host
if you want a host who is On Top of It, but he exudes warmth,
charisma, and ease—and, as I watch him flail around and engage
casually, easily, with his guests, who range from idols to actors to
musicians, many of them veterans in Korean entertainment, I'm
reminded of the mid-2000s, when I loved him and wanted to be
his twin and took on a riff of his name as my online ID. We're
only two months apart in age, after all, and neither of us really
takes anything seriously, and we both love to cook, though he
really needs to cut down on how much sugar and MSG he puts in
his food. We'd probably fight a lot over that.

05
아이유 IU
Yellow C-A-R-D
이 선 넘으면 *If You Cross This Line,*
침범이야 *You're Encroaching*
IU, "삐삐" (BBIBBI)
BBIBBI, 2024

As far as I'm concerned, IU (birth name 이지은 [Lee Jieun]) is the closest to a perfect human being we are getting in this world. She's impossibly beautiful, and she can sing and act equally well, and she has great stage presence, *and* she has a positive reputation.

Currently managed by EDAM Entertainment, which was established specifically for her by Kakao M in 2020, IU debuted in 2008 from LOEN Entertainment at age fifteen. Her road to debut was difficult—her family had gone through financially turbulent times when she was young, so she lived with her grandmother, away from her parents, for a period. She was rejected more than twenty times from auditions, and, when she finally made it and debuted to a decent amount of attention as a singer-songwriter, her debut song, "미아" (Lost Child) on Lost and Found (2008), was considered too dark and moody for Korea, and the mini-album did poorly. She had to redo her image and come back with more cutesy, digestible pop that slotted her into the mainstream.

IU has since gone on to become a mega-popular, mega-talented artist. She contributes to writing and producing her music, she acts, and she models, racking up major advertisements and establishing herself as a CF queen. She's beautiful and successful and still so young, just thirty in 2023. When I look at her, I often think, *Wow, what's it like to be her?*—but even IU isn't free from the pressures of impossible beauty standards. For five days in the early 2010s, in the lead-up to a comeback, IU infamously ate an apple for breakfast, two sweet potatoes for lunch, a protein shake for dinner, all to lose five kilograms, roughly eleven pounds.

— — —

was born and raised in the United States and have been to Korea a total of four times. The first time I visited, it was December 1997, and I was in middle school, still innocent and unaware that I existed in a body. My family stayed for roughly two weeks, and it was the freest I felt in Korea because it was before the body-shaming started.

The second time hardly counts because it was just a few days, for my paternal grandfather's funeral, but the third time was a disaster.

It was summer 2012. I was on my first solo international trip after graduating with my BA and had just spent three weeks backpacking around Japan, and it was my first time back in Seoul since December 2001. This was also my first summer in Korea, in the stifling humidity that was so different from the dry heat I was accustomed to in suburban Los Angeles.

It was my first time back since the body-shaming had started.

I am not thin and never have been, though my body is fairly average by American standards. However, as a child of 1.5-generation immigrants who was raised in a predominantly Korean community, I was held to Korean standards, and beauty was no exception. Korean beauty standards start with thinness, and, because I wasn't thin, I couldn't be pretty, nor could I amount to much as a human being. For over fifteen years, the message was drilled into me—I had to lose weight. I was an embarrassment otherwise and would remain so until I could bring my body in line. My weight was a direct reflection of my character, and no one would hire me or date me or want to be my friend because I was a Miss Piggy, and who wanted to be around someone who was so lazy and undisciplined?

I knew my body wasn't "right"; it didn't look like the bodies of the K-pop idols and Korean actresses I'd grown up admiring. As an adolescent, I marveled over their double-lidded eyes and pale skin and envied them for their bodies, their thin arms and legs and tiny waists. As shame seeped into my brain and started breaking me down, I internalized this envy, fully accepting that my inability to whittle myself down to thinness was a moral failing.

By 2012, I had already endured twelve years of this. The main reason I wanted to visit Korea again was to see my favorite band, Nell, perform at a rock festival, so I tried not to think about the

Body Thing, even as I was hugely anxious about it. I knew how vicious and, frankly, rude Koreans could be. Once, as friends and I were eating samgyupsahl at Honey Pig in LA's Koreatown, the ajumma cooking our meat freely offered me dieting advice as she cut our pork belly into bite-size pieces. I wish this had been an isolated occurrence.

Korea was so much worse than I had anticipated. Everywhere around me were women who looked like me but thin and put together, in perfect makeup and styled outfits and coiffed hair, even in July humidity. They were pretty in the way that yeonaein are, their faces touched up, their ssangapool perfect, V-lines sharp, cheeks plump and filled out. Seoul—at least in her trendy neighborhoods—was filled with the type of women I'd seen only through my phone and computer screen.

In Korea, though, I wasn't just watching them; they were watching me. As I went up escalators, I'd catch ajummas going down and giving me the up-and-down and shaking their heads. I'd stand on the subway and feel people's eyes on me. I'm five-foot-eight, taller than your average Korean woman, and I already stood out as a gyopo, a Korean American, from the clothes I wore, my tanned skin, and my makeupless face. In the suffocating humidity and heat, sweat rolled off me constantly, making me feel even more self-conscious as the thin Korean women around me didn't seem to sweat at all.

I didn't want to eat anywhere or be visible in any way. I had meant to stay in Korea for three weeks and do some traveling outside of Seoul, but, after ten days, after I had gone to the rock festival and heard Nell live, I fled the country.

— — —

Pop culture is often seen as low-brow, the realm of teenage girls and, if you loop in K-dramas, silly housewives and young adults. That's a whole discussion in and of itself, but I often think that one reason for this insistence on downplaying the influence of pop culture is that it lets people, whether they are producers, writers, media executives, or anyone involved in the industry, off the hook for how they contribute to perpetuating toxic perspectives on body image, gender, and overt politics. It's possible to disavow responsibility for propaganda only when you don't acknowledge the medium of education as consequential.

(It particularly makes me cranky when Christians discount media and novels and pop, as if Christ himself, with his parables, didn't recognize the power of storytelling.)

There's a fair amount of Korean media that harps on weight as a bad thing, focusing on how shedding weight transforms an overweight female character into someone worth acknowledging, and one of the most formative K-dramas of my youth was 내 이름은 김삼순 (*My Name Is Kim Samsoon*), which aired on MBC in 2005. The drama starred Kim Sunah as the titular lead, Kim Samsoon, the youngest of three girls who was impulsively named Samsoon by her paternal grandfather in exasperation at having three granddaughters and no grandsons. Samsoon is an old-fashioned generic name—삼 for three, 순 for girl—and she feels she is the unlucky one of her sisters, the least successful, single, and chubby.

Kim Sunah made headlines for gaining weight for the role. When the drama aired, I expected to see an overweight woman, but she was just, well, average, maybe a little chubby by Korean standards, but even then, barely so. Her face was a little round, and maybe her arms were a little soft, her stomach not concave—

but the way the drama loved to call attention to her body and her weight made it seem like she was horrifically obese.

Twenty years later, I don't actually remember how I watched *Kim Samsoon*. This was after the days of going to the video store at the Korean market every weekend to pick up VHS tapes but before the days of streaming, before Netflix and DramaFever and Viki. I can't remember if *Kim Samsoon* aired during the time of BitTorrent or the days when people would cut up video files and upload the pieces to sites like MediaFire for viewers like me to download individually and then stitch together using an app like WinRAR. I don't think I watched *Kim Samsoon* on Dailymotion or Vimeo, but somehow I watched it every week, getting my hands on the episodes the day after they aired in Korea, lucky that I understood Korean so I didn't have to wait additional days for fans to provide subtitles.

Kim Samsoon hit two of my sore spots—first, that I was actually overweight, and second, that I, too, would have loved to be a pâtissier, like Samsoon. I loved food, and I loved baking, and I was bigger than Samsoon was. If Kim Sunah was seen as frumpy and huge for gaining a measly fifteen pounds for the role, what hope did I have?

■ ■ ■

IU herself starred in a drama as the fat girl who gets skinny and wins her love interest. In *Dream High* (KBS, 2011), Kim Pilsook is a gifted singer with perfect pitch, but she'll never actually become an idol or a performing artist because she's fat. She actually shows up to the audition for Kirin Arts High School in the sushi mascot costume of her parents' restaurant to hide her appearance, and, when she goes to school on orientation day, a boy holds up her plus-size skirt and makes a joke about it. She's mortified, but she can't hide anymore. She's also instantly demoted to the basic classroom because it doesn't matter that she has a beautiful voice, good technique, and perfect pitch—her body means she will never debut.

We know the story, though—the girl gets motivation to lose weight because she has a crush on a boy. The boy (Jason) is kind to her, and *Dream High* takes care not to paint her love interest as a superficial asshole. When Pilsook finally works up the determination to lose weight and tells Jason, he encourages her. Jason has been selected by Top Entertainment to debut and will be going off with the other chosen students to train for two hundred days, so that will be the deadline. He agrees that, if she successfully loses weight in that time, he will hear her love confession.

This is portrayed as a kindness on Jason's part. Shortly before this, Pilsook had been chosen to sing the jingle for a CF, excitedly telling her parents that her voice will appear on television. Unknown to her, though, she was providing the voice for Ria, a pretty girl who had also been scouted alongside Jason for her visuals even though she couldn't sing. Pilsook obviously wasn't on set when the CF was recorded, but Jason was and overheard Ria reassure the producer that no one would know that the voice wasn't hers. The voice belonged to a girl named Pilsook, and Pilsook would never debut because she's too fat. Ria's secret would be safe.

Hilariously or not, this is the very theme of another film, 미녀는 괴로워 (*200 Pounds Beauty*), released in 2006, starring actress Kim Ah Joong in the role of an overweight singer who provides the actual voice of an idol—like, she sings in a little room behind the stage, watching videos of the idol *on* the stage who is lip-synching along as if the voice the audience hears is hers. (Korean media went through a stage where live performance was required to appear on major music shows.) During one performance, Kim's character jumps along with the idol and breaks the platform she's standing on. As she realizes she'll never win the attention of her love interest, she leaves, undergoes full-body plastic surgery, and spends months in isolation, exercising and dieting, until she emerges, thin and beautiful, to entrance the world with her visuals—and her voice, I suppose.

This whole narrative of a fat girl losing weight to become beautiful and realize her potential is irritating in all contexts, but it particularly annoys me in Korean media. In *Kim Samsoon*, Kim Sunah isn't even *fat*, and, in *Dream High*, the whole thing seems even more ludicrous because IU is beautiful—we all know it—and the fat version of Pilsook looks so *sad*, her potential literally saddled with her weight. IU checks off all the features desired by Koreans—big double-lidded eyes, a straight nose, a narrow jawline—without having a generic face, and she isn't only pretty but also multitalented. She's a unique K-pop star, one who's managed to break out of the mold and solidify herself as a singular talent with global fame and popularity.

Since adolescence, I've looked at Korean idols and actresses like IU—and, later, diasporic Asian fashion and lifestyle influencers and YouTubers—with wonderment. Life must be so easy for girls with faces and bodies like theirs. The world must just open up for them, and it must be so much easier to stay skinny when you're already skinny, to love to eat the "right" foods and enjoy working out for hours a day.

As I got older, that morphed into a reluctant admiration of their diets and workouts, and I went so far as to begrudge them the discipline an eating disorder necessitates because I never had that willpower. In my darkest periods, I wished I could starve myself down, but I loved food too much to give it up. Food was too interesting, even in my adolescence and early young adulthood—it was one of the very few things that could get through the darkness in my depressive brain and light a tiny spark. Back then, I hated myself for it—I wanted to be like K-pop stars like IU, to be able to eat as little as they did, work my body to the brink of breakdown, and finally be thin and pretty. I just didn't have the perseverance these girls did, and wasn't that what was wrong with me?

— — —

U, of course, isn't the only K-pop star to go on a dangerous diet, and public reaction to these diets is performative horror—these diets aren't safe; they're not healthy! However, if you search on YouTube, you'll find numerous videos of young women trying "the IU diet." It's taken as a challenge, and, though many of the videos carry disclaimers that the diet is unhealthy, the YouTuber isn't advocating that anyone actually try it, et cetera, the existence of the videos alone betrays how we generally think about bodies. If you can make it all the way through the challenge, you're disciplined. You're good because thin is good, even if it is achieved through unhealthy means, and fat—or even average—is bad.

This is enforced, again, by what we're taught in media. Halfway into Dream High, Pilsook commits to losing thirty kilograms (over sixty-five pounds) in two hundred days. She seeks the advice of one of the teachers at Kirin, and Maeng-ssaem is impressed, saying, "Appearance is skill. Because, if you try, you can change it. In the world, there are no ugly women, just lazy ones."

Starting that very day, all Pilsook has to do is be diligent, starting with how she eats. Maeng-ssaem breaks down Pilsook's new meal plan pithily: in the morning, eat like a queen—rice, soup, banchan. For lunch, eat like a commoner—a hard-boiled egg, half an apple, a salad. For dinner, eat like a beggar—a sweet potato with milk.

For exercise, Pilsook should jump rope for thirty minutes every day. At Pilsook's weight, she can burn two hundred kilocalories each time—and, with that advice, we're off on a montage of Pilsook on her diet, jumping rope, eating sweet potatoes, and sticking the cap from the day's bottle of milk to a calendar that counts down the promised two hundred days.

To this day, I can't decide if it's inspirational or not, though that kind of discipline feels very Korean, the kind that we would call 독하다—intense or poisonous (독 is poison)—for how extreme and singularly focused it is. I've always been stubborn as hell, but I could never muster up that kind of intense willpower; instead of avoiding food, I started baking in high school. At the time, it was something my Sunday school classmates and I liked to do, so I didn't think much of my interest in food, never mind that I rapidly deviated from the usual cookie baking to tackle French macarons, opera cake, and palmiers. At the same time, I spent all of high school on one kind of diet or another, going to the gym every night to log my requisite hour of cardio and weight machines. Baking was an acceptable hobby only because it was church-centered, not for my personal enjoyment. I only allowed myself to taste, taking just a bite or two of what I'd made.

When I went to college, I had to learn to structure my life, which felt impossible with what I know now to be an ADHD brain. Away from family and the set schedule of high school, depressed and terrified of socializing, I gained weight—a lot of it. This was additionally distressing because I had lost a significant amount of weight the summer before my senior year of high school, spending months going to my local Jenny Craig every Saturday to get weighed, chat with my counselor, and pick my food for the week. While my family ate home-cooked meals, I microwaved my daily selections, supplementing them with the acceptable salads and low-calorie dressings (also provided by Jenny Craig). I was the thinnest I've ever been in my life, the thinnest I'll ever be, the weight my parents still reference as preferable today.

Unfortunately, all it took was a few months at university to gain back all the weight I'd lost and more, and, for the next ten years, I constantly battled my weight. I restricted, counted calories, kept daily food logs of everything I'd eaten. I worked out to net a daily intake of 1,200 calories. I cooked a lot of chicken breasts in the blandest way possible, ate a lot of salads, and obsessed over everything I would eat on "cheat days"—burgers, Korean fried chicken, toast. I marinated in self-loathing every time I fell off the diet bandwagon, which happened too often too quickly. I detoxed, starting by drinking juices then nothing but water, feeling great as the water weight dropped out of me and my face started looking lean and my tongue got furry and my skin got super soft as the "toxins" seeped out of me. I'd walk miles from campus to my apartment because, yes, I did genuinely love walking and wasn't it nice that there was a workout I could do without really thinking about it, even if it was in the nineties in Southern California and the sun was directly overhead?

All my efforts to diet came to nothing, though. I never was able to keep any weight off because I always came back to food—I loved food. I wanted it too much to eat only an apple, two sweet potatoes, and a protein shake a day, but I wished I had the discipline to stick to something so intense. If I must love food, I wished I could at least have the ability to make myself throw up before the food could turn into calories, into fat, into weight.

Because, if appearance was a skill, I didn't have it, and maybe I wasn't an ugly woman, but I was a lazy one. Weren't ugliness and laziness the same thing?

— — —

When you fail to manage your body in a communal culture like Korea's, it becomes the moral task of the people around you to bring your body in line. I was always told that the criticism of my body was done out of love, and, even now, I don't doubt that people's intentions fundamentally came from a good place. Their actions were horribly misguided and destructive, of course, but there wasn't necessarily malice behind the shaming, not from the people who loved me, at least. It wasn't their fault the world was cruel, that, as a girl in a bigger body, I would be ostracized and rejected for how I looked.

My trip to Korea in 2012 verified everything I'd been told for years. As I tried to hide my body, to press myself into corners on the subway and in cafés and restaurants, I kept thinking that my weight, my ugliness, really must be my fault. If only I could control what I ate, if only I could try harder and go without delicious things for a while, then maybe I could fix myself.

I know there's only so much I can say about how anti-fat society is. I might be fat when it comes to Korean beauty standards, but, according to US medical standards, I am considered overweight, on the tipping point of obese. I'm five-foot-eight and wear a size 12 to

14. I can shop in your average store. I struggle with finding bras, but that's a different story altogether. I sit in an airplane seat fine, and my body doesn't impede me from existing out in the world.

Fat-shaming is a real thing, and fat people deal with a tremendous amount of stigma every day. I do not claim to represent that experience because it is not mine, and for me to do so would not be right.

What I can speak to, though, are body-shaming and dysmorphia. In my lived experience, neither of those really has to do with your actual, physical body but more with how you are perceived according to society's standards of beauty—and how you perceive yourself. My community told me that I was too big to amount to anything, and I believed that because I could see that my body was different from the bodies of other Korean girls, whether idols or not. My stomach bulges and forms rolls when I sit. My thighs jiggle when I walk, and my upper arms are soft and make me look even wider than my broad shoulders already make me look. My face isn't round like the faces of K-pop stars who get fillers but in a way that makes me look like an overstuffed mandu.

I was even told that I walked funny because of my weight, my toes pointing outward and making it look like I was slapping my big feet out in an unseemly way—so I changed the way I walked and tried never to be seen running and wore a lot of black and baggy jeans and sweatshirts even in the Valley's hundred-plus-degree summers. I was told I looked gross and disgusting, so I started hiding, stopped socializing, and told myself for years that I was an introvert and a misanthrope who just needed her books and K-pop. I believed everything I was being told about my body, about myself.

And then there was this: in middle school, when I was obsessed with H.O.T., my church youth group was also into K-pop, so we'd often end fellowship nights by playing performances recorded on VHS tapes and trying to replicate their choreography. Very few of us were any good at it, but the point was to have fun, to laugh and sweat together.

One Sunday night, though, an adult from the Korean congregation pulled me aside and told me harshly that I should stop. I looked like an idiot, and everyone thought I was embarrassing, and they were all laughing at me. I don't know how true that was, if people really were mocking me, but he was someone I trusted and respected, and his words had their desired effect. I stopped dancing, not just that night or at church but for good. I started to feel self-conscious, as if there was something wrong with me, but I didn't know what, exactly—just that something was wrong with me, with my body, and that made me an embarrassment.

The body-shaming started in earnest a year later. It took place on all fronts—from family, from my Korean community, from the media. As I quickly learned, it doesn't matter if you have the right face, the right double-lidded eyes or straight nose or V-line—if you're not thin, you cannot be beautiful, and, if you cannot be beautiful, then, as a woman, what worth do you have?

\- \- \-

For better or for worse, I was never able to whittle myself down, and trying to heal my relationship with food and stop thinking of it as "right" or "wrong" has been a process. Every year, it seems to be something different—in 2016, I made Asian sponge cakes ad nauseum while writing a blog that blended food writing and book criticism. In 2017, I started making pasta by hand; 2018 passed as a blur because I had a new puppy to feed and love and train; and, in 2019, there was Momofuku Kāwi with the chef's inventive takes on Korean food. Throughout 2020, when COVID-19 kept us in our homes, I took on various cooking projects to keep me balanced and busy, re-creating Momofuku's take on bing, rolling lots of kimbap, even milling my own rice flour to try making garaeddeok.

I can't point to an exact moment when I stopped putting so much pressure on myself about my body. It helped to move away from Los Angeles in 2012, across the country to Brooklyn, putting a literal country between me and the source of my trauma. It helped to start finding a community of my own, cobbled together from people I met at Redeemer (when I was still going to church) and people I met via the book community online. It helped that I started having to take care of myself, seeing a psychiatrist, getting on an antidepressant, and meeting with a therapist. It helped that I got a puppy who taught me that I have a deeper capacity for love and joy than I'd thought. It helped that I was able to become financially independent and buy clothes I wanted and try to become a person I liked.

As my relationship with food normalized, I started to find myself. Healing doesn't mean that I necessarily love myself or am happy with my body as it is. Even today, years into my "healing journey," every time I walk into a grocery store or a restaurant, every time I make a choice about what I put into my mouth, I confront the same demons. When I look at myself in the mirror, I'm filled with that familiar self-hatred and disgust. I make conscious decisions not to look at nutrition labels or think about calories, and I grapple with the softness clinging to my face and body, my fluctuating weight, the jiggles in my upper arms.

I still look at K-pop idols like IU and wonder what it's like to be like them, to be thin and pretty. I look at Suga in shorts and wonder how I would feel standing next to him, my thighs and calves probably twice the size of his. I don't want to date anyone shorter than I am because I'm already big-boned and will probably be, well, bigger, so I also don't want to be taller, though this is moot because I'm in my late thirties and still haven't dated. To be honest, the idea of being intimate with someone, getting physical, and letting someone see and touch my body—that is a level of healing I have yet to reach. When I was in high school and active in youth group, my body insulated me from purity culture; I was considered unable to be tempted by boys and sex and desire because, unlike my thin friends, I existed in a body that wasn't desirable, anyway. I have not yet been able to shed the belief that that is true, especially when it seems to be verified by the fact that no one has expressed a romantic or sexual interest in me in my almost four decades of being alive.

Whenever I talk about body-shaming, though, I am careful. I didn't call this trauma until, maybe, four years ago when Stephanie Foo's *What My Bones Know* was published, and I recognized some fundamental commonalities in our experiences. Foo's memoir blends journalism with personal writing to explore complex post-traumatic stress disorder, which stemmed from being physically and emotionally abused by her parents since childhood. My parents neither abused nor assaulted me, but there was a lot I recognized in her post-traumatic self, in her deeply negative self-perception, in the ways she wrapped herself in work as a way of hiding from herself, in her dysregulated emotions. I resonated with her struggle to heal and learn to become a functioning social person in the world, able to handle conflict without imploding, to protect and cherish herself, and to *accept* love.

Even now, I think "abuse" is such a strong word to attach to body-shaming, even though that is what body-shaming is. If I had connected the dots ten years ago, I might have embraced it wholeheartedly because I was still so angry then, so furious and confused and broken, so eager to have a label for what I'd experienced and how I felt.

The anger may have faded to the background of my life, but the effects of trauma are ever present. I grapple, daily, with self-loathing, with looking myself in the eye in the mirror and not cringing. I struggle with maintaining a sense of worth, with believing that friends are friends because they like me and not because they pity me, with being okay as a human existing in a physical body. I went back to Korea in spring 2023 and was more terrified than excited because it was Koreans who had told me over and over and over again that I would be worth nothing if I couldn't make myself thin.

It lives on in my writing—I cannot tell stories of myself, be vulnerable about myself, without talking about shaming, about trauma, about rage, because body-shaming shattered the very foundation of who I am. I can't tell you about my love for K-pop without talking about how it reinforced the crap about my body I was hearing every day. I can't tell you about my love for food, even though it was a much-needed escape, without telling you how I blocked myself off from love for over a decade, and I can't tell you about my need to write without sharing how writing was the only thing that gave me a sense of confidence, of purpose, so much that I can no longer love it or find joy in it because I resent it. There are people in my life who tell me I should "get over it," but, when the center of your life is blown out by trauma, there is no defining yourself or seeing the world without it, even when the anger has burned out.

The anger does, at least for me, burn out—or maybe it's more accurate to say that a part of healing is processing that anger and learning to move past it. Sure, the trauma is still a part of my life, and I struggle daily with self-loathing and resentment, but I no longer hate myself. I also no longer hate or resent the people who did this to me.

I don't think I'm grotesque or monstrous anymore, though I do still think I'm lazy—I still can't be bothered with makeup and barely blow-dry my hair. I no longer believe I am undeserving of love and have built myself small communities of friends who are good people, who make me want to show up for them, who do not talk about diets or restrict or count calories but approach food in a more balanced, thoughtful way.

In *Dream High*, Pilsook undergoes a dramatic transformation, emerging from her two hundred days thin and beautiful. The drama doesn't leave things there, though—Pilsook's weight comes back over and over again, as does her fear of gaining the weight back, to the point that, when she's hospitalized for hepatitis B, she eats some samgyupsahl her mother sneaks into the hospital, gains weight, and bundles up in a coat to jump rope outside in winter. As she gets ready to debut, her past comes to haunt her when TV producers unearth photos of her during her "fat days," congratulating her on her discipline. They expect her to be ashamed of who she was, but Pilsook has a different perspective—she doesn't want to hide her past self.

When her love interest gently suggests that she delete her past photos from her mini-home page, Pilsook says, "I should, right? But that's kind of disappointing. To be embarrassed of and erase pictures from those days. Even when I was eighty-two kilograms [about 180 pounds], I was pretty happy. I got into Kirin Arts High, stood on a stage for the first time, met a lot of good friends—and met you, too. But, when people look at those photos, they'll say I'm disgusting and point fingers at me, won't they? For me, it was a happy period, but I'm afraid I'll start hating myself from then, too."

At first, I wished I had that perspective, but the years I was body-shamed were the loneliest years of my life. I tried to hide myself away, and I never really developed as a social human being, and it's only in the last seven years that I've started to emerge from that, to piece myself together and make an effort not to hate myself. It's been a painful journey to break down the barriers I'd built to protect myself against the messages I received and my fear of potential rejection. I told myself so many lies, convincing myself that I was a misanthrope and an introvert, when the truth is that I love people and enjoy being around people and want people to like me. In some ways, the hunger from dieting and restricting and physical self-loathing was easier than making myself vulnerable and open to the world. Trying to whittle my body down was a physical goal; I could attach numbers to it; I could work toward it. Dealing with the emotional hunger underneath, though, with the want that lay beneath it all—that was and continues to be more painful.

Much like Pilsook, though, I have also arrived at a place where I wouldn't want to erase my past self. Even if those years weren't happy years for me, they are still *mine*.

And then there is the truth that erasing them would also erase the time and work I have put into becoming who I am today, and it would undo the work my family and community have done to make our relationships better. There is still a lot of work to do on all our ends, but, over the last seven years, I think it's fair to say that we have all tried as best as we could, and we have, yes, come so far.

— — —

I still hate cauliflower, though.

It has nothing to do with the vegetable itself but what it represents to me—a certain waiflike woman who eats cauliflower rice and cauliflower pizza because the worst thing that could happen to her is that she eat a carb and gain weight. I recognize cognitively that this isn't necessarily fair of me (to the cauliflower), but it's an association that's burrowed deep in my brain.

I have largely removed myself from the toxic world of diet culture, but it alarms me constantly how we've so normalized disordered eating. Today, people hide it more deftly behind "health and wellness" and personal choice, claiming they want to lose weight for themselves, they want to gain muscle, they want to do this for their health—health, health, health!—when what they're really doing is restricting and attaching moral values to different types of food.

As a society, we tend to glamorize eating disorders and disordered eating because we do still, at our core, value thinness. It's normal for celebrities to share their frankly insane-sounding diets and workout regimes, the lengths to which they will go to stay thin, and, for plebeians, we mask any disordered eating behind wanting to be "healthy" and "fit." It's hard to criticize someone who wants to diet and work out because she claims to want it for herself, whether for "health" or aesthetic reasons, and there's often no examining why we have ideas of what "looks good" or who, exactly, is deciding that these beauty standards are what are desirable.

In 2014, IU appears on *Healing Camp*. She opens up about struggling with an eating disorder during a period in her life when she became consumed by anxiety and fear that all her present popularity and success would be taken from her. To cope, she would binge eat, then throw everything up. She passed those days sleeping, eating, throwing up.

Realizing that she was in a bad place, IU got treatment, and she says she's doing better now, though her disorder hasn't gone away entirely. Eating is still how she manages stress. She's made changes, though, trying to be healthier about her eating choices and exercise habits. She's still thin—she was always naturally thin—but now she looks healthier and happier with herself.

To be honest, I've never quite known what to do when thin pretty girls share stories of their own struggles with body image because I'm not sure if I find it relatable or not. At the end of the day, they're still thin and pretty, and I'm still jiggly and pudgy and not pretty, but I suppose I appreciate the honesty and hope that the more open and genuine women are willing to be about these issues, the more we can strip unreasonable beauty standards of their power.

As for me, my relationship with food is still complicated and disordered, and I still don't look in the mirror and like what I see. I still look at K-pop stars like IU and wonder what it's like to be thin and beautiful, even knowing the struggles she herself has with her body and self-image, and maybe this isn't the ending someone wants to hear, but it's the only true one I have to offer. Shame and dysmorphia don't just go away overnight, and they take daily effort to manage, but they *can* be inoculated against.

In 2021, IU releases the song "Celebrity" as the prerelease to her fifth studio album, *Lilac*. In the chorus, she sings,

왼손으로 그린 별 하나	*A star drawn with a left hand—*
보이니 그 유일함이	*Can you see? That uniqueness,*
얼마나 아름다운지 말야	*How wonderful it is.*

As part of her promotion for the single, IU shares a video showing her makeupless face and non-glammed-up self and launches the "Celebrity Challenge," encouraging listeners to share videos of their natural selves behind their cultivated social media images. Other celebrities participate in the challenge, including actor Kim Soohyun, Girls' Generation's Yoona, and Red Velvet's Yeri, and IU takes the time to view and comment on posts by fans who use the hashtag. There's a sweet earnestness to her attempt to spread positivity and celebrate people's individuality with so many difficult things happening in the world, and it reminds me that being pretty and successful doesn't make you immune to being a woman in the world with immense pressure to look "right" and act "right." I'd love to live in a world where we've discarded these unrealistic, impossible standards, and *that* feels like an impossible dream—but who knows? There is a current trend in Korea where women are throwing out their makeup and cutting their hair short in protest of Korea's rigid standards. I don't expect all women to do so (and neither do I *want* all women to feel like they must), but maybe that's the more realistic world to aspire to, one that allows for difference and celebrates beauty in all shapes and forms, where even those of us who look like crooked stars can have the room to shine.

06

소녀시대 GIRLS' GENERATION

- - - - - - - - - - - - - - - - -

소원을 말해봐 *Tell Me Your Wish*
소녀시대, "Genie"
Genie, 2009

01

소녀시대 (Girls' Generation) was one of *the* girl groups, if not *the* girl group, of second-generation K-pop. They debuted from SM Entertainment in 2007 with nine members, and I couldn't stand them, thinking they were so fake and manufactured with their saccharine-sweet image, freakishly synchronized choreography, and supposed plastic surgery. I thought Yoona looked vapid, Tiffany like a manipulative fox, and Jessica like a flirt, and I treated them scathingly, mentally accusing them of flirting with labelmates TVXQ and

Super Junior because I was jealous that they got to interact with Jaejoong and Heechul, these nine girls with their long legs and aegyo. Everything about Girls' Generation felt, to me, artificial and manipulative, playing into the kind of demure innocence that Koreans, particularly Korean men, find appealing.

For years, I simmered in this as if my beloved boy bands weren't just as manipulated and manufactured, though, in my defense, thanks to gendered double standards, things *are* different for boys.

When I finally get into Bangtan and their mountain of content in 2022, I feel simultaneous joy and sadness because I know that girl groups are still not allowed the range of expression and respect that Bangtan gets. Girls aren't allowed to be known for their songwriting or producing talents, and they don't get the kind of critical acclaim that lets them be seen as artists. Girls are still expected to show a lot of skin, to display their long, thin legs, to wear heels, short skirts, and pleasant smiles. Girls can only hide in baggy clothing for brief concepts; they must be svelte and show off their figures; and they must be giggly and feminine, even if they are loud and outspoken—being an exception is acceptable as long as it is delivered with an underlying sweetness.

The members of Bangtan don't sexualize themselves. Until they enter what they call "Chapter 2," when they're on hiatus before enlisting in the military, they don't show a lot of skin, their production team going so far as to edit in stickers of their animated characters to cover up any accidentally exposed stomach or back on their self-hosted variety show, *Run BTS!* Where other boy bands go shirtless onstage, as Bangtan becomes more famous, they hardly even show their bare arms. They're praised for writing and producing a lot of their music. They speak out about the difficult parts of fame. They share so much of themselves, recording content with faces bare and puffy from sleep, and they win respect for their authenticity, positivity, and vulnerability.

Girl groups are still not allowed this amount of freedom or self-expression, either by their companies or by the public.

02

Korean culture is a shame-based culture, and it's one that likes to emphasize purity. As someone who grew up in a conservative Christian church in Los Angeles, I tend to view the notion that girls should be pure and innocent through the lens of Western purity culture, an idea that weaves together Christianity and misogyny to enforce double standards on girls. I've long assumed that Christian values were also why Korean society has clung, at least on the surface level, to conservative, gendered, prudish expectations. Sure, both men and women were meant to be chaste, but girls and women were meant to be pure and innocent. For example, it is acceptable for a man to frequent hostess bars or to participate in booking at clubs, which means he points out a woman to the waiter, who then brings her over, sometimes physically grabbing her and forcing her to join the man. It's unseemly for the woman to go along happily (and many women, unsurprisingly, find the practice misogynistic and abusive); she is expected to resist but, still, ultimately go along with it.

While this expectation that girls be innocent likely is inflected with the influence of Christianity in Korea today, historically it's a little more complicated. During the Joseon dynasty (1392 to 1897), Korean society was arranged in a strict hierarchy, with the royal family at the top, the upper-class yangban right below, then the merchant class, then the lower class. Your social status mattered, and women from yangban families were expected to be "pure," hidden away in homes surrounded by walls and, even within those homes, sequestered within the inner chambers, literally 안방 (an-bang) for 안 (inner), 방 (room). Young, unmarried women were called agassi, easily distinguished in public by the long single braids they wore and by the hanbok skirts they carried to cover their heads and shield their faces. Agassi of yangban families didn't go anywhere unaccompanied.

Once girls were married, they put their hair up and became the property of their husbands. Women in the Joseon dynasty, which brought in neo-Confucian principles, including Confucian patriarchy and misogyny, didn't have legal status on their own, couldn't inherit property, and were always tied to a man—their father, then their husband, then, if widowed, their sons. Yangban women weren't formally educated and were not taught the classical Chinese characters that would allow them access to the public sphere.

But then there was another class of women—gisaengs.

Sex work has long been a dominant part of Korean culture—as it has everywhere, given the adage about the world's oldest profession—from gisaengs to sex workers in postwar Korea who were encouraged by the government to have sex with American GIs in order to bring American dollars into the poverty-stricken country. Gisaengs are common characters in historical dramas, portrayed in their colorful hanboks and elaborate hairstyles, often playing the gayageum or serving drinks while flirting and laughing with yangban men. They've also been portrayed as playing active roles in revolutions and rebellions, providing both financial support and physical cover for independence movements, in contrast to yangban women characters who spend their time on fancy embroidery.

Gisaengs, unlike other women in Joseon Korea, were classically literate. They were cultured and, to a degree, educated because they had to converse with yangban men, placing them in a position from which yangban women were excluded, sequestered away in their inner rooms and walled courtyards. Gisaengs sat at an intersection of knowledge (as gisaengs) and invisibility (as women) that made them hiding spots and sources of financial support.

Some might draw lines from gisaengs to idols and entertainers, and there have always been rumors about sexual favors passed between the media elite and entertainment companies. I grew up hearing unsubstantiated claims that companies like SM kept a cadre of trainees who would never debut but would keep media heads happy, providing the double service of offering sexual bribes and keeping the trainees who *would* go on to debut, essentially, clean. I think that the atrocious part of that isn't that the rumors exist but that I would believe there is a degree of truth to them.

That isn't to say that idols are free from harassment—there's a video of Girls' Generation onstage, standing around with other groups as well as people from the broadcasting station. Jessica is standing next to a much older man when she moves away from him abruptly and whispers something to Hyoyeon, who looks over at the man with disgust and puts her arm around Jessica, placing her body between them. We can't know exactly what happened on that stage, but the implication is clear.

Of course, these are just allegations, and there's never anything truly explicit and open about sexual exploitation in entertainment. I feel like we simply take it, to a degree, as inevitable, a byproduct of an industry that dangles fame and stardom in front of the young and ambitious.

But then, in 2009, Jang Jayeon, an actress who had finally gained a foothold when she was cast in the Korean adaptation of *Boys Over Flowers*, the popular Japanese manga, died by suicide. She was twenty-nine years old. In her suicide note, she allegedly wrote about the years of sexual favors she had been forced to provide to media executives, directors, and CEOs for promises of acting roles, supposedly also providing a list of names. Neither the note nor the list was made publicly available, but, for a while after her death, there was some noise around an investigation, and the former head of her management agency was arrested and extradited from Japan to Korea where he was charged with physically abusing Jang (sentenced to four months in prison, one year of probation). Police spent a few months investigating the people allegedly named on her list, but, ultimately, nothing of consequence came of her death.

03

What is considered sexual is also cultural. BoA was in her prime in Asia at the same time that Britney Spears was active in the US, and she was often called the Korean Britney—just more wholesome. While Britney performed in bikinis and showed off her body, BoA was more conservative, more age-appropriate, and she didn't do a "sexy" concept until she released "My Name" as the title track for her fourth album in 2004. The song and choreography were a departure from her usual style, a marked difference from the perky, youthful "Atlantis Princess," the title track of her third album. "My Name" took on a moodier, more sultry tone. BoA still didn't show much skin; she dressed in long, fitted pants and tailored shirts and jackets; but she did show off her bare midriff with a belly button ring. Her hair was pulled back and away from her face instead of in the long layers that had been her default style for years, and her makeup was smokier. She was eighteen.

Similarly, when Girls' Generation debuted, their concept focused on their youth and girlhood—their debut tracks, "다시 만난 세계" (Into the New World) and "소녀시대" (Girls' Generation), were anthemic and hopeful, announcing their entry into, well, the world. The music video for "Into the New World," particularly, introduced the nine members as young, active girls brimming with potential and excitement—each was assigned a hobby, from Seohyun practicing ballet to Tiffany spray-painting a moped pink to Taeyeon and Sooyoung trying to get a plane in the air (seriously). They weren't presented overtly as objects of desire, though of course their innocence would quickly be sexualized, just in the more subtle (and maybe more unsettling) ways preferred by Korea in the late 2000s. Girls' Generation didn't show a whole lot of skin necessarily, but we were always very aware of how they looked. With "Gee," the title track to their second album, *Oh!* (2010), Girls' Generation became iconic for their brightly colored skinny jeans and for the length and shape of their legs, accentuated by the high heels they wore.

All of this tracks with what is typically still permissible in Korea now. We've been seeing more cleavage in Korea, along with, I assume, an increase in the rates of breast and butt augmentation, but Koreans still tend to be more conservative with their tops (no bare shoulders or deep-cut Vs!) while wearing short skirts and short shorts that show off their bare legs. Korea isn't necessarily a prudish society, but it still presents itself as fairly conservative, so, when female idols deviate from that and showcase more overt sexuality, there is often some kind of hell to pay.

(04) SEE ALSO: STELLAR

Stellar debuted in 2011, a girl group managed by The Entertainment Pascal. They released their first album as a three-member group who had generated some buzz in the lead-up to their launch, because Eric, the leader of first-generation boy band Shinhwa, was reportedly involved in producing them. Stellar, unfortunately, never really hit it big; they were a middling girl group at best, switching up members until their agency did a hard pivot with their image and started aggressively and overtly sexualizing them.

After three years in relative obscurity, they released their single, "Marionette." Gone was the cutesy image, and here were four young women in leotards, one with both side panels cut out, dancing provocatively. In the music video, all four are shown in sexually suggestive situations—the video opens on one of the members in bed, seemingly naked and covered in a sheet, the camera panning over her bare thighs. In the next scene, another member, nineteen years old at the time, goes to the fridge in a white camisole and underwear, bending over as she pulls out a bottle of milk. She sits on the counter and takes a sip, the milk leaking down her chin, spilling onto her breasts then onto her bare leg.

The video was marked as mature and not suitable for viewers under nineteen by the Korean government and YouTube. The choreography had to be modified for Stellar to be allowed to perform it on music shows, and, one part, when the girls turn around and rub their butts, was still deemed too provocative. "Marionette" was Stellar's first commercially successful song.

Delighted that this extreme presentation of sex sold, even as it attracted controversy, the company turned it up another notch for their next album. In "Vibrato," the girls are styled in short dresses, one side slit all the up to midwaist, exposing their black boyshorts. The choreography is blatantly sexual (at one point, the girls roll onto the floor and thrust their hips against it in a clearly sexual manner), and, at certain points in the music video, the video is cropped to focus on their butts or crotches or breasts, literally reducing them to their body parts.

There's obviously nothing wrong with women portraying sexuality or performing choreography that's meant to be erotic and simulate sex, and I am not here to judge anyone for wearing clothing that shows off their body—if that's their choice. The problem with Stellar, though, is that they had no say or agency in their concepts or how they were presented to the public.

In their promotional images for "Vibrato," the four girls wear short red dresses, cut up to midwaist on the left. Instead of the black boyshorts in the music video, the high slits expose strings. Later, in an interview with *Insight* in 2018, former member Gayoung shared that she and the other members were highly uncomfortable with how they were styled and that they had protested their outfits with the string bikinis, but their company insisted on taking a few photos before letting them change and continuing on with the photoshoot. The girls were horrified to see their company use the shots with the string underwear as their promotional material, just as they were deeply uncomfortable with their highly sexual image, concepts, and choreography, but their company ignored them, even threatening to disband the group before their contracts expired, which would force them to pay hefty penalties. The sex appeal might have helped their songs chart better and sell more records, but it also opened them up to pervy fans and to controversy and criticism, which, in itself, laid bare the general hypocrisy around girls' sexuality. The public pilloried them for their highly sexual image, but they were also happy to consume it. Shinhwa's Eric was quick to clarify that he had only been involved before the girls debuted and had departed the project long before their image change.

Stellar would try to soften their image after "Vibrato," going for a still-sexualized but sweeter girlfriend concept with "Sting," but they wouldn't get the same attention again. When their contracts finally expired, none of the members renewed, and the group officially disbanded in 2018. All the members left the industry: one became a YouTuber, and Gayoung opened a coffee shop while trying to become an actress. In the seven years Stellar was active, Gayoung reported in the same interview, each member was paid only $9,000.

05

When Christianity started to enter Korea in the late nineteenth century, it was suppressed. The ruling family was suspicious of the new, Western faith, but the religion spread partially because of the Korean social rules that secluded women, allowing them to evangelize quietly and even hide a priest who had snuck into Korea for years.

I ask myself constantly: If Joseon-era ideas of purity and womanhood came down through neo-Confucianism, what about modern Korea's?

Protestantism in Korea is interesting in the ways it wove in Korean beliefs like animism and shamanism—or kind of created equating lines that would make Protestantism feel less foreign and more attuned to Korean practices. This weaving of Protestantism into culture is maybe more clearly demonstrated in the twentieth century, starting with the Japanese occupation. Christianity became intertwined with the Korean independence movement, with Protestants and Catholics both taking leadership roles in organizing rebellions and protests. This would continue after the war, when Korea was a struggling war-torn country, and Protestant leaders started to tout nationalistic slogans and embrace the prosperity gospel as a means of rallying Koreans to bring the country out of poverty.

This is a generalization, but Koreans tend to attach Confucianism to notions of the traditional when it comes to Korean culture.

The thing, though, is that Korean culture was massively disrupted from the late nineteenth century on, from Japan's occupation to the division of the peninsula to the war, which all had deep impacts on Korean culture and identity. Even what we consider traditional Korean food today has been affected, as much of what we—whether my parents' generation or mine (as second-generation Korean Americans)—know has come from Korea in its poor and hungry postwar period. Nevertheless, Koreans still hold to the idea of Confucianism as "traditionally" Korean, and elements do live on in modern Korean society, from its patriarchal culture to its misogynistic, controlling views of women. Combine that with Protestantism, and you have modern notions of female purity and sexuality in Korea.

06

Purity culture isn't really about sexuality, though; it's about control, most dominantly of girls and women. Sure, there's the side of it that also tries to control boys, but a trait of toxic masculinity is that boys are expected to have sexual urges. It's acceptable, borderline expected, for them to be "animalistic," to think about sex and want it and seek it out, and wrangling that is part of their Christian struggle. There's still a gender binary that teaches us that only boys watch porn, and part of being a girl is learning to accept that there's just this crude side to boys. We also see it when Christian men get caught having affairs—their wives are often advised by their pastoral leadership to forgive and accept. Their husbands are men. Men have urges they can't control. They are still the heads of the household, the figures of Christ in the home.

Again, though, this isn't about sex or sexuality, but about control. The same goes for the fight over abortion—people who are anti-abortion aren't pro-baby, and the so-called pro-life movement isn't about life at all. If the men in power can make women nothing more than receptacles for birthing children, then women can be saddled with children and kept within the home. If the powerful don't provide for maternity leave or encourage better workplace policies to make space for women to have both children and professional opportunities, women can be made to be dependent on men and therefore under male control. Patriarchal society continues on.

Sometimes, I feel like a conspiracy theorist when I try to draw these lines, but Korean history itself is an example of just this. Yangban women were kept at home. A popular game among girls of the upper class was the seesaw, where they would take turns jumping up and down in order to look past the walls of their homes. They weren't allowed to be their own persons; they were able to exist only when attached to a male figure.

But to bring this back to K-pop: Where do we start to think about consent and female agency in an industry so fixated on youth? Where idols debut at such young ages? When Girls' Generation debuted, Seohyun, the maknae, was fifteen. Krystal, the maknae of girl group f(x) (managed by SM and debuting in 2009), was also fifteen at their debut, as were Changmin of TVXQ (SM, 2003) and Taemin of SHINee (SM, 2008), the maknaes of their respective groups. Yeri, the maknae of Red Velvet, was sixteen when she was added to the group.

Time will tell how committed SM is to this, but, briefly, the company seemed to indicate a shift with the debuts of aespa (2020) and RIIZE (2023)—Ningning, the maknae of aespa, was eighteen when the group debuted, and Anton, the maknae of RIIZE, was nineteen, while ages, however, seem be skewing younger elsewhere in K-pop. The maknaes of NewJeans (ADOR, 2022) and Baby-Monster (YG, 2023) were both fourteen when they debuted.

When I was younger and closer in age to idols, I admit that their youth didn't bother me much, although it's probably more accurate to say that I was never really conscious of their ages at all, except when the idol was particularly young—like BoA. BoA, though, wasn't sexualized when she debuted—yes, she did sometimes show her tummy, but she looked like a girl in her teens, just one who happened to dance incredibly well.

Now idols seem so young. Even eighteen seems too young, but it doesn't surprise me that entertainment companies like young, not only because youth sells or because there's this idea that youth is so fleeting that it must be exploited at its prime moment, but, also, and maybe more importantly, because youth can be more easily controlled.

(07) SEE ALSO: GAIN

Brown Eyed Girls debuted in 2006 from Nega Network, a four-member girl group who didn't slot into idoldom but were known more as vocalists. It wasn't until 2009 that they shot to mainstream fame with "Abracadabra" (Sound-G), a dance/electronic song with choreography that featured a hip-swaying move that quickly became a trend, nicknamed "Arrogant Dance." "Abracadabra" was all over K-pop that year, even parodied by members of boy bands 2AM and 2PM, but it was also controversial because of its provocative music video, an image change for the group.

During the dance break, Gain is featured on her own with female backup dancers. She's wearing a leotard with cutouts, and the break starts with her at the center, the dancers running their hands up and down her body, even cupping her breasts at one point. I remember thinking how sexy she looked throughout but how everything still seemed tasteful—Gain was twenty-two at the time, young still, but at least an adult, and the other members were twenty-eight. They didn't look like young girls trying to sell adolescent sexiness.

It's common for members of groups to release solo work, and Gain's "피어나" (Bloom), released in 2012 as part of her second EP, *Talk about S*, was a sensation. The song is catchy, bright, and effusive, and the music video was over-the-top and, well, bright and effusive, but then there was this—it depicts Gain, then twenty-five years old, masturbating on a kitchen floor, her hand in her jeans.

The song is about a woman coming into herself as she has sex for the first time, and it centers female sexual pleasure. In the video, Gain has sex with a faceless man, and it centers her—we see *her* face, *her* desire, *her* pleasure. She is the one in bloom, and the video takes delight and joy in this.

I thought Gain would be seen as controversial for this, and she was. She also got a lot of positive attention, though, and continued on this path of embracing her sexuality, with her subsequent solo releases being just as sexual or open about sex. Maybe it helped that "Bloom" centered a woman's pleasure, performed not for the male gaze but to celebrate a woman's joy, in such an effervescent, almost innocent and pure way. Maybe it helped that Gain was older, that she didn't debut in an idol group but as part of Brown Eyed Girls, who largely avoided the image of youthful innocence because of their bigger voices and older ages. Maybe the soft sexiness of "Abracadabra" made Gain's sexiness seem more natural and not so forced or contrived.

Surprisingly, it wasn't Gain's sexual image that brought her solo career to a close. In 2020, she was fined roughly $865 for using propofol in 2019 and consequently had to step out of the public eye. She has been quiet since.

08

What *does* it mean to take agency over your own sexuality as a woman, though? And how much agency do any of us really have when we live in a patriarchal world, constantly confronting images of what a woman "should" look like and being told how a woman should be?

It's similar to how we've so normalized eating disorders by hiding them behind "health" and "wellness." We don't go on diets anymore to be thin; we restrict and exercise obsessively to be "healthy," never mind that *healthy* is still synonymous with *thin*. When a woman claims she's counting calories and avoiding carbs for "her health," it's difficult to argue with that. When she claims she wants to lose weight for herself and her self-confidence, it's hard to criticize that. She's doing this for *herself*, not for a man, not for society, so why is that so bad?

YouTube personality and content creator Kristin Chirico, one half of *The Kitchen & Jorn Show*, addresses why this is fundamentally problematic, tweeting that ultimately, yes, we can make choices for ourselves. We can choose to watch what we eat and how much we exercise, just like we can choose what we wear and who we sleep with and how often. Those *are* women's choices, and we firmly believe and stand for that.

However, it is disingenuous to act like we live in bubbles, immune to the influence of the world. Whether intentionally or not, we internalize the messaging we receive, messaging about how we should look and behave. If you look at K-pop as a young woman, you're still told that you need to be thin, that you should preserve your innocence and cuteness, but that you should also have sexual allure to make you appealing to men even if you are a teenager. There are limits to your agency, especially when you're young and under the control of your company, which determines whether you'll debut, the style of music you'll do, the role you'll play in the group. You can grasp a measure of control over your image, your creativity, your individuality only when you finally reach a certain age or degree of success—but even then there are limits, and the limits are narrower if you're a woman.

Many female idols remain in a prolonged state of youth, but it feels particularly true for Girls' Generation, who kept being given infantilizing, cutesy concepts all the way to their tenth anniversary, when they were all in their late twenties.

In 2014, Jessica Jung posted on Weibo that she had been forcibly removed from Girls' Generation. The other eight members were on their way to Thailand to film a music video for their upcoming comeback when she was reportedly told that she was no longer a part of the group. They were photographed at the airport visibly shocked and distraught, hats pulled down low to hide puffy faces.

We never got a clear answer as to why Jessica had been removed. There were plenty of speculations—she was in a serious relationship with Tyler Kwon (whom she had allegedly been dating since 2013), and there had been rumors for a while of infighting in the group between her and Taeyeon. According to some netizen speculation, the two hadn't spoken in months, and Taeyeon was behind Jessica's removal. Other rumors pinned the blame on SM, which could have been unhappy with Jessica's relationship (though Sooyoung was in a serious relationship with actor Jung Kyungho by then, too). Jessica launched her own fashion brand, Blanc & Eclare, just a month before she was kicked out, so many speculated that SM had concluded that her entrepreneurial ventures would interfere with her ability to focus on Girls' Generation. By then, though, Girls' Generation had been active for seven years. Jessica was twenty-five years old. SM had decided, for whatever reason, that Jessica—who had joined SM at age eleven after the company had aggressively recruited her, convincing her parents to let her and her sister Krystal move to Korea from San Francisco to train to be idols—was no longer worth retaining. She could no longer be controlled.

09

And then there is also that fantasy that is part of K-pop—there's a meme of gathering together photos or clips of idols being "boyfriend/girlfriend material," which amuses me because Koreans have a weird relationship with sex. Korean culture is prudish on the surface, given that many Koreans tend to live at home with their parents until they get married, a norm in a culture that's centered on the social unit of the extended family, while, at the same time, sex isn't that uncommon but open, even expected. To get private, intimate time, unmarried couples (or couples having affairs) go to love motels or love hotels, places where they can rent a room for a few hours or overnight to have sex. Korean men, in recent years, have also become some of the primary participants in sex tourism in Southeast Asia.

And yet, there is a lot of shame around sex for women, who are expected to be pure and virginal while also sexually desirable and available. Women just cannot win.

10

n 2024, a blowup between HYBE and Min Hee-jin, the CEO of ADOR, a subsidiary of HYBE, went *very* public. It's a complicated mess, but, basically, HYBE decided to audit ADOR on the speculation that Min was trying to take over the company and break away from HYBE. The conflict ended up in court, with HYBE formally requesting that Min step down from her role, and Min took things public by staging a press conference during which she went on a personal tirade against HYBE, accused another HYBE subsidiary of plagiarizing her, and dragged in other idol groups including Bangtan, Le Sserafim, and aespa.

Formerly a creative director at SM, Min Hee-jin had a reputation in the industry both for her aesthetic perspective and her seeming oversexualization of her talent—the shoot for SHINee's fourth EP, *Sherlock* (2012), is famous for having made both the boys and their parents incredibly uncomfortable with how the concept sexualized them. Min left SM in 2018, after sixteen years there, and joined HYBE as chief brand officer in 2019, and, in 2021, HYBE set her up as CEO of the subsidiary ADOR, where she would be given the resources and creative freedom to launch and debut a girl group. In 2022, NewJeans, a group of five girls, aged fourteen to eighteen, debuted to almost instant mega success.

NewJeans also pretty quickly became controversial for seeming too sexualized for girls so young. One of their early singles, "Cookie," was criticized for being sexually suggestive—the lyrics are ostensibly about a cookie the girls have baked and are offering to a love interest, but the innuendos are all there. Around the same time, Min shared posts on Instagram of her studio space, which included photos of sexualized minors, allegedly as visual inspiration, framed and hung on the walls. No one who had followed Min's work at SM was necessarily surprised; she already had a reputation for fetishizing and sexualizing youth, wanting Taemin (the maknae of SHINee, who was barely eighteen during *Sherlock*) to maintain his slim, youthful figure and telling Krystal of f(x) to find inspiration from a young Brooke Shields.

In an unusual move for K-pop, ADOR published a verbose essay in defense of "Cookie," essentially blaming the audience for any sexualized interpretations by claiming that, if anyone interpreted the song sexually, that meant that they were the pervert, they were the problem, not ADOR. NewJeans then did a hard pivot in their styling, shifting to nostalgia and schoolgirl innocence, not only referencing the members' own youth but hearkening back to the warmth we sometimes imbue the past with, even collaborating with the Powerpuff Girls for their second EP, *Get Up*, which featured characters designed to represent each member of the girl group on their album design and in official merch, really leaning into those nineties aesthetics.

Netizens were split on the "Cookie" controversy. Some commenters on Soompi claimed that NewJeans should be allowed to pursue their careers however they liked, that it wasn't fair to police them just because they were young and they were girls. I find that horrifically disingenuous: these girls weren't even of age, and it was their company that assigned them songs and decided their image. They were literal teenagers. And they were under the control of Min Hee-jin.

NewJeans, unsurprisingly, has been caught in the middle of this HYBE versus Min controversy, and I'm sad that they will likely be the ones to lose the most from it, with their very young careers on the line. Kakao messages have been leaked left and right, with Min calling out how HYBE chair Bang Sihyuk wanted her to create a girl group to "step on aespa," who had debuted in 2020 from SM and were doing well. Then a YouTuber found leaked messages sent by Min in which she insulted NewJeans and tried to take all the credit for their success. The mess is ongoing in 2024, and netizens, again, have had interesting opinions. The fact that NewJeans debuted so young means they entered as K-pop trainees at even younger ages, and it isn't difficult to argue that they have likely been influenced from those young ages by Min, who has historically fostered close, friendly relationships with her idols. The girls apparently submitted a petition to the court in support of Min, which has riled up some members of the public who think the girls are old enough to know better—but the youngest is now *sixteen*. What is a sixteen-year-old who has been in the K-pop bubble for years supposed to know about the real world, about consent, about the dumb politics of corporations? How much agency or control is a teenager supposed to have in an industry that wants to profit off her?

All this does is prove to me how little people actually know about consent—and how much people just want to perv over teenage girls.

(11) SEE ALSO: MAMAMOO

Mama, *Mama, Mamamoo*, the four-member girl group croons when they introduce themselves. A third-generation group known for their vocals and range, Mamamoo debuted in 2014 from WA Entertainment, which merged with Rainbow Bridge Agency in 2015 to become RBW. They are made up of Solar (leader), Moonbyul, Hwasa, and Wheein, and they stood out in K-pop for their vocal power, willingness to play with different genres and boundaries, and their contributions to writing their own music. They also have a significant LGBTQ+ fan base, having won the demographic's loyalty with their positivity and openness, though none of the members identifies as queer, at least not publicly, but this is Korea.

Mamamoo generally exists within gender norms and Korean beauty standards, though Hwasa's and Moonbyul's visuals aren't super typical—Hwasa with her cold appearance and narrow eyes, Moonbyul with her deeper voice and tomboyish look. Solar has played with beauty standards, though, sporting a unibrow for one of her solos, and, in one of Mamamoo's early songs, the foursome went for an androgynous look that leaned more masculine.

These sound like small things, but rebellion isn't always done in loud, daring strokes. Mamamoo's presence in the K-pop mainstream, their popularity despite debuting from a small company and pursuing a musical style that deviated from more accepted pop is a clear sign that K-pop has been changing as it has become bigger, as Koreans themselves have gone more global.

And then, in 2023, Hwasa was reported to the police for a supposed "indecent" performance. As one of the hosts of the tvN show *Dancing Queens on the Road*, she took part in a summer festival at Sungkyunkwan University, performing "주지마" (Don't), a song she released with Zico in 2018, when she improvised on the choreography, miming licking her fingers and gesturing toward her vagina while wearing short shorts and performing a move that required squatting low with her legs spread. Even though the performance was at a university, where it would be safe to assume that the audience was of age, online forums lit up with netizens commenting on whether Hwasa, who was twenty-seven years old, had crossed a line. In July, the Student Parent's Rights Protection Union reported Hwasa to the police, arguing, interestingly, that her sexually suggestive performance made her audience feel shame.

The festival had taken place in May, and, in September, police actually brought Hwasa in for a three-hour interrogation as part of their investigation into whether she had committed an act of "public indecency." Ultimately, she was cleared.

12

Of all the major girl groups in their generation, Girls' Generation is the only one that remains active. 2NE1 (YG) disbanded (though, in 2024, they announced a reunion tour), Wonder Girls (JYP) split up, T-ara (MBK Entertainment) imploded from within, and Girl's Generation is still together, despite having been subject to the black ocean, where everyone in the audience of a concert who wasn't a SONE turned off their light sticks and stood in silence. Sure, they're missing one member because Jessica was kicked out, but they're still an active entity.

In 2022, Girls' Generation stages their fifteenth-anniversary comeback. It's been five years since their last album, since three of the members left SM, and it's nice to see them together again. They've all been pursuing different things as individual women over the last five years—Taeyeon has been thriving as a soloist, Tiffany debuted in the US, Sooyoung, Yoona, and Seohyun have been growing their acting careers. Yuri has her own cooking channel on YouTube. Hyoyeon rebranded herself as DJ Hyo and always looks like she's having fun in her sporadic solo releases. Sunny has been quiet, but, in 2023, she also leaves SM and, in 2024, launches a new camping show with Hyoyeon on JTBC.

When they come back for their fifteenth anniversary, all the members are in their thirties. Some of them are dating; the public wonders when Sooyoung and Jung Kyungho will finally get married. True veterans of the industry, they all look freer and more relaxed, comfortable and secure in their skin.

They're also allowed to be the women they are. Gone are the cutesy, wide-eyed girls of their previous selves, and, now, fifteen years in, they're just women, each with her own personality and style. As women in the media, they're aware of how to carry and present themselves, yes, but now it seems less artificial and more a part of their reality.

Looking back, as I watch them on their variety show, *Soshi Tamtam* (JTBC, 2022), laughing at their ridiculousness and camaraderie, I wonder why I was so annoyed by Girls' Generation in those early years. They were so young then, and they had so little agency. Why did I hold it so against them? Is it that I, too, was young, in a situation I couldn't control, with my own community bearing down on me and telling me I had to look a certain way, want a certain life, be a certain woman, wife, mother?

And I wonder what it is about women that society fears so much—because I do believe that this desire to control and repress women is rooted in fear. Girls' Generation was a bunch of young girls who wanted to sing and dance and who were very good at what they did, and I think it's a pity that we never got to see them grow, really, from girls into women because SM was too concerned with keeping them locked in girlish innocence for so long.

I'm glad we get to see them more as they are now, though, as veterans in an industry that still seeks to control and sexualize young girls while demanding they appear and act demure and innocent. They don't seem to give a shit about playing that role anymore, and it has been a joy and privilege to see how they've bloomed.

ANONYMOUS

- - - - - - - -

I Don't Care

네가 예뻐라 안 해도 *If You Don't Tell Me I'm Pretty*

난 예뻐 예뻐 *I'm Pretty, Pretty*

aespa, "Yeppi Yeppi"

Savage, 2021

This is an essay I do not want to write.

It feels impossible to write critically about plastic surgery without it sounding like a moral judgment of people who get plastic surgery, though that is never my intent, especially not here. I wonder constantly about how this balance is possible—*if* it even is—because I do fundamentally believe in personal choice. I believe everyone has the right to make decisions about their own appearance, but personal choice gets complicated because it is inevitably influenced by the world we live in, one that prioritizes a certain face, a certain body, a certain aesthetic. Insofar as we exist in the world, we are exposed, daily, to these expressions of beauty, advertised to constantly about how to fix supposed flaws in the pursuit of unrealistic, often false depictions of beauty, thanks to Photoshop, phone apps, and social media filters.

In the end, what is personal choice? Where does personal choice end, and where does external influence begin? How do you write critically about an *act* when that requires talking about people who participate in that act?

This is further complicated in the world of K-pop, where aspiring idols are expected to maintain their appearances obsessively. Idols are weighed regularly and put on unreasonable diets that stress their bodies, all to keep them at the desired weight and thinness. Plastic surgery is commonplace and accepted, so how do we call out K-pop's obsession with plastic surgery without acknowledging that it is still unfortunately necessary for success, especially when your appearance is part of the fantasy you're selling? Where does free will come in when you are a young person subject to the demands and expectations of an agency that can decide not to debut you simply because you refuse to conform? And how many of our decisions as private citizens are really based solely on something we desire for ourselves when we live in this world of unrealistic expectations and standards?

And what does it say about us that we do hold up as examples those who apparently didn't get plastic surgery? We praise celebrities like IU, Jeon Ji-hyun (Gianna Jun), and Song Hye-kyo for looking exactly like their childhood photos, and we admire Bangtan for seemingly not conforming. This duplicity exists even in me—I say that I don't judge anyone for getting plastic surgery, but I still feel relief when I see photos of, say, Suga over the years and see that he is aging "naturally," his face structure untouched, his asymmetrical eyes unaltered, the corners of his eyes starting to wrinkle when he laughs. I feel disappointment as Taeyeon's jawline disappears and her body shrinks down to extreme thinness, though my disappointment has less to do with her than it does with SM, and it is dwarfed completely by concern given her history with depression and the number of losses she has had to grieve in recent years.

What does it say that I'm trying to put off this essay as much as I can, wanting to cushion myself from how deeply uncomfortable this topic makes me? I think we need to talk about plastic surgery, but I don't want to be the one to do it. Even as I write these words, I brace myself for doubt and second-guessing, but I sit here doing the work because I believe strongly that we need to talk about beauty and unreasonable beauty standards, because I'm tired of living in a world where we ruin people who can't or don't conform, because I have been there—I am an example of how unrealistic beauty standards can destroy a person and set back a life.

■ ■ ■

I had blepharoplasty the summer before my senior year of high school.

I was born with monolids, which I got from my monolidded mother. My mother felt insecure about her monolids her whole life, saving up to get blepharoplasty when she was younger, only to be talked out of it at the time, and, when I was in high school, she was more than happy to pay for me to "fix" my eyes.

At the time, I was three years into the body-shaming and went for it gratefully; I was also on Jenny Craig then and dropping weight, so this would be perfect, I thought—I would go into senior year as a new self and, the year after that, enter college as a better-adjusted person, in the correct body with the correct eyes.

Nowadays, blepharoplasty is barely considered surgery, a gift commonly given to high school seniors as incentive to study harder for the college entrance exam. There are two types of blepharoplasty: a simple tuck-and-pin that creates a crease in the lid and a more involved procedure for more hooded, thicker lids that requires removing a part of the eyelid to allow for the fold. The former has a shorter healing time, while the latter takes more stitches and a longer time to settle and look "natural."

So much of K-beauty is dedicated to this pursuit—to look "natural." The best plastic surgery doesn't give itself away. The preferred makeup style in Korea is still the "no-makeup makeup" look that requires applying layers of makeup in a way that makes women look like they aren't wearing any. It takes a lot of effort, and I think it betrays a lot about what Koreans value in beauty and how Koreans think about plastic surgery, despite it being so common and, even, to a degree, expected.

■ ■ ■

What *is* the standard Korean face? Big, double-lidded eyes, a narrow nose with a straight bridge, a V-line jaw. Pale skin. Full cheeks, aegyosahl under the eyes, straight eyebrows. Thinness. Double-lidded eyes can be achieved via blepharoplasty, and rhinoplasties these days can be done with tiny incisions in the nostrils or even via injections to temporarily reshape the bridge. V-lines are achieved by shaving down the bones of squarer jaws via small incisions made under the ear. Idols like Tiffany (Girls' Generation) or Lisa (BLACK-PINK), who came from other countries (the United States and Thailand, respectively) and had tanned skin, debuted with pale skin, likely thanks to skin bleaching. Fillers give idols' faces youthful fullness as well as the soft plumpness of aegyosahl, and straight eyebrows are simply grooming. We've also been seeing more breast implants among idols and actresses, and I'm sure more butt procedures, as Koreans aren't genetically very blessed in that area.

These, to me, have become fairly standard procedures, and my discomfort sets in primarily when it comes to procedures that are controversial in other parts of the world because of their potential harm—like calf reduction. Koreans genetically tend to have muscular calves, which are seen as undesirable because, well, the thickness detracts from the svelte, slim figures desired by Korean beauty standards. Calf reductions literally remove *muscle*, requiring patients to learn how to *walk again*, and this is a procedure that's actually banned in the US. It is legal in Korea, though, and that is one reason I have long worried about Luna of girl group f(x). Throughout her career, she received brutal shaming and bullying for how thick and muscular her legs were—because she's a *dancer*. On an episode of SBS's *Strong Heart* in 2011, Luna shared that she felt insecure about her legs, aware that online search engines paired her name with terms like "horse thigh" or "horse muscle," and, in 2016, when she appeared in public with significantly slimmer legs, I immediately felt alarm bells going off in my head. It isn't necessarily that I thought she had gotten surgery but that her legs, now lacking their muscular dimension, were evidence that the shaming had fully gotten to her, that she had taken whatever extreme measures she needed, whether it be an insane diet and workout regimen or surgery, to attain this look that wasn't natural to her or her art form. In 2018, she released a video on her YouTube channel, *Luna's Alphabet*, showcasing intense massaging techniques to "make muscular legs into straight legs," which finish with binding her legs in bandages for twenty minutes. At the end of the video, she says that the one who endures is the one who wins, and I want to ask, *But what is it that you win?*

Idoldom is a world in which appearance trumps everything else. Even Taylor Swift, whose choreography isn't nearly as close to the intensity of K-pop idols' routines, said in her documentary, *Miss Americana* (Netflix, 2020), that she learned how much of a difference it made to eat regularly while on tour, having gained weight after her eating disorder days. Food is sustenance, and musculature helps support us, not only in our day-to-day lives but even more so in the rigor of singing, dancing, and performing. Sometimes I wonder if SM's preference for vocalists with thinner sounds has to do with wanting their idols to maintain their necessary thinness—like, it doesn't surprise me that there are no big voices in K-pop, especially as the idols seem to get thinner and thinner.

Basically, I find beauty to be superficial and disingenuous, and I find the disingenuity to be hugely hypocritical and irritating because it contributes to the near-impossibility of having a candid conversation about the topic. Some people condemn plastic surgery outright, while others say they respect any individual's choice while secretly (or not-so-secretly) judging people for getting it. Those who do get it also fall into different camps, some (like actress Lee Siyoung) readily admitting that they went under the knife, others (like actress Park Min Young) admitting only to getting their eyes and nose done, the two most accepted procedures, while the vast majority of celebrities say nothing at all. Netizens try to unearth photos from celebrities' pre-fame days to compare and either praise (*omg she's so natural!*) or ridicule (*look how much work they got done; being pretty really is about money*). In my humble opinion, plastic surgery doesn't have to be so fraught; there is fundamentally something impressive about the dedication required to manipulate the human face and body, from the skill practiced by surgeons, both aesthetically and medically, to the pain people are willing to endure (and the money and time they're willing to invest), all to be beautiful.

Fans also have differing responses to their idols' purported surgical procedures, and it can be amusing to scroll through comment sections on articles, social media, and Reddit to see the ways fans will bend over backward to make up excuses for their "favs," citing lymphatic swelling or weight loss or weight gain or better posture or extreme makeup, when it seems clear that the underlying structure of someone's face has changed, or that someone's lips have puffed up to the point of looking like a distended balloon, or that someone is basically unrecognizable. The defensiveness only serves to maintain the shame and stigma around plastic surgery, as it betrays social preference for the "natural" and places it on a higher pedestal, allotting higher social value to those deemed unaltered. This, too, is a way of enforcing a social hierarchy; it's why the term 얼짱 (uhl-zzang) exists, short for 얼굴짱, literally meaning best (짱) face (얼굴).

Anecdotally, I find there to be a lot of judgment against plastic surgery. When men have it, it's seen as emasculating; when women do, they're written off as superficial and vain and frivolous, never mind that both mentalities are dripping with misogyny and hypocrisy. As a society, we want to uphold ideals of beauty, ideals that have likely always been impossible to attain, and we punish those who dare to be open about how they achieve and maintain beauty. There's a classist element to it, too, and one of the reasons I have so much contempt for beauty influencers on social media is that they shill skin care products as if their clear skin isn't due to facials, skin treatments, and regular upkeep, all of which cost money.

Because the thing is that beauty, whether in the realm of celebrity or online influencing, is about upholding the illusion of effortlessness and attainability. No one wants to see the effort it takes to maintain the perfect body, face, and image. Beauty should come easy, and all it should seem to require are personal discipline and self-love. It shouldn't be something to take seriously, though, lest we be seen as shallow. Beauty should be *fun* because the fantasy isn't simply to be beautiful and to live a perfectly sun-filtered life—it's to have all that without having to try.

▬ ▬ ▬

And then there's age.

In general, whether we're talking about Korean society or Western, we're *weird* about women aging. Once an actress hits a certain age, her roles diminish to maternal ones. In 2024, Anne Hathaway played a forty-something single mom in the rom-com *The Idea of You* (Amazon Prime), and the internet lost its mind over how she looked, the most common refrain being that Hathaway couldn't play a forty-something-year-old when that was exactly what she was.

K-pop can be even weirder because, I argue, there's a sense that we are supposed to age out of pop, whether we're fans or idols. Pop is still seen as the realm of teenage girls, and, as a fan, you're supposed to grow up and mature and find more "serious" pursuits. As an idol, you're supposed to become a more "serious" musician or pursue another field; it's fairly common to see idols segue into acting jobs, gigs as variety show regulars, or, even now, YouTube show hosts—it's so common, in fact, that it's rare to see a singer like Taeyeon who's in it to sing and perform and little else.

Taeyeon, though, is now (in 2024) thirty-five, only three years younger than BoA. BoA is an icon who has done more for K-pop than any other idol until Bangtan or BLACKPINK, but, in 2024, as she tried out acting and launched a comeback with the single "정말, 없니? (Emptiness)," BoA had to deal with massive online criticism for her appearance. It's arguable that she's had more work done in recent years—her jawline, historically more squarish, is disappearing into the desired Korean V-line—but netizen comments got so bad that she took to Instagram to call them out and stated point-blank that she might simply retire when her contract with SM expires at the end of 2025. I don't expect BoA to be nearly as active a pop star as she approaches forty as she was in her twenties, but her retirement from K-pop would be a loss.

As I get older, I find myself more drawn to idols and yeonaein who are either around my age or slightly older. Being around the corner from forty is a strange place to be, though, as I am too old to take cues or inspiration from idols in their teens and twenties, and society at large doesn't know how to handle aging women. We marvel over women who seem to be aging "well," but what does that really mean? Anne Hathaway and Jeon Ji-hyun are both in their early forties, and, yes, they both look beautiful, but they're also celebrities—even if they are aging "naturally," they are still very well maintained, with regular facials, skin treatments, and possible fillers or Botox. I look at BoA, who is only one year younger than I am, and wonder what I look like compared to her—do I look "my age"?

As much as we like to dismiss and talk down pop and celebrity culture as frivolous and inconsequential, the truth is what we consume matters. I often see a lot of hand-wringing over the effect of social media on young people today, the deleterious impact that, say, beauty influencers can have on impressionable youth by promoting highly curated, manufactured lifestyles, but isn't entertainment the same? Because the thing is that beauty standards and expectations, as embodied by industries like K-pop, don't simply affect how we, as plebeians, think about our own appearances; these harmful ideals of beauty bleed into everything—I know this firsthand. When you don't feel comfortable in your body, with your appearance, it's hard to feel confident in anything else. When you feel like you don't look good enough or that you're not thin enough or pretty enough—when you feel wrong—it eats away at who you are.

I find it difficult to express clearly exactly *how* much body-shaming ruined my life and destroyed me. I've blocked out a lot of it, so, when I try to put it into writing, it all seems so small and inconsequential. So what if people called me names and commented at every meal that I was eating so much—wasn't I full yet? What was the big deal that there were eye rolls every time I displayed an interest in food, like, no wonder I looked the way I did? Why did it matter that people told me I needed to be skinny before I could be loved or wanted or valued—shouldn't I have been smart enough to know that was all just hyperbole?

Who cares that, after I got my blepharoplasty, I was asked over and over again, now that my eyes had been "fixed," why couldn't I lose the weight? Wasn't I so lucky that only my eyes needed to be "fixed"?

■ ■ ■

Officially, any conversation about plastic surgery is speculation. No one can say authoritatively whether someone has actually had surgery, but I find it disingenuous to pretend that plastic surgery hasn't been normalized across the industry. It is not only encouraged for idols but expected. Former Girls' Generation member Jessica even spoke of being required to get surgery if she wanted the lead role in the musical *Legally Blonde* when it came to Korea. There are so many actresses or singers I flat out didn't recognize because their faces have changed so much. I've been watching as BoA's face has changed, as both her and Taeyeon's jawlines have disappeared, and there's an idol whose name I don't even want to say because I'm afraid her addiction to plastic surgery has much more sinister roots in insecurity and self-loathing.

I don't want to shame anyone or make them feel bad for their choices—they are ultimately their choices, and I want everyone to be happy in their bodies as they are on their own terms. However, I do think it is possible to respect someone's individual choice while also acknowledging that we do not exist in bubbles, that our choices are the result of outside influences, that there is a need to question the toxic system that is the K-pop machine—an industry that requires a certain image of perfection, of conformity to a beauty standard that is largely unattainable without some external force, whether that be surgery or an absurd diet. These beauty standards have physical consequences, and they are unfortunately borne by young girls and boys during times of physical and psychological development.

I mean, as a civilian, I think about plastic surgery often. I want to get liposuction to remove the fat from under my armpits so I can wear bras and shirts and not look weird and lumpy. If I weren't so terrified of rhinoplasty going wrong, I'd love to raise the bridge of my nose and narrow the tip and fix whatever it is inside that makes me snore. If I had money to waste, I'd get dimples.

If it were possible, I'd get my blepharoplasty reversed.

Of all the plastic surgery I'd want, it's the last that I do think most seriously about. I have thought of at least going in for consultations to see if it's possible to reverse because, as far as I know, it likely isn't. As I've written, there are two types of blepharoplasty: the first is an easy tuck-and-pin that could potentially be undone, but the second requires cutting away part of the eyelid. Mine was the latter, my eyelids too thick and heavy, so I doubt it's possible to undo the fold in my eyes, although I would love to chat with plastic surgeons in Korea about it.

It isn't that I regret getting my eyes done, not really. Part of it is that monolids have become more accepted and considered beautiful in more recent years, and I miss mine. My eyes hadn't even been considered small. I distinctly remember my surgeon happily assuring me that he wouldn't have to make incisions at the corners of my eyes to make them wider—my eyes were as wide as Caucasian eyes, he said; what a relief that must be for me because that would also help my new double lids look more "natural."

The other part, though, is that I wish I'd cared more about

my appearance twenty years ago, like, genuinely cared, instead of just being ashamed of how I looked. I wish I hadn't so eagerly gone along with the procedure simply because my mother offered it to me, thinking that, if I could at least "fix" my eyes, maybe the rest of me would be okay. I believed, then, that if I had the "right" eyes, maybe Koreans would see something about me that satisfied at least one of their beauty standards, and maybe they would be more inclined to accept me as one of their own. It obviously didn't work that way because the body-shaming went on for years after I got the desired folds in my eyes, and I still sometimes wonder— what if I got more plastic surgery? What if I fixed this, what if I fixed that?

That, maybe, is the thing that makes me most sad. I know that surgery won't fix my broken self-perception or the body dysmorphia I still live with. I know there is no such thing as perfect; I could get my liposuction, rhinoplasty, breast augmentation, but there would always still be something wrong with my body. I mean, idols are meant to sell the fantasy of perfection, but there is always something people will find to criticize about their appearance and denigrate them for because this is the world we live in.

So, in the end, my experience with beauty standards has led me to this: the people who love you should build you up. They should be a soft place for you to fall, to provide you a cushion where you can be tender, sad, and, honestly, maybe ugly. They should guard you *against* the cruelty of the world, instead of inflicting paper cuts on you as a way to make you tougher.

The people who love you shouldn't reinforce the lessons we learn in media, that we are worth something only if we fit into a mold. We shouldn't be respected as musicians or writers or whatever else only if our bodies meet the unrealistic beauty standards demanded by society, and the people who love you should teach you to grow your confidence in who you are and what you can do instead of tearing you down for how you look.

In the end, I feel angry on behalf of idols forced to go under the knife. They're young people who just had dreams of being onstage, of singing and performing and, sure, maybe, becoming famous, and there's something supremely depressing about capitalizing on young people's ambitions and hopes just to mold them into something they may not even be sure they want.

I was seventeen when I chose to alter the shape of my eyes, and, yes, I would say that I did it out of my personal choice. At the same time, when I look in the mirror, I often wish someone had been around to talk some self-love into me twenty years ago. My brain wasn't even fully formed at that age, and I had no idea who I was, already so broken down from shame. I wish someone had been there to say I could wait on this, that, no, there was nothing wrong with wanting to get my eyes done to get that desired fold—wanting double-lidded eyes has no moral value attached to it—but it was just plastic surgery. It wasn't life or death. My appearance was just one part of who I was, and I could decide what value to attribute to it.

T.O.P

T.O.P (born 최승현 [Choi Seunghyeon]) of boy band Big Bang was an anomaly in my K-pop experience, a brief dalliance, might I say, but one that was intense in its short lifespan.

Big Bang debuted from YG Entertainment in 2006, a hip-hop-styled group led by G-Dragon (born 권지용 [Kwon Jiyong]), the prodigy rapper the group was built around. Big Bang's music wasn't my preferred style, and I was mostly intrigued by their debut because Park Bom (of 2NE1) featured in their first music video for the song "We Belong Together" (*Big Bang*, 2006). Park was one of my most anticipated idols after her appearance in Samsung's promotional video "Anystar" in 2006, alongside K-pop legend Lee Hyori (formerly of first-generation girl group Fin.K.L) and actor Lee Junki, and I wanted to see more of her, wanted YG to debut her already. I probably would have gone on being uninterested in Big Bang had I not seen them perform live in Los Angeles as part of the annual Korean Music Festival that ran from 2003 to 2018 at the Hollywood Bowl. Big Bang made an appearance in 2007, and T.O.P got me with his deep voice. I'm a sucker for deep male voices. I knew he had a deep voice because I'd listened to some Big Bang songs by then, but hearing something live can often shift an experience.

Because they came from YG, the five-member group was decently popular, but, later that year, they would release their first EP with the lead single "거짓말" (Lies) (*Always*, 2007), with an electronic dance sound that would ripple across the entire industry to become a major musical trend and catapult them to mass fame. In May, though, at the Hollywood Bowl, I was smitten as T.O.P ran past our box, rapping in his deep voice. My dalliance would last a few years until I finally became exhausted with Big Bang's cultural appropriation and toxic masculinity and kind of fell out of K-pop.

Arguably, all of K-pop is cultural appropriation, given that Western-style pop was brought into Korea. After all, the westernization of music in Korea really got going after the war, and the club scene around the American base in Itaewon in particular was heavily influenced by the music of Black American GIs. Several of the would-be big figures in mainstream K-pop got their inspiration from these clubs.

From the start, YG was the company with more of a hip-hop influence, managing groups like Jinusean (1997) and 1TYM (1998) who focused on rapping and often featured Korean American members who emulated the language, style, and swagger of Black Americans. Teddy, the leader of 1TYM, would go on to be one of YG's biggest producers, working with Big Bang and defining 2NE1's sound, which he would continue with BLACKPINK.

It was through Big Bang that I learned how much I despised YG, which also debuted 2NE1, the four-member girl group counterpart to Big Bang. Yang Hyunsuk, the founder and former CEO of YG, would comment publicly about how 2NE1 was ugly, and he was so terrible at managing the group that fans started to refer to the "YG basement," wondering sarcastically online if YG would let 2NE1 or other trainees out to release new music and perform. I also don't think YG was ever competent to handle the scale of fame and influence Big Bang and 2NE1 reached, and both groups eventually imploded in their own ways. For years, 2NE1 was put in the "basement," until Park Bom's "drug scandal" (she was caught bringing Adderall into Korea, where it's illegal) dealt the final blow to the group. Big Bang knocked itself down with individual scandals—G-Dragon was accused of smoking weed in Japan, Daesung was involved in an accident that resulted in the death of a motorcyclist (who had been driving under the influence and was already lying on the street from a previous accident), T.O.P got tangled up in a weed scandal that involved a troublesome trainee, and Seungri was exposed for his allegedly kinky tendencies (according to a Japanese tabloid, he reportedly liked choking women during sex) before being arrested as part of the Burning Sun scandal that rocked Korea in 2019. The scandal was named for a Gangnam club, of which Seungri was one of the directors, and it implicated numerous actors, singers, and entertainers in charges that included rape, prostitution, and spy cameras. Seungri was arrested, charged, and tried on charges of procurement of sex services, mediation of prostitution, and embezzlement, among others. He was originally sentenced to three years in prison but won an appeal that reduced his jail time to eighteen months, and he was released in February 2023.

Sometimes, when I think about Big Bang and 2NE1, I get really sad. From the beginning, YG has come across to me as a company that overtly celebrates a certain kind of male ego. For example, the only reason Seungri made it into Big Bang to begin with is that he petitioned Yang personally, asking not to be cut from the lineup. Yang apparently liked this attitude, even though Seungri didn't seem to have any particular skill that would make him an asset to the group. YG tries to model a certain kind of male swagger that steals heavily from Black American hip-hop but lacks its gravitas (which is no surprise, cultural appropriation being what it is), and I tend to think that kind of posturing is unsustainable, especially when you are unable to care for your stars.

YG, of course, isn't the only company guilty of cultural appropriation, but its hip-hop style makes it a more obvious and visible target. Taeyang, the main vocalist of Big Bang, sported cornrows from the beginning in "We Belong Together," and, in a photobook released in 2016, he fetishized Black pain and suffering, writing in a caption, "I'm not Black, so I'll probably have to have more experience and go through more pain if I want to express the sentiments, emotions, and soul that Black people have through my music. That's why I believe that pain and suffering will make my music richer."[2] This is doubly laughable given that twentieth-century

---

2 "Fetishizing Black Culture: Taeyang on Being Black," https://seoulbeats.com/2016/12/fetishizing-black-culture-taeyang-on-being-black/.

Korea is a nonstop record of pain and violence that he could easily tap into to "make [his] music richer."

G-Dragon, like many other Korean rappers and idols, has used the Korean 니가 (you) as a way of saying the N-word without *technically* saying it. Formally, 니가 is written as 네가 and pronounced *nega*, but, as it is a near-homonym for 내가 (me), pronounced *naega*, Koreans tend to say it with a long *ee* to avoid confusion when speaking. Context clues make it clear when the rapper is trying to get away with saying the N-word, most obviously when the word is just tossed out of nowhere.

I do want to stress that YG wasn't (and still isn't) the only offender perpetrating cultural appropriation and racism in K-pop. Actors on *Saturday Night Live Korea* have performed in blackface in skits multiple times, even into the late 2010s. When Shinhwa performed "Yo!" (*T.O.P.*, 1999) on Yoon Do-hyun's music show *Yoon Do-hyun's MUST* in 2012, they kept the N-word in the chorus (even though the lyrics shown on the screen removed it). SM Entertainment has welcomed Black songwriters and producers to songwriting camps and happily taken their music and even choreography, sometimes without proper credit or pay, as with Micah Powell's work on Super Junior's "Devil" (*Devil*, 2015).

I started to lose interest in Big Bang around 2008, when they released *Remember*, their second studio album. By that point, Big Bang had become too big, in my opinion, going through that phase where idols struggle, in subtle ways, to adjust to their outsize fame and adulation. Their music videos became flashier, leaning more into the visuals and attitude of Black hip-hop and rap culture, and my interest flagged.

In some ways, I think it was a blessing, because that means I missed Big Bang's *MADE*, their third studio album, released in 2016. They produced a video for each of the eleven songs, some of which are genuinely fun and cute (like "맨정신" [Sober] and "We Like 2 Party"), but the music video for "뱅뱅뱅" (Bang Bang Bang), in which they lean heavily into their imitative swagger and machismo, featuring lots of chain jewelry and big vehicles like tanks and bouncing cars, as well as a Native American headpiece worn by Seungri, epitomizes why Big Bang has been so problematic throughout their career.

K-pop fans—in general, not only of Big Bang—love to defend away cultural appropriation by claiming that *all* art is, to some degree, derivative. That, however, is not the issue at hand—yes, part of being an artist, whatever your medium, does entail finding inspiration in other art, sometimes from other cultures and races, but appropriation is about power, essentially about finding something shiny that belongs to another group of people and has cultural and sociopolitical significance, and trying to make it yours, as if you are entitled to it just because you think it's shiny. For a very obvious example, a hairstyle might just be a hairstyle to some of us, but Black people are regularly discriminated against because of their hair, with Afros, braids, and locs considered unprofessional—so a K-pop idol like BLACKPINK's Lisa wearing braids, as she did in the video for "Kill This Love" (*Kill This Love*, 2019), or Korean reggae duo Stony Skunk (YG, 2003–2008) sporting locs is questionable and out of touch at best, especially when Korean entertainment is happy to take from Black and Latin cultures without actually seeing Black and Latin people as equally human.

At the same time, I don't think it is always fair to expect K-pop idols to have an understanding of racism because that is just another way of imposing a Western-centric perspective on K-pop. K-pop might have gone more global in the last two decades, but, much like the director Bong Joonho famously calling Hollywood a local industry, K-pop, too, is local. It is a domestic industry where the primary target audience is Korean. Most idols were born and raised in Korea, which is a homogenous society that has been impacted more by imperialism, colorism, and classism than racism. The argument that idols should Google more and be more conscientious of the sociopolitical struggles of people of color in the West is, frankly, irrational, especially when many Americans who were born and raised in the United States within its rampant systemic racism are themselves often ignorant of how deep the problem runs in our own country. Just as women internalize misogyny, people of color internalize racism, and it's a learning process to undo that toxic thinking that ultimately keeps white imperialism in power.

I don't say this to excuse Korean media, because I absolutely believe that Korean entertainment companies should, by this point, be more aware that they are part of a global world, and K-pop, as a whole, really needs to do better and be more respectful and inclusive of its Black fans. I do want to challenge international fandom, though, because I'm frankly over the West centering the West and looking at K-pop through that lens. The same West-centric attitude has caused misperceptions about East Asian history because using the European nation-state paradigm to study China, Korea, and Japan misses their unique interactions with each other, which were viewed with more cultural fluidity within a sociopolitical hierarchy than those in Europe.

But to go back to Big Bang: Big Bang had a huge influence on K-pop, bringing hip-hop and electronic dance music into the mainstream, and G-Dragon and T.O.P together were one hell of a charismatic, dynamic duo. At the same time, 2NE1 was one of the biggest girl groups of second-generation K-pop, the biggest rivals of Girls' Generation, and they could have become so much bigger had YG managed them competently. I think Big Bang got as far as they did only because G-Dragon and T.O.P were involved in producing and writing their music, in pushing boundaries and finding their style, whereas 2NE1 wasn't given a similar opportunity despite CL, the leader, particularly, wanting more chances to make music, work with other producers, and get onstage.

Thus far, YG hasn't done much to redeem itself. BLACKPINK— 2NE1 part two (but pretty, according to Yang)—has been active since 2016 but has a pathetically tiny discography, especially compared to other idols in the K-pop system who "come back" every year. To this day, out of K-pop's Big Four management companies, YG is still the one I openly despise, and it seems incapable of debuting a girl group who isn't just another version of 2NE1 (BabyMonster, 2024, is part three). I'm sure YG will be fine, though. K-pop, unfortunately, has shown over and over that cultural appropriation is an excellent way to make money.

아이린 IRENE

I'm Original Visual
Red Velvet, "Psycho"
The ReVe Festival: Finale, 2019

n every K-pop group, there is the Visual. The Visual has their own set of skills, but they are meant to be the face that appeals to the mass [Korean] public, with the ideal Korean features—big eyes, straight nose, narrow jaw. Beyond good looks, though, the Visual should embody the words 착하다 (to be kind) and 순하다 (to be innocent). In other words, there should be a sweetness to the Visual, a kind of pureness, and they should exude trustworthiness and wholesomeness. Examples include Girls' Generation's Yoona, Bangtan's Jin and Taehyung, BLACKPINK's Jisoo, aespa's Karina, and Red Velvet's Irene.

The Visual looks like they could be your friend, and they're inoffensive and come across as friendly and sweet. A male Visual looks like he would give up his seat on the subway to a halmoni or offer to carry your bag, while a female Visual appeals to Korea's gender roles and looks like she would smile while peeling fruit after dinner. The Visual is someone you would bring home to your family, someone who isn't meant to have isolating opinions, even more so than pop idols in general.

The Visual certainly doesn't associate herself with something like feminism.

In March 2018, Irene, the leader of Red Velvet, casually mentioned that she had just finished reading Cho Nam-joo's novel, *Kim Ji-young, Born 1982*. She didn't say anything *about* the book or her thoughts on it—and yet the backlash was immediate and extreme, as a corner of Red Velvet's male fandom exploded in outrage.

Irene had shown herself to be a feminist, and this was not acceptable. These male fans disavowed her, allegedly going so far as to burn merchandise and photos of her because, if she was going to be a feminist, she stood for a world that opposed them and, therefore, needed to be taken down.

— — —

Red Velvet is a five-member girl group from SM Entertainment who sing pop music and perform choreography, but their sound is a little more experimental than their labelmates, Girls' Generation, with their more standard, bubbly pop.

Their name actually isn't taken from the cake but is meant to represent the two sides of the group—"red" for a brighter, poppier sound, "velvet" for something more moody and atmospheric. Their releases tend to alternate between the two—for example, *The Red Summer* (2017) is a red album, while *Perfect Velvet* (2017) is velvet—and Red Velvet's music videos tend to be thought through with high concepts and elaborate designs. While I don't think Red Velvet has hit the soaring heights that Girls' Generation did—which is not a criticism or meant to sound like a detraction—they've had a very steady career with consistently positive critical acclaim for their vocals and sound for more than a decade with no signs of stopping.

In general, I think SM does very well in creating groups who sound really *pretty* together. Each company in the Big Four has its own musical preference, vocal color, and choreography style that generally acts almost like a foundation for their idols. YG is known for its hip-hop/electronic sound and can't seem to variegate beyond the badass girl crush image; HYBE's choreography style, in my opinion, is best described as bouncy; and SM tends more toward the controlled and precise, having originated the concept of 칼군무 (knife choreography). Of the Big Four, SM also has the strongest reputation for selecting vocalists and investing in vocal training for idols, and it doesn't tend to go for big, rich voices, but those with thinner sounds. Each group has a lead and main vocalist who have a more unique color and stronger technique, and they're supported by the other members who may have more basic voices that round out the group. In Girls' Generation, the lead was Taeyeon and the main was Jessica, and, in Red Velvet, the lead is Wendy, and the mains are Seulgi and Joy. Red Velvet fits SM's general sound of smooth voices that meld together sweetly—all five members have fairly thin voices, but they come together to create a pleasant vocal color, with Wendy's warmer tones and Joy's thinner, more nasal, unique sound. They're really nice to listen to.

■ ■ ■

Cho Nam-joo's *Kim Ji-young, Born 1982* is a slim novel that goes quickly. It's hard to think of it as fiction; Cho tells the story of Kim Ji-young's life from childhood to adulthood in a mechanical cadence, interspersing the narrative with statistics and footnotes to make clear that Ji-young's life experiences are grounded in reality. "Ji-young" was one of the most common names for girls in Korea in 1982, and she's meant to represent the average modern woman in metropolitan Korea, following her expected trajectory in life—school, college, a brief job, marriage, motherhood. She experiences the restrictions of Korea's patriarchal society, which affect how she and her sister are treated at home (as opposed to the coddling their younger brother receives), her ability to find a job after college (how much harassment and gender discrimination will she swallow?), and the physical and professional sacrifices she is expected to make to have a child to appease her in-laws (compared to her husband's sacrifice of coming home earlier from after-work social events). Kim Ji-young's story is not meant to be remarkable. As evidenced by her name, Ji-young is not meant to be unique; it is her averageness and the familiarity of her story that are important because she is a stand-in for Korean women, representing their lives and experience and demonstrating the gendered expectations placed upon them.

Published in Korea in 2016, *Kim Ji-young* became the number-one-selling book in 2017, selling over a million copies. At the same time, the #MeToo movement was gaining traction in Korea, with women speaking up about sexual harassment, the wage gap, and gender inequality. Male politicians, filmmakers, and writers came under intense scrutiny, and the notion of feminism started to gain more traction in both positive and negative ways, bringing more attention to the shit Korean women have had to endure in Korea's patriarchal society while also riling up the discomforts of men who found themselves supposedly losing their rights.

I read *Kim Ji-young* when it was published in the US in 2020, translated by Jamie Chang. The book is written in flat, detached prose. It's not that there's no emotional charge in the novel, but I don't know that I really felt like any of the characters, including Kim Ji-young, was meant to be truly three-dimensional. Rather, each represents a certain type of person in Korean society. As exemplified by her inclusion of statistics and citations, Cho didn't want Kim's experience to be written off as fiction or as singular— again, Kim represents your average Korean woman. That also may be why the novel didn't necessarily leave a strong impression on me—I'm familiar with patriarchal Korean culture, so nothing in the novel was new to me: it was the same tired, heteronormative, gendered Korean thinking I know so well.

That is likely why the book was so popular in Korea. It hasn't been common to see this experience so bluntly represented or reflected in media or culture, and the novel resonated strongly with the public, especially as women were starting to make their voices heard.

And then there was this: on May 17, 2016, a man sat in a stall in a public restroom at a bar in Seochu-gu, Seoul. A few men came and went, and he waited, and then a woman entered. He stabbed her to death.

He didn't know the victim and later allegedly claimed that he had murdered her because he hated women for humiliating and rejecting him. It didn't matter who the victim was; she just had to be a woman.

It was a horrific event that shook the whole country, but it wasn't as if violence against women was some rare, uncommon thing in Korea. The country is apparently rife with hidden cameras that are placed in all kinds of spaces, from public restrooms to store changing rooms to individual homes, recording women in their most private moments and, when these recordings are released for public consumption, ultimately making the world less safe for them. The punishment for sexual assault and violence is laughable. Despite being the twelfth-largest economy in the world, with a high literacy rate for women, Korea has one of the largest wage gaps in the developed world (70 percent in 2022), and there is a rigid ceiling that prevents women from advancing professionally. A woefully low percentage of women make up the National Assembly or are executives in Korean companies. To put it shortly, Korea is not a country friendly to women, but there is still a prevalent fear among men that society is changing for the worse for them, a mentality on which Yoon Suk Yeol, the thirteenth president of South Korea, built his 2022 campaign, stoking men's misogynistic belief that they are being unfairly targeted by liberal "wokeness," similar to Trump's fearmongering in the United States.

We cannot seem to avoid the patriarchy wherever we are.

— — —

Korean history before the twentieth century is roughly broken up into three historical eras: Goguryeo, Goryeo, and Joseon. Joseon-shidae, which spanned roughly from the 1300s to Japan's annexation of Korea in the late 1800s, is what we commonly think of when we think of "traditional" Korea, from the royal courts depicted in sageuks to how we define "traditional" Korean food (which is basically royal court food) to Confucianism.

The notion of traditional Korea, though, is a complex one, an idea that has been cobbled together post-Occupation and postwar. Korea was torn apart (figuratively and physically) in the twentieth century, and Koreans today are generations removed from what was once "traditional," that sense additionally distorted by the Japanese attempt to erase Koreanness and by the introduction of Americanness-as-aspirational after the Korean War.

Before Confucianism entered the Korean peninsula and became the defining ethos of elite Korean society during the Joseon era, Korea, then known as Goryeo, was more heavily Buddhist—and more egalitarian and less patriarchal or patrilineal. We can't go so far as to say that Goryeo was a shining example of gender equality, but women weren't relegated to being just a man's daughter or a man's wife or a man's mother. They could inherit land and had a place in ancestral lineage. Maternal grandparents were provided the same ancestral rites as paternal ones. Mothers and maternal grandparents were recorded in family registers, and husbands tended to move into their wives' homes after marriage. Because daughters were considered equal in familial inheritance, women had strong ties with their siblings, and there wasn't much shame around divorce or remarriage after widowhood. Men did tend to take plural wives, but these wives didn't always live in one compound but often in multiple cities.

But then Confucian patriarchal principles were introduced via China, and, gradually, over decades, women were relegated to the privacy of their homes. Under Confucianism, which in Korea was adapted to the classism and social hierarchies that organized society more than they did in China, women's social standing was defined entirely by their relation to men. This patriarchal slant has continued through Korean history into the present day, when Confucianism has come to stand in for traditional East Asian values. Clinging to Confucianism and, in connection, to Joseon Korea as the "traditional" representation of Korea is awfully convenient for the patriarchy. In some ways, it does make sense because Joseon was, of course, the last dynasty before the Occupation, war, and division, but Confucianism in Korea is more complicated than I originally thought as someone who was born, raised, and educated in the West. I thought of Confucianism as a fairly monolithic, shallow, sociopolitical force that more or less spread patriarchy throughout East Asia, but, as I learn through reading and research, the representation of Confucianism in the West has been, unsurprisingly, colored and defined by Western missionary colonialists, specifically, in this case, the Jesuits.

■ ■ ■

Marketers say it takes an average of seven touches to convert a lead into a customer. I think that also applies to human change and learning how to be "political," a term I put in quotes because it's kind of like the word "feminist"—they both have negative connotations attached to them.

I have lived my entire life as an Asian American female in a racist, misogynistic world, but that doesn't mean I grew up really *aware* of what that meant. Sure, I was unhappy having to help with the cooking and cleaning every time my parents hosted their church group or our extended family, and I was annoyed by how my female Sunday school classmates were expected to get married young and have kids. I wanted to throw my Bible at male pastors and leaders who delivered heavy-handed sermons on Ephesians 5:22–23 (rendered in the New International Version as "Wives, submit yourselves to your own husbands as you do to the Lord. For the husband is the head of the wife as Christ is the head of the church, his body, of which he is the Savior"), but I didn't really know what those feelings of distaste meant or what to do with them.

Gender is a social construct, as is the value placed on gender. Historically, as men were responsible for upholding the morals of the state, they were also responsible for the raising of children, given the thinking that children were an extension of the state, but that changed in the early twentieth century when (1) sanitation started becoming a focal point during the Japanese occupation and (2) the fertility rate started to drop. As the colonial government began to implement reforms around hygiene, the role of women began to shift to one seen as maternal, and the proper raising of children fell under their domain—moral women raised moral sons who would facilitate the functioning of a moral state, the thought went. This also coincided with the entrance of women into the medical profession, as a practical need for women nurses and physicians rose, given the separation of men and women in upper-class society.

The notion of family itself has been of governmental concern throughout Korean history. In the mid-twentieth century, the government rallied for families to have *fewer* children because of postwar poverty. Today, we see the extreme effects of that policy as Korea has one of the lowest birth rates in the developed world. In the last quarter of 2023, the rate dropped to its lowest, 0.65 births per woman. Korea, along with its neighbor Japan, is an aging society.

As a woman, albeit a Korean American woman, it's been frustratingly amusing to see the Korean government's clumsy efforts to encourage women to have more children, which generally simply involves throwing cash incentives at heteronormative couples to reproduce. To me, the solution seems pretty obvious—create a more equitable society, one in which women are able to have equal professional opportunities with equal pay, and, also, in which men are encouraged to take paternity leave and be more involved with their families. Provide access to affordable childcare, housing, and public spaces, and stop placing motherhood on a toxic, gendered pedestal. Forgo toxic masculinity, and life becomes better for everyone.

What I find most frustrating is that the predominant male reaction to the idea of an equitable world is fear. This isn't unique to gender; it is a common response when it comes to any group in a position of power. An equitable world might entail some loss of power for the majority group, but it leads to a better world overall, including for the majority. It's a pity that people are often too shortsighted to recognize that—or maybe it's just easier to want the status quo because that allows the majority to continue succeeding without putting in much effort. In the end, mediocrity wins, and, as a society, we lose.

■ ■ ■

The funny thing, maybe, is that I learned how to be political at church, after I graduated from high school in 2003. I credit the pastor and his wife of our English Ministry for that—they welcomed debate and conversation about current affairs, including the war in Iraq, abortion rights, and gay marriage, and they weren't judgmental or forceful about upholding or molding us to a conservative Christian agenda. I'm sure I was annoyingly aggressive and forceful then; I was still deep in the body-shaming and all the accompanying insecurities, fears, and lack of social awareness; but I felt safe in our long conversations during Friday night meetings or post–Sunday service chats. A few of us would regularly gather around and talk as we were waiting for parents and siblings, and I remember that I didn't feel like I had to present a certain type of thinking and that I was free to ask questions about abortion and homosexuality, even though I definitely still skewed *very* conservative then.

If I got started at church, social media was my way into learning how to be more political in a more open space. I started using Instagram in 2010, first on my iPad because the iPhone hadn't come onto Verizon yet. At first, social media was a casual curiosity, but, then, once Instagram got on Android, I started using it a bit more. By the time I was traveling in Japan in 2012, I had been on the platform for a brief while, long enough to make a few friends through it. Attitudes toward social media were more suspicious than they are today—it was weird for me to be meeting people "off the internet"—and I remember my parents being intensely wary of it, worried about my safety and wondering if I was okay if I was trying to meet people, just friends, online. Nowadays, of course, even my parents encourage me to get on dating apps to meet someone, so I can hurry up and have children.

Once the iPhone got on Verizon, my family switched, and I started getting more active on Instagram. In the early to mid-2010s, Bookstagram—as the book community on Instagram is called—was a new thing, and we were a small, tight-knit group. Publishers started wanting to tap into social media, and I started connecting with more book people—readers, authors, publicists—as I posted about what I was reading, using Instagram captions to supplement my Tumblr and blog posts.

As I learned to think more critically both about the books I was reading and the K-pop I was consuming, I was able to start dismantling the misogyny I had already internalized, and it's actually only within the last ten years that I've educated myself when it comes to women's rights. I grew up in a predominantly Korean community in suburban Los Angeles, within patriarchal Korean culture whose worldview was reinforced by the conservative church I grew up in. Even while I resisted the gendered expectations placed on me, I still internalized all that patriarchal thinking and misogyny.

"Feminist," to me, was a dirty word. It's a word I eschewed for much of my twenties because I didn't want to get looped in with the stereotype of feminists as angry, man-hating women. I went around saying that I was a "humanist," that, yes, I wanted equal rights for everyone, but wasn't it only natural for men and women to be different and have different roles in society? Men and women were *physically* different, after all; it just made sense!

When it came to K-pop, this internalized misogyny came out as a dislike of the Visual. When Girls' Generation debuted, I didn't like the group in general, but I especially didn't like Yoona. I found Jisoo the least interesting member in BLACKPINK. I glossed over Red Velvet's Irene as generic—pretty, yes, but with the standard, desired Korean face. I associated that kind of prettiness with superficiality, fakeness, and duplicity, because in dramas, it's usually the pretty woman who's the 여우 (fox), the one who uses her looks to get what she wants. The Visual is not often the lead vocalist or the main dancer or the rapper. The Visual is pretty; ergo, she must be empty; she must be there because of her face, not her talents.

K-pop is a machine; companies like SM Entertainment, which manages Girls' Generation and Red Velvet, essentially manufacture and maintain every facet of an idol's image. To succeed, idols, including the Visual, must play their parts—I've known this for a very long time, but it took me well into my twenties for that awareness to turn into self-interrogation, which led to a change in mentality. What's wrong with being the Visual? Is it the Visual's fault that she's placed in this role, when every girl group needs a Visual to pull in mainstream male appeal? I would get so angry over the gendered expectations placed on me as a young woman; how must an idol feel?

Because K-pop, too, is a system of power, and women—young girls, really—wield very little of it.

— — —

Feminism in Korea has, in recent years, gone from being a dirty word to a dangerous word, a label that can have severe consequences for young women. Unsurprisingly, Irene isn't the only female K-pop star who has been targeted for being a "feminist." Naeun, of girl group APink, posted a photo of her phone in a case gifted to her by Zadig & Voltaire that said "girls can do anything" and faced a barrage of criticism for promoting feminist ideals. Her agency had to issue an apology, and the photo was taken down from her social media page.

One of the most tragic victims of this horrible mentality, though, was Sulli, formerly of the girl group f(x). Sulli was a child star who grew up in the industry, and she was one of f(x)'s most popular members until she formally withdrew from the group in

2015 after years of burnout and bullying. She still remained in the public eye, though, as she focused more on acting.

Most notably, she was in a relationship with Choiza, fourteen years her senior. They met when Sulli was fifteen; when their relationship was exposed, she was nineteen. Sulli left idol life and started to share more candidly on Instagram, posting photos of her kissing her boyfriend, not wearing a bra, and speaking about menstruating. The public response was vicious, slut-shaming her, accusing her of taking drugs, and calling her a hypocrite, to the point that Sulli had to publicly address the comments and accusations being hurled against her, even going so far as to host a television program, *Night of Hate Comments*, where other celebrities would appear as guests and read hateful comments and address them.

The heart of the hate directed at Sulli was that she was a young woman who refused to conform to the image of the sweet, innocent girl. Instead, she was a "feminist," open about her sexuality, daring to go about publicly without a bra, and standing up to her bullies instead of deferring to them.

In October 2018, after years of vicious bullying, Sulli took her own life. She was only twenty-five years old.

■ ■ ■

To be a K-pop fan is to bear witness to a whole lot of contradictions. Double standards run rampant—for example, while all K-pop idols are forbidden from dating in order to maintain the fantasy of an idol loyal to the fans, if they *do* get caught, the woman is shamed, while the man gets away with it (see: Taeyeon and Baekhyun).

It reinforces everything I learned just being a daughter in a Korean family. I was expected to help cook and clean and peel fruit while my brother could slip away after dinner to play games. It was always assumed that I loved kids and couldn't wait to get married (to a man) and stay home to serve my husband and family. I was expected to be demure and fit Korean beauty standards, and I was bullied and shamed when I couldn't get my overweight body to comply.

One effect is that, for much of my life, I wished I could be a Visual, that someone might see me on the street and breathe, *Wow, you're beautiful.* Life seemed easier if you were pretty, and I begrudged pretty girls their looks and their thinness, resenting how little they seemed to have to do to gain access to better opportunities, to be liked, to be offered so much—attention, fame, success.

Cognitively, I know there's also the other side to beauty—the viciousness, the misogyny, the disordered eating—and K-pop also showed me that. It took a while, though, for things to begin shifting in my brain as I finally started to draw the lines between my own personal frustrations as a young woman living in gendered Korean society and the dark side of K-pop that so exploited the dreams and ambitions of young women. It was frustrating to watch Korean dramas where women were pitted against each other, while "bromances," friendships between the male characters, were fawned over, especially when I personally knew how strong and impactful female friendships could be. I finally started to ask myself why the narratives about women were so toxic, why my mom would warn me against girls who wore short skirts and heavy makeup, why I was so dismissive of the Visual for relying on her looks because she didn't have the vocals or the dance abilities to flaunt instead. I started to like groups like Girls' Generation for their resilience and success in an industry that skewed male, to see Irene's personality come through along with her adaptability as an artist, and, as I began to break free from the toxic mentality I'd grown up under, I stopped hiding from the word *feminist*. I still don't love the label because it's too tied up with white feminism, which has its own slew of problems—namely, well, racism and anti-transness—but I've luckily moved past the internalized misogyny.

It's encouraging to see changes within Korean society, too. The fact that #MeToo gained traction in Korea is incredible, that accusations against even respected auteurs like Kim Ki-duk and politicians like Park Won-soon, the former mayor of Seoul, have been brought to light and taken seriously. It's to the credit of the women of Korea who have been risking everything to speak up, to demand more equitable treatment, to stand up for themselves.

Unfortunately, Korea's also regressed in ways similar to the United States, most notably with the election of Trump in 2016. In 2022, Korea elected to the Blue House Yoon Suk Yeol, an incompetent garbage fire, in my opinion, who ran on a platform that appealed to disenchanted young men and conservative, misogynistic older people. Yoon promised to dismantle the Ministry of Gender Equality and Family, and, when he narrowly won the presidency, many Koreans, especially women, responded with despair. The Ministry of Gender Equality and Family wasn't there just to protect women but also to do things like raise awareness and support for paternity leave.

Even though Korea seems to be moving backward in some ways, I am still encouraged. I can't actually quantify *why* I feel that way when Korea doesn't have an antidiscrimination law, technically made abortion no longer illegal but never codified it as legal, and has a huge, vociferous Christian population that will get loud over things like Seoul Pride, coming out en masse to line up along the parade route and hold up signs about Jesus and how they, as parents, would never accept a gay child.

Maybe, though, it's that I recognize that change might be slow but that doesn't mean it isn't happening. In 2017, for their tenth anniversary comeback, Girls' Generation featured drag queens prominently in their music video for "All Night" (*Holiday Night*, 2017). K-dramas like 응답하라 1997 (*Reply 1997*, 2012), 갯마을 차차차 (*Hometown Cha-Cha-Cha*, 2021), and *Nevertheless* (2021) have featured openly queer characters, not as punch lines but as fully realized human beings who hope, thrive, and fall in love. Variety shows like 슈퍼맨이 돌아왔다 (*The Return of Superman*, 2013–present) and 아빠! 어디가? (*Dad! Where Are We Going?*, 2013–2015) centered and highlighted the importance of fathers' roles in their children's lives beyond being financial providers. In 2020, Seoul National University elected its first openly lesbian student body president.

Nowadays, there's a lot of hand-wringing over the ills of social media. There's a lot of cynical chatter over how performative it all is, and there are indeed *very* valid criticisms to be made of social media, like how these platforms privilege the white and heteronormative, can be settings for bullying and abuse, and are often unregulated and therefore easily exploited for perpetuating fake news or soliciting illicit sexual favors. The ways social media allows us to curate narrow versions of ourselves for a certain kind of public consumption can contribute to people's own self-distortions and can exacerbate consumerism and capitalism as people try to mimic the shiny, curated lives of the influencers they follow on Instagram, TikTok, and YouTube.

Ultimately, though, social media is a tool that isn't inherently good or bad, and I do think it can be a good way to learn to be a person in the world, someone who is plugged in and cares and refuses to look away, no matter how hopeless the world seems. It takes practice to be political, to care, to learn to think critically instead of blindly consuming, in a similar way that it takes practice to figure out what your voice and perspective are as a writer, a musician, an artist of any form, and what I hope for people is that they have safe spaces where they can try on new perspectives. I don't care for the hand-wringing over social media and its accompanying cynicism, but I do think that one of the things that is indeed regrettable about the internet in general is the flattening of nuance that doesn't allow people a whole lot of grace.

Of course, not every toxic thing can be forgiven, and not everyone can be redeemable, but, in general, I do believe that people *can* change—I am proof positive of this. I went from stupid statements like *I believe in humanism, not feminism* and blaming rape victims for their clothing choices (*maybe she shouldn't have worn such a revealing outfit*) and personal decisions (*why was she walking home so late?*) to understanding what the fight for equal rights actually entails and recognizing what sexual assault victims go through when they try to seek justice. It took years to break through the conservative, patriarchal mindset I was so entrenched in, and, to this day, even now, my knee-jerk instinct might still be to question a victim, but that is something I at least am now able to cut off immediately. We are products of our environment, but, just like we can halt the flow of generational trauma, we can also inoculate ourselves against environmental toxicity.

That's not to say I'm perfect; I still have a lot to learn, especially about race. I grew up in suburban Los Angeles, and I was six years old when the LA riots broke out in Koreatown in April 1992, following the lenient sentencing of Soonja Du after fatally shooting Latasha Harlins in the head for allegedly stealing a carton of orange juice, and the acquittal of the white police officers who had beaten Rodney King. I grew up with the casual racism of Koreans against Black people, and I know that xenophobia and racism run rampant through Korea and the diaspora, with K-pop idols being no exception (for example, Taeyeon once commented that Alicia Keys was pretty for a Black woman, and Seungri of Big Bang said it was lucky that he wasn't shot when he opened the door to the wrong van upon arriving in the US one year). K-pop is horrifically guilty of cultural appropriation; blackface continues to show up on Korean variety shows, and K-pop fandom can be hostile to Black fans—and, even today, I don't think either the industry or the fandom is equipped to handle conversations about racism and anti-Black prejudice. I mean, we can barely talk about misogyny.

At the same time, this is one reason I find international K-pop fandom so maddening. I am a second-generation Korean American who was raised and educated in the West. Despite my culture and ethnic history, I have so many gaps in my knowledge, and I view the world, pop culture, and more through my Western lens. I wish more Western fans had the humility to recognize this about themselves, to stop perceiving K-pop through that Western-centric perspective, and instead acknowledge that they are being invited into another culture, and that culture isn't perfect and still has a long way to go, but, honestly, so does the West, so maybe Korea deserves some more respect and grace.

━ ━ ━

M y love for K-pop is, unsurprisingly, complicated, particularly because of gendered standards and what is allowed male idols versus female idols. Take Bangtan: when I look at Bangtan, I think a girl group could never be like them—not because a girl group doesn't have the talent and skill that Bangtan does but because a girl group would never be allowed the freedom or given a similar kind of outsize veneration.

When I first come into the fandom at the end of 2022, I notice that the members are seen as more liberal or progressive, supportive of LGBTQ+ rights and gender equality, and expressive on mental health issues, and I think, okay, that's cool, but where is the proof? It's easy to see where the mental health stuff comes from—Suga, RM, and Taehyung have all written songs about depression, anxiety, or suicidal thinking—but, as far as LGBTQ+ rights and gender equality go, I'm still puzzled. Bangtan's production team is pretty much all male, what we see of their friend groups are all male, and the groups they tend to publicly support are also all male. It takes eleven episodes of *Suchwita*, Suga's YouTube talk show, for Suga to have a female guest, and, over the show's first-season run of thirty-one episodes, he has only four. To draw a somewhat unfair comparison, given that there is a generation of K-pop between them, it took Jaejoong of TVXQ three episodes to feature a female guest when he launched his YouTube talk show, 재친구 (*Jaechingoo*) in 2023, and he has consistently featured women since.

In the end, Bangtan's progressive image ultimately seems like one that is heavily projected onto them, something that isn't granted to female idols—or other idol groups, really. After all, when Irene simply mentioned that she had read a feminist novel, fans destroyed merchandise and slandered her online. It isn't that

Bangtan hasn't done good things—they did donate $1 million to the Black Lives Matter movement in 2020, and the members individually donate regularly to causes both domestically and internationally—but I would still argue that Bangtan got increased positive boosts when their fans, international ARMY, matched their donation, coordinated to disrupt a Trump rally in the run-up to the 2020 presidential election, and flooded a Texas app set up to collect videos of protestors with fancams of K-pop performances instead. The latter two actions, both initiated and taken on by the *fandom*, not endorsed by Bangtan, could arguably be seen as yet another example of men being raised up by the actions of women.

The irony, I suppose, is that it is also the fandom that contributes to the maintenance of gendered barriers in K-pop because idols of opposite genders can't interact without rumors and malicious comments blowing up online. Suga and even RM have spoken about wanting to be mentors to younger idols so they don't have to feel as isolated as Bangtan did in their early years, and I think that's really cool of them—in theory. The reality is that, in practice, their nice gesture ultimately only serves to reinforce and perpetuate the patriarchal slant of K-pop because that mentorship, that networking, is only available to boy bands. Bangtan doesn't extend the same public mentorship to girl groups as they do, for example, to labelmates TXT. Generally, Bangtan's interactions with girl groups or female idols are relegated to dance challenges.

I understand that one reason for the public segregation is to keep fandoms happy—to which I say, blow the fandom up. Forget about the fandom if the fandom is being used to maintain these patriarchal, misogynistic systems that keep men in power and bar women from access to the industry at all levels, not simply public-facing idoldom.

Maybe it's time to stop pandering and for the fandom to grow up.

■ ■ ■

But, then, I suppose, the question becomes: Whose responsibility is it to change things in the industry? Is it the artist's? What if the artist is a puppet of the company and doesn't have any power? Is it the company's? What if the company is simply reacting to the fandom because that's the market? Is it the fandom's? What if the fandom is at the mercy of what the company wants to offer of its idols? At what point does the hot potato of responsibility stop being tossed around?

And in the world at large, what is worth defending? Who is worth seeing as having more value?

As women, we've heard the argument over and over again. Men who are put on trial for sexual assault are defended with the question, *Why should we ruin their lives because of a mistake? He's apologized. He's expressed remorse. Must he lose out on all his potential? Must we lose out on his potential?*

Men are always seen as having more to offer the world, even when they've committed crimes.

■ ■ ■

Gender, though, is one thing that makes SM interesting to me, even outside of my company loyalty as a good bbasooni.

As a general rule, SM is as rigid and heteronormative as companies come, and it isn't great at managing its female groups. It kept Girls' Generation locked in perpetual girldom into the members' thirties, and it's historically been more than willing to exploit its idols' youth and innocence without paying them adequately. It's terrible at providing adequate security for its idols, leaving them open to physical assault and danger, as is clearly depicted in any video taken of SM idols moving through airports. No one on SM's roster is or has been publicly out.

At the same time, SM is the only entertainment company in Korea with four generations of female idols. The second group it debuted was S.E.S., a three-member girl group, one year after H.O.T. debuted in 1996. You could argue that HYBE is the youngest of the Big Four, but it's been around (starting as BigHit) since 2005, and it never successfully managed a girl group. Instead, they built it into company lore that Bangtan struggled so much partly because BigHit had tried to debut a girl group, GLAM, in collaboration with Source Music in 2012, but had to disband them after one member became embroiled in controversy when she blackmailed actor Lee Byunghun. The first girl group it actually debuted was Le Sserafim in 2022, via its subsidiary Source Music (which was acquired by HYBE in 2019).

Fall 2023 was a fun time to be an SM fan, as Red Velvet, aespa, and Taeyeon all released new music, so we got not only a wave of new releases but also a clear look at how each group has its own brand identity and sound, while still fitting in with SM's overall style. Red Velvet's *Chill Kill* leaned more into creepy, Halloween-esque vibes, with the slightly off-kilter sound we've come to expect from their music. aespa's *Drama* featured the stronger, more badass electronic sounds and tones that are aespa's signature—aespa's vocals hit a harder edge than Red Velvet's softer colors, while still retaining the general prettiness of SM's vocals. Taeyeon continues to play around with different sounds within the broad R&B/pop genre, and *To. X* highlighted the smoothness of her voice (and SM's continuing penchant for weird English and punctuation).

SM also has a history of pushing boundaries, particularly when it comes to gender presentation. Amber, of girl group f(x), was styled in a very masculine way, in direct contrast to the extreme femininity of her fellow members. Taemin has played with the boundaries of gender presentation over his fifteen-year career as part of SHINee. When Sulli left f(x) and openly dated a much older man and refused to wear bras or desexualize herself, SM didn't kick her out; instead they produced a single ("Goblin," 2019), in which she talked about multiple personality disorder. SM's idols have spoken about living with depression, Taeyeon even admitting that she was getting treatment and taking medication for it a few years ago, and the so-called Milk Club is fairly well known after it was first disclosed by Super Junior's leader Leeteuk in a 2009 Cyworld post, describing it as a "gathering of depressed souls" and listing Taeyeon as the "manager" of the club. Since his debut, Heechul has been dealing with gossip and rumors that he's gay because of his more effeminate appearance and flamboyant personality, and SM never tried to tone him down or counter the gossip. In 2020, Heechul finally addressed this, confirming that he was, indeed, straight but that he didn't feel the need or desire to clarify this vehemently because to do so would be to imply that there is something wrong with being gay. aespa's Karina had an ask.fm account during middle school in which she expressed a love and admiration for other girls that could code as queer even by Korea's standards, but SM didn't scrub it before she debuted.

I don't list any of these to say that SM has been better than other companies because, as I've stated before, SM is the company I know best, so I can't compare and contrast it fairly with other companies. In recent years, though, SM seems to be imploding due to bad executive management—as of June 2024, Kakao, one of Korea's top conglomerates, owns a majority stake in the company, and SM founder Lee Sooman was unceremoniously ousted in 2022 in dramatic fashion. HYBE purchased his shares in what seemed to me would have been an FTC violation if it had happened in the US, as a SM/HYBE merger would completely topple the balance of the Korean entertainment scene. Lee Sooman's departure seems to have had a ripple effect because, despite SM's general lack of management of its artists, many of the remaining first- to third-generation idols had been brought in and created by Lee Sooman, and many of them have spoken warmly of him. In 2024, Red Velvet's contract renewals were under question, and SHINee members Onew and Taemin took their solo careers to smaller companies. For all of SM's flaws, I do personally want the company to continue to thrive—again, it is the only company of Big Four to have four generations of female idols and a female producer and songwriter (Kenzie) who has been with the company for years. SM doesn't necessarily do *well* by its women, but it *has* consistently had women, a ridiculously low bar, yes, but one not all companies clear.

SM also raises the most questions when it comes to how much a company is responsible for the mental health of their idols, especially as, in 2017, Jonghyun of SHINee dies by suicide. In 2019, Sulli, formerly of f(x), dies by suicide.

K-pop is a business, and I tend to think of entertainment companies as employers and idols as employees, but things get complicated when you consider how young idols are and how much control companies have. Then you add in how idols are seen as products and expected to behave as such by the public, who might be quick to love and adore them but are equally as quick to turn on them, to hold them to unreasonable standards. It's even harder when you're a girl. When idols are the commodity being sold and consumed, who protects their humanity?

■ ■ ■

These days, I think a lot about Karina.

At twenty-four years old (in 2024), Karina (birth name 유지민 [Yoo Jimin]) is four years into her career in the public eye as the leader of SM's four-member girl group, aespa, but, as a human being, her brain is still forming. She's also the Visual of her group, and, when I first saw aespa when they debuted in 2020, I thought that, back in my time, we would have called her an 얼짱 (face best). Karina has the huge eyes Koreans love, a small face that ends in a narrow, pointy chin, and she might have had subtle work done, given that she debuted from SM, but she was still beautiful as a middle and high school student, which led to her being scouted by SM (via a DM on social media).

At first, in 2020, I don't listen that much to aespa and can't decide if I like their concept. SM, with aespa, is clearly trying to create a virtual world, and aespa debuts as four members who each have a virtual counterpart, an animated avatar, all of whom live in this world called Kwangya. I'm honestly surprised that SM hasn't launched a full-on video game set in this world yet, but I suppose the attempt to turn SM into Kwangya has failed given that aespa has been recently moving away from their avatars and virtual world concept.

aespa debuts during the COVID-19 lockdown, and, at first, they feel a little flat, which is maybe expected given that they aren't able to perform live or interact with an audience in a real, physical way, which inevitably stunts their growth as performing artists. The girls are clearly talented, embodying the girl crush image made popular by 2NE1 and BLACKPINK, opting more for a tough attitude than innocent cutesiness. Their music is heavily electronic-influenced, and their sound is stronger than SM typically tends to lean with their girl groups but still fits within the company's sonic universe—f(x) was also an electronic-influenced group, albeit one with a softer sound. aespa feels like their sassier younger sisters.

Four years in, as the world has opened up and aespa has gone on tour around the United States and Asia, the members seem to be more comfortable onstage and in public. They have live performances under their belt now and a greater ease onstage, and, as I watch clips of Karina in particular, I find myself drawn to her because she's clingy and hilarious and freakishly strong.

She and fellow aespa member Winter are selected to represent aespa as part of the company unit GOT the Beat, a supergroup formed by female idols from all four generations at SM. BoA is the center, and the seven-member unit also pulls in Taeyeon and Hyoyeon from Girls' Generation and Seulgi and Wendy from Red Velvet. They release their first single, "Step Back," in December 2022, and the song itself is fairly lackluster, the lyrics feeling a little backward as it falls into the age-old trap of pitting girls against each other over a boy, but the videos that come out of the promotion cycle are adorable and honestly pretty special, as we get to see four generations of female idols interacting with each other in rehearsals, on sets, and backstage.

As I watch more of Karina, this girl fifteen years my junior, I hope that K-pop is able to protect who she seems to be—a kind, bubbly girl who picks up watermelons like they weigh nothing and posts encouraging messages to her classmates on her ask.fm. I hope this industry, from the companies to the fandom, changes to be kinder to our young people, to not box them up in toxic heteronormative, gendered standards, but to let them be who they are—and, most of all, to stop seeing them solely as products to mold and profit off but as creative human beings with something to share.

That may be grossly and naively optimistic, but, as I watch the behind-the-scenes footage of GOT the Beat—these four generations of K-pop idols laughing and interacting as they practice choreography, work their photoshoots, and promote together—I think that maybe it is okay for me to have hope. K-pop today isn't what it was when it first got started thirty-ish years ago because, here, look at this room of women, some of whom have been here for decades, some of whom are just getting started. Look at the stories they hold, the challenges they have faced and overcome over their collective decades in this industry. Here is K-pop's present and past, and, here, too, is its future. May we continue hoping and fighting for them.

09

방탄소년단 BTS

- - - - - - - - - -

Run, Bulletproof, Run, Yeah, You Gotta Run
BTS, "달려라 방탄" (Run BTS)
Proof, 2022

N ames in K-pop can often be confusing. Many idols take
on stage names, which are sometimes riffs on their
government names, sometimes not, and fans will often
oscillate between calling idols by their stage names and
by their government names. Then, to add to that, Koreans like to
nickname idols by shortening their names and attaching common participles to them to make them cute.

    For example, take Bangtan's Kim Taehyung. His stage name
is V. Fans affectionately shorten his name to Tae or Tete. I tend
to call him Tete and often forget what his stage name is because
I never call him that, even in this book. RM originated as Rap

Monster, which was often shortened to RapMon, then became just RM as Namjoon (his government name) outgrew his adolescent moniker. Sometimes, when I'm feeling soft toward Namjoon, I call him 준이 (Joonie). Jungkook becomes 꾸기 (Kkookie) because he's the maknae and twelve years younger than I am. Suga is sometimes Suga and sometimes Yoongi (his government name) because Yoongi is mine and Yoongi is actually not a name that nicknames naturally.

How much I am joking when I regularly text a friend that 윤기내꺼 is up for anyone's interpretation.

THE TRANSLATOR: 김남준 KIM NAMJOON

◇◇◇◇◇◇

Stage Name: RM

Birthday: 1994 September 12

Hometown: 일산 Ilsan

The summer before Bangtan debuts, Psy's "Gangnam Style" blows up around the world. I'm in Korea when the song is released, but I don't register its existence until I'm back in the States and have moved to Brooklyn to start law school in August 2012, with every new person I meet asking me breathlessly, *Oh my god, you're Korean?! Do you know "Gangnam Style"?!* while crossing their wrists and bouncing up and down in the now-infamous horse dance.

The Western reaction to the song irritates the hell out of me, and I can't decide if I prefer that response to my Koreanness over the asinine question *Are you North or South?* that "Gangnam Style" has temporarily replaced.

Much is made of the song's reception in the West, but I find it outsize and overblown. Yes, the song is popular, and, yes, people love doing the horse dance, and, yes, Westerners now have more of an awareness of Korea in some way or another—but that doesn't mean actual respect. It doesn't mean white people are willing or able to see Koreans as equal because Psy's "Gangnam Style" really just becomes another way for white people to consume our culture without seeing us as human.

Unfortunately, even with the global rise of Bangtan, I don't think much has changed, other than my increased irritation over how people like to sentimentalize this naive idea that music is a universal language. I suspect that RM, the leader of the seven-member group, would agree with me, to a certain extent.

■ ■ ■

Bangtan debuted in 2013, as part of what we consider the third generation of K-pop. This was after SM brought its collective SMTOWN concert to the US for the first time in 2010, after Big Bang went on a world tour that drew eight hundred thousand audience members in the Americas and Europe in 2012, and after Psy's "Gangnam Style" took over the West. This was also after K-pop heavyweights BoA and Se7en both tried (and failed) to launch solo careers in the West, Girls' Generation gained minor traction promoting "The Boys" in the United States, and Wonder Girls opened for the Jonas Brothers on their North American tour.

For over twenty years, I have watched K-pop grow in the US

from a niche interest limited to the Korean diasporic community to something so much bigger. To watch Bangtan sell out stadiums around the world and perform in front of tens of thousands of screaming non-Korean fans has been both cool and amusing.

I'm not so naive as to consider Bangtan's massive popularity some great movement that will somehow save us from racism. The way Bangtan is written about in the West largely reinforces the racist narratives pushed upon us as people of color, from the way Bangtan is treated as a solitary phenomenon (which, sure, the sheer scale of their fame does make them unique, but as a group? Not so much) to the way K-pop, in general, is oohed and aahed over, criticized in broad strokes for the prominence of plastic surgery to the notorious slave contracts that control every element of K-pop idols' lives. K-pop is still dismissed as formulaic and unoriginal, and the way Bangtan's fans try to set the boy band apart by leaning into how members RM, Suga, and J-Hope produce and write much of their material also feeds into this narrative by highlighting the impulse to make Bangtan a unicorn.

It isn't that I necessarily disagree; I love that the members are actively involved in their music and am floored by their creativity—and I, too, have used that argument to hype up my favorite boy band in the past. H.O.T. was unique not only for being the first K-pop boy band; they were also writing and producing their music and choreographing their dances from their third album on. In their lyrics, they criticized the Korean education system, the government, and the strictness of society, much like Seo Taiji, who immediately preceded them, did.

The thing, though, is that making Bangtan exceptional removes them from their greater context and isolates them on a pedestal to put them in faux proximity to whiteness, which is still the standard.

It's like the Asian model minority myth—Asian Americans have long had their Asianness weaponized by being made to seem atypical in contrast to other communities of color, but all that does is create a false sense of exceptionalism that allows the white majority to sow distrust and conflict between Asian Americans, Black Americans, and Hispanic Americans. The Western impulse to disconnect Bangtan from K-pop at large and hold them up as superior to the rest of the industry only weakens them, which is actually pretty standard white imperialism at play.

— — —

I have ranted plenty of times on Instagram about how much I hate the Bangtan narrative. Much of Western writing likes to focus on the records Bangtan has broken on Billboard charts and whatnot, and, every year now, there's some kind of drama during Grammy season, with ARMY, Bangtan's official fan club, posting all over social media about how the Grammys are corrupt or whatever when, yes, we've *long* known the Grammys are political and racist—and I'm sorry to say, Namjoon, you haven't won one not because you're in an idol group but because you're not white. The fact that Beyoncé has not won a Grammy for Best Album of the Year, losing out to Harry Styles of all basic white people in 2022 (who then had the *audacity* to go onstage and say, "This doesn't happen to people like me very often" with a straight face), is all anyone needs to know about what the Grammys stand for.

(Also, never mind that Bangtan's English music loses everything that makes Bangtan so special. The first Bangtan song I listened to was "Dynamite," and I thought it was so superficial, it kept me from listening to Bangtan for another two years. "Butter" is insipid. I've heard "Permission to Dance" a few times but can't remember what that song sounds like to save my life.)

But maybe this is one of my controversial opinions—people love to say that music is a universal language, that it transcends spoken language, but I find that idealistic. There's a tendency to romanticize music as if it can somehow break down barriers and create more mutual understanding between disparate groups, and I'm not going to say that that's *entirely* untrue. It's just sentimental, like claiming that readers are more empathetic, open-minded people because reading is good.

Neither music nor literature is inherently good or bad, and people can and often do very much consume culture and content in bubbles. Liking K-pop doesn't somehow make someone less racist or prejudiced—it's like the West's love for Japan, which has Cold War propaganda roots from when the US needed an Asian country to hold up as a shining example in contrast to bad Communist China. Oohing and ahhing over another culture, making a spectacle of it, fetishizing it, and using one's supposed love for it as an excuse to barge into spaces that don't belong to you—that's Othering and toxic and suspect.

I do think Bangtan themselves are aware of this, RM probably more than others. As the member fluent in English, RM has acted as the de facto translator for the group when they've made media appearances in the West. He has a lot of patience, in my opinion, not only as the one caught in the middle and having to work twice as hard as everyone else but also as the one who (we assume) understands the most of what is being said around them when Bangtan is abroad. RM is often praised for having a high IQ and, in general, for his intelligence, which is most prominently exemplified in the wordplay in his lyrics, and I appreciate that he seems like a thoughtful person who is generally aware of the privilege he has, of the platform and influence he wields.

In a vlog recorded on September 7, 2020, in the lead-up to the release of their fifth studio album *BE*, RM talks to the camera about interviews they've been doing, quoting himself in English, "Music truly transcends every barrier, like language"—and then he immediately follows by admitting that he's been questioning how much he actually believes that. On one level, lyrics are a big part of music, but, sometimes, you don't need to understand the lyrics to understand the heart of a song, while, other times, knowing the lyrics helps enhance the song—or vice versa. The lyrics can also bring down a song.

In the end, RM concludes that it is enough if Bangtan is able to bring people comfort with their music because music is, first and foremost, an auditory experience. As I watch the clip, though, I still wonder how much he really believes that music *transcends* barriers, because is providing comfort enough? What does it truly mean to communicate via music, to connect with people in that medium? Should that carry through in how Bangtan is regarded? Because Bangtan has invariably had to put up with a lot of racism and condescension while doing media interviews, and my favorite part of them participating in the Western media circus has been seeing how little Bangtan seemingly cares about it all. The way the seven members are seated in their appearance on James Corden's *Carpool Karaoke* in February 2020 never fails to crack me up—Jin, Suga, and Taehyung, the three members who care the least about pandering to the West, are all the way in the back, with Jimin, J-Hope, and Jungkook, who engage happily and enthusiastically but in limited capacity because of the language barrier, in the middle. RM, as the leader and English speaker, sits in the passenger seat.

RM's position, though, also reminds me that he arguably carries more responsibility than the other members as the leader of the group. Sure, the role of "leader" might not mean much in terms of actual responsibility because the company exists for that, but the leader of any K-pop group is still the one who has to act as an anchor for the others, wrangling everyone and keeping them in line. It feels like too much to place on the shoulders of people who debut so young—RM was nineteen years old when Bangtan debuted. Our human brains aren't even fully developed then. He has had to carry so much, not only in K-pop but on the global stage, having to navigate cultures that aren't his, all while Bangtan's fame essentially puts a target on his back and opens him up to criticism from all these people around the world who are so happy to consume him and what he has to offer without seeing him as an equal human being.

In general, I believe music is political, in the ways that food is political and literature is political, the ways that our identities are made political simply by virtue of not being white (or straight). We live in a world where heteronormative Western imperialism has its poisonous fingers in everything, and, insofar as Westernness, as whiteness, maintains its position of power—and whiteness has built the world to maintain its position of power—we are, by virtue of our ethnicity, made political. To attempt to deny that is to play into white supremacy.

At the same time, though, I recognize that music has a power that other artistic mediums might not, which is why it's easy to subscribe to the sentimental notion that music is a universal language. I grew up in the church, and there is a reason so many church ministries, like Hillsong, invest heavily in songwriting and worship teams. Tim Keller once said in a sermon at Redeemer that music goes straight to the heart, that it will take a belief you have in your head and convert it into faith in your heart, and that is why music is a key part of Sunday service. There is also, I argue, a reason worship music and hymns tend to be catchy, repetitive songs that are easy to plant in our heads. This is the power of music. This is why we want to believe so much that it is somehow able to break down racism and other systems of power simply by virtue of being music, while discounting the very big factor of human nature.

I am neither idealistic nor naive enough to believe that white people listening to K-pop or eating Korean food or even learning Korean will somehow eradicate racism against Asian people.

Insofar as our culture is seen only as something to be consumed, we can only be a spectacle.

THE HYUNG: 김석진 KIM SEOKJIN

◇◇◇◇◇

Stage Name: Jin
Birthday: 1992 December 4
Hometown: 안양 Anyang

I wish I had a friend like Jin.

As the eldest member, Jin is the 맏형 (maht-hyung) of Bangtan. He was reportedly scouted on his way to class at Konkuk University, and, as he tells the story (to the stone-faced expressions of the other members), the scout fawned over his face, saying the company needed a Visual and he would be perfect—wouldn't he join?

Jin is indeed very good-looking. When a friend finally got me to pay attention to Bangtan, I kept asking her who the good-looking one was. He had reportedly been recruited by SM Entertainment but turned them down, and I'm glad he never signed with SM—Jin's face isn't perfectly symmetrical, and SM would have "fixed" it, taking much of his natural charm away.

Jin isn't the strongest vocalist in the group, and he acknowledges that he's one of the weaker dancers—it takes him extra time to learn choreography. There are probably detractors out there who criticize him for just being a pretty face, but it's impossible to think of Bangtan without him. He's the hyung; that's his role. He is just as crucial to Bangtan as RM or Suga with their songwriting or Jungkook with his vocals.

Pop isn't about musical genius, and I don't say that to insult pop stars at all. One of the things I love about pop is exactly that—that it isn't weighed down or burdened by arbitrary notions of "greatness" or "brilliance." As K-pop idol groups have demonstrated over four generations, a successful group isn't made up of all musically inclined people but a few stellar vocalists and dancers and, more importantly, a range of personalities that mesh well together, and being a pop star is about being a pop star, not about being *the* musician. There's a reason each group is built on the same formula, with different members selected to slot into particular roles. Some sing well, some write songs, some are consummate performers. Some are personalities who shine on variety shows, and some are Visuals.

At the same time, I do recognize the frustrations of being written off as an idol group or a pop star, but I think that's more telling of society than of pop. In a similar way, I have little patience for commercial writers who complain about not having literary critical success—you kind of can't have both. You can have the commercial, financial success that comes from appealing to the wide mainstream or you can have the niche critical acclaim that's understood by a smaller audience and doesn't necessarily come with money. It is not possible to have it all.

In 2020, in a collaboration episode of *Run BTS!* with Channel Fullmoon, run by Na Youngseok (known colloquially as Na PD), they play a game in which they each admit a character flaw. Jin says, "저는 생각이 별로 없어요"—as translated, "I don't really have many thoughts," or, to put it another way, I'm very simple-minded. He admits that he kind of just tends to do something without really overthinking it, and I can see that, as far as his public persona goes. Jin tends to laugh easily, doesn't really take much too seriously, moves about the world with an easy confidence that doesn't come across as arrogant or egotistical, simply the ease of a man who has figured out how to make peace with his life. As a member of Bangtan, Jin does not know "normal." He can't be nobody. He can only be himself within the cage of fame and global attention.

One day, while browsing my explore page on Instagram, I see a video of clips a fan has assembled of Jin displaying his athletic prowess. Jin is lean and tall but doesn't really come across as someone who might be super athletic, and I'm surprised by these clips—he's just so *bendy*, quick on his feet, his body seeming to move in instinctive reaction to things, whether it's a ball coming at him or a water-gliding contraption twitching in a random way, and he moves in such a natural fashion that doesn't feel so much trained as born. From the way Bangtan is presented, you would think that Jin is kind of the flail-y member and Jungkook the super athletic, talented one.

And yet Jin doesn't make a thing of it. In one episode of *Run BTS!*, the members do an elevated obstacle course, and, as I watch, I think Jin is deliberately going slower, ultimately so Jungkook, as the maknae, can win. In another episode, the members are making kimchi, and Jin is the one patiently working away and getting RM and Taehyung to focus. In so many videos taken back-stage, on *Run BTS!*, on vlogs, Jin is often heard saying, "형이 할게!" (hyung will do it!), while reaching out to feed a member, help with whatever activity they've been assigned, or just provide support in whatever capacity a member needs, moving first before they can even ask.

And, every time, I think, This is why Jin is the hyung . . . even though, hilariously, he is the maknae in his family.

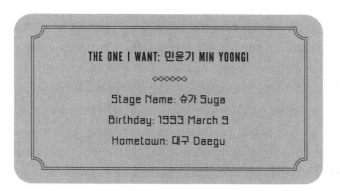

THE ONE I WANT: 민윤기 MIN YOONGI

◇◇◇◇◇

Stage Name: 슈가 Suga

Birthday: 1993 March 9

Hometown: 대구 Daegu

Suga is quite possibly the only idol I have actually been intensely, genuinely attracted to. Sure, I thought Jae-joong was beautiful and T.O.P was hot, but Suga is the only one whom I would theoretically date. Maybe it's that he's that perfect blend of masculine and feminine, and he has a deep, slightly gravelly voice, and he has broad shoulders and a round butt and mandu cheeks.

Even as I write these words, I think this all sounds absurd. Suga is a stranger, a celebrity who lives on the other side of the world in a version of reality that is vastly removed from mine. I have no idea who he is as an actual human being, as Min Yoongi, and yet I have built an idea of him in my head, a character, essentially, who is flawless and not real, and I have spent a ridiculous amount of time and money consuming content and playing with this version of him.

I wonder, constantly, what it is that makes me so susceptible to fandom. I resist it, too, in ways—I don't call myself ARMY and, in fact, have never really aligned with an official fandom, though I suppose I would still join Club H.O.T. if I could. Part of the reason is that I didn't grow up being able to participate in fandom, the internet being so new and K-pop so domestic during its first- and even second-generation days. Content was harder to come by and required a lot more effort than simply going on the internet. To watch music videos or performances, you had to wait for your parents to make their weekly trip to the Korean video store and hope a VHS was rentable (and viewable). To get CDs, in Los Angeles, you had to get to Koreatown Plaza in all its pink-tiled glory to go to the music store on the third floor while your parents were grocery shopping downstairs. You could purchase magazines at ArtBox a few months after they were published in Korea. Being able to go to concerts and see your favorite idol live in the US was unheard of.

As the world became more wired, participating in fandom was still a challenge if you had a Mac because most Korean programs were built for Windows. To add to that, most Korean sites required a Korean registration number, the equivalent of a social security number, just to register, which meant that it was difficult, if not impossible, to join fan cafés, have a Cyworld mini-hompy, or access Clubbox if you weren't a Korean national. As K-pop became more global and companies started to realize there were more fans around the world than before, things became somewhat easier, and, as K-pop grew, even in niche communities, thanks to SMTOWN, Big Bang, and the Wonder Girls, international communities sprang up on forums, LiveJournal, and Tumblr, with fans providing translations of lyrics, interviews, and variety shows.

K-pop is such a different thing today than it was in the late 1990s. Fandom was simultaneously a lonelier and more intimate thing then. It was less polished, less intense, and, at least, from across the Pacific, less aggressive. My experience being a bbasooni of Tony was so different from being a bbasooni of Suga—I didn't know much about Tony. There was less information readily available, and I had to dig things up in Korean. When I get into Suga in October 2022, there is so much information easily available, and I don't even have to Google. I can just post something on Instagram Stories and people I have never known or interacted with online are ready to provide me answers, recommend Suga-centric songs, squee with me over how hot he is. I can go on YouTube and spend hours watching video clips of performances, interviews, and, of course, *Run BTS!* Maybe the difference between my platonic love of Tony and my obsession with Suga comes down to something as simple as access—I "know" so much about Suga, and, even if that knowledge is built upon what is fundamentally an illusion and a fantasy, it is still a way of knowing. It is still intimate because of its fantastical nature and pure desire.

— — —

When Jin, the oldest Bangtan member, enlists on December 12, 2022, the media starts to announce that Suga, the second oldest, has allegedly received permission to fulfill his military service as a social service worker. This means that he wouldn't be an active-duty soldier but would work a desk job, which doesn't surprise me. Suga has a well-documented shoulder injury that he sustained in a car accident when he was twenty years old and has caused him chronic pain since. For years after Bangtan debuted, he got by on injections and adrenaline, until he finally got to the point when he couldn't even lift his arm, and, in 2020, he underwent surgery, which took him out for a few months to recover properly. The other members often carried around a photo of Suga to their public events and called him on speakerphone on *Run! BTS* episodes and at awards shows.

Suga isn't the first celebrity to be assigned desk duty because of an injury sustained in an accident, and he won't be the last. In 2011, when Super Junior member Kim Heechul enlisted, he was also assigned to a desk job because of an accident in 2006 that left him with steel rods in his legs. Actor Lee Minho also served at a desk because of injuries sustained in an accident. To take it a step further, in March 2024, Pledis Entertainment confirmed that Seventeen member S. Coups had been granted an exemption because of a knee injury. Nothing about the speculation about Suga's service should have surprised or shocked anyone, but it also didn't surprise me that it would bait negative feedback.

The lack of critical thinking irritates me. Even Heechul had to publicly address critics, although his 2006 accident had made headlines. On a realistic level, there is also *zero* incentive for the Korean government to grant Bangtan any favors when it comes to military service. Its refusal to grant them an exemption alone displays the government's desire to set a precedent when it comes to celebrity enlistments, and, given the scale of Bangtan's fame and the criticism they invite, the government wouldn't risk being seen as going "soft" on Bangtan.

Of course, though, it is easier for people to sit at a computer or on a phone and shout crap thoughtlessly into the void. Fandom does it; why shouldn't haters? The media does it as well, failing to contextualize things properly in order to get their clicks and chatter. In Korea, when it comes to yeonaein, it's about getting views, even if the "news" being reported has been unverified, even if there might be no grounds for whatever is being speculated upon—it is more convenient for the media to stoke netizens' outrage and give them something to criticize, never mind that the criticism is thoughtless and misguided and there is a real human being at the center of the maelstrom.

Suga enlisted in September 2023 after doing a solo tour across the United States, Southeast Asia, and Japan before closing with six total concerts in Seoul. Unlike the other members, who have occasionally posted on social media when they have access to the internet, Suga has more or less disappeared—there are no Weverse messages or Instagram posts or photos released of him in uniform at military ceremonies. He was already less active on social media than the other members, but I assume that part of the reason for his total lack of visibility while in gundae has been to keep as much criticism at bay as possible, which I understand but am still bummed out by. Irritation at public stupidity aside, I miss Yoongi.

— — —

For Bangtan fans, 2025 has become a kind of mantra. RM, Jimin, Taehyung, and Jungkook were the final four to enlist in December 2023 (J-Hope had enlisted in April 2023), which means that all of Bangtan will be out in July 2025 when Yoongi is discharged. (Yoongi's service is the longest because he's serving desk duty; active-duty soldiers serve roughly eighteen to twenty months, while those assigned to social work serve for closer to twenty-four.) That leaves less than half a year for them to record new music, get back into performing shape, and so on, but that tight timetable doesn't stop the fandom from holding on to 2025, as if the big comeback will happen so quickly.

Maybe I'm just old. I've avoided behind-the-scenes footage of Bangtan's concerts because I've seen clips of Jungkook being supported backstage, held up by staff members, of Jimin holding onto his chest, of the boys clutching mini oxygen tanks to their faces. Some fans commend this as a positive sign of Bangtan's dedication to their jobs. I personally hate it. You get one body in this one life. No job is worth pushing yourself to that extreme. No fame, no success, no fandom is worth that, and I'm already dreading the feeding frenzy when Bangtan comes back.

THE BRAND: 정호석 JUNG HOSEOK

◇◇◇◇◇

Stage Name: J-Hope
Birthday: 1994 February 18
Hometown: 광주 Gwangju

hen I finally get into Bangtan in October 2022, I'm genuinely stunned by how much content they have. Sure, they've been around for almost ten years at that point, but, even so, compared to other groups, their body of content, largely self-produced by BigHit, seems almost excessive, from their behind-the-scenes vlogs posted on YouTube to concert documentary series released on various platforms, including Disney+, to their own variety show, *Run BTS!*, released on the digital platform Weverse. They also have themed spin-off variety shows that take them camping (*In the Soop*) or on trips in foreign countries (*Bon Voyage*), the members left to their own shenanigans as cameras follow them around and record their every movement.

In June 2013, the timing couldn't have been more ripe for a group like Bangtan, one that tried to counter some of the dominant expectations of idols, rejecting surgically fine-tuned faces, pretty boy aesthetics, clearly manufactured personas. Bangtan was also early to get on YouTube and Twitter, and they ran their own blog, supposedly posting content themselves, instead of opting for shinier, company-managed methods of introducing themselves to the public. According to Bangtan's own narrative, that wasn't necessarily by choice—BigHit simply didn't have the resources or financial support to generate the manufactured content that companies like SM or YG might, and all this combined has helped develop Bangtan's brand as a group that is "authentic," though that word has become such a part of marketing jargon through the late 2010s and the early 2020s as to be virtually meaningless.

And, I mean, it worked. Branding and narrative are as important in K-pop as in any other industry, and I would argue that Bangtan's popularity did come about significantly through their content, especially because, as I watch *Run BTS!*, I can see where the charm comes in. The boys seem unfiltered and "real," though to varying degrees. RM carries more obvious self-consciousness as the leader, knowing there are lines Bangtan must exist within. He's often pulling back Suga, who is more open and less guarded about things—in a 2018 interview with *Billboard*, writer E. Alex Jung notes that RM has stepped back his public opinion about gay marriage, whereas Suga doesn't hesitate in continuing to publicize his support for it. In another video, Bangtan encourages students in Korea during the national university exam, and, as Suga keeps talking about how the 수능 isn't *that* important, Jungkook starts playing with Suga's hair and RM speaks up to make him stop.

As I watch more of their content, seeing how they constantly have to be turned on as public figures, given how much they record of themselves, I feel like all the members have come up with different ways of placing boundaries around themselves and figuring out how to blend their "real" selves with their public-facing personalities. Members like Jin and Suga seem to have built personas that blend the two fairly naturally, allowing fans to feel like we actually know them more. Jin, for example, is very blunt, loud, and kind of obnoxious in videos, but he seems to be that kind of unfiltered person, just taking things up many notches when he's being Jin of BTS and laughing louder, leaning more heavily into his dad jokes, and playing at being one of the maknaes instead of the hyung by goofing around. Jimin seems more guarded, yes, but also like his gentle public persona reflects who he is. Taehyung, with his alien spaciness, and Jungkook, as the golden maknae who can do no wrong, seem the most natural, the most themselves even in the public eye.

J-Hope, though—J-Hope, to me, always comes across as J-Hope.

In my mind, he is always simply J-Hope, maybe Hobi if I'm feeling warmer toward him in a given moment, but he is never Hoseok or any other version of his name that might feel more personal or affectionate. J-Hope feels like a public persona, full stop. Fans love to speculate on discussion boards or social media about which idols are most genuinely themselves in public or who might be an asshole, and, out of Bangtan, J-Hope is, in my opinion, the wild card, the member who could be anyone in real life because he wears the most rigid public mask, the most aware that he is a brand. On some level, I very much commend that because I believe that boundaries are crucial when you're as famous as Bangtan is, but admittedly it also makes him feel less knowable to me.

THE TARGET: 박지민 PARK JIMIN

◇◇◇◇◇◇

Stage Name: 지민 Jimin
Birthday: 1995 October 15
Hometown: 부산 Busan

S talking. Hate-filled comments left on websites, articles, message boards. Black oceans. Messages telling you to die, that your group would be better off without you, that the world would be. Hacked phone numbers and personal information.

In 2023, it was exposed that an employee of the national Korean rail system, KORAIL, had been accessing and leaking RM's personal information, including his phone number, address, and even national registration number. Later that same year, a stalker was arrested in the elevator of Taehyung's building; she was allegedly holding an application for a marriage certificate for herself and Taehyung. Jungkook has asked fans repeatedly during Weverse lives not to show up at his gym or send food delivery to his apartment.

Most of this is par for the course when you're a yeonaein, but Jimin even had a deranged Brit get plastic surgery after plastic surgery in attempts to look like him while claiming to be "transracial," a term that, when used correctly, applies to children who are adopted into families of another race. Then, there was the wrath brought on by shipping—in Bangtan fandom, one of the most prominent ships pairs Taehyung and Jungkook (called TaeKook) together. Given that Jimin, Taehyung, and Jungkook make up the maknae line in Bangtan, Jimin is close with both, but he's become a target in the past whenever he interacts with either member, accused of interfering in TaeKook's relationship and trying to come between them.

There is something to be said about K-pop's dependence on building and nurturing parasocial relationships between idols and fans. This has existed since the beginning of K-pop, by providing fan service (idols refer to their fan clubs as a collective and will play up how much they love their fan club, *here's a finger heart for you, here's some aegyo, here, swoon for me*) and not dating publicly, but I do think the flip side to Bangtan's "authenticity" is the further blurring of these lines between idol and fan, and I don't know how I feel about that. There's something unnerving about catching a glimpse of numerous staff with cameras following Bangtan members around *constantly*, so they can make vlogs and post content to provide fans access.

Bangtan had more than their fair share of antis when they debuted—the hate they received from VIPs (Big Bang fans) and EXOLs (EXO fans) is written into their origin story, along with netizens leaving vicious comments on articles and message boards, media companies blacklisting them, and show organizers making them wait to perform then deciding they didn't need Bangtan after all and leaving them to perform for their fans without fancy concert lighting or stage design. They, too, were black oceaned—twice.

On the other end of fandom is antifandom, though I honestly think they're just two expressions of the same kind of intense, obsessive love. Both types of fans scream *notice me, notice me*, and both pay focused attention to the object of their affection. Both types of love often seem misguided and distorted, one expressing itself in possession and adulation, the other in contempt and loathing, but, still, love. Hate, after all, is not the opposite of love (that would be indifference), but the other side of the same coin.

Sometimes, I think Korean culture is set up for this kind of obsession because of how extreme daily life is. Young Koreans call Korea Hell Joseon because the competition is so brutal—to get into a good university, to get an office job, to be able to afford the huge deposit required to rent an apartment—and I can see how fandom—or antifandom—becomes an escape, a way to vent stress either by cheering madly for your bias or by ranting about your antibias. That makes me wonder, though: What is it that I seek from fandom? Why is it so satisfying to stan some stranger I'll never meet? And, on the other side of things, why is it stress-relieving to rant about a gasoo or yeonaein I can't stand for whatever dumb reason? These are actual people who happen to live public lives, but that alone shouldn't be reason enough to make them targets, either for my obsessive affection or for my irrational hatred.

But what is it that makes fandom or antifandom feel so . . . human? And how much is too much?

Bangtan, obviously, isn't the first idol group to be targeted by antifans, and they won't be the last. In October 2006, Yunho, the leader of TVXQ, was poisoned when he drank a bottled beverage that had been spiked with super glue then somehow resealed and given to him by a supposed fan as he was leaving an event. The antifan had no reason for the attack other than that she didn't like him. In 2009, Kan Miyoun, a member of first-generation girl group Baby Vox, received box cutters in the mail with notes telling her to kill herself from fans of H.O.T.'s Moon Heejun because there were rumors the two were dating.

In 2018, Bangtan was scheduled to make an appearance in Texas, and Jimin received death threats so serious that local law enforcement actually took additional protective measures. In 2024, BigHit released RM's second album, *Right Place, Wrong Person*, while he was in gundae, and antis started hate trains on Twitter, declaring him the ugliest man in the world.

While I understand the impulse to want to gossip about celebrities, where is the line? And what is it that makes some people cross it in such awful ways?

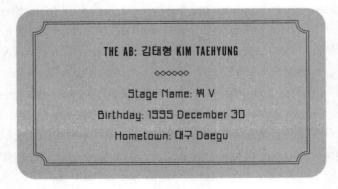

THE AB: 김태형 KIM TAEHYUNG

◇◇◇◇◇◇

Stage Name: 뷔 V
Birthday: 1995 December 30
Hometown: 대구 Daegu

Yoongi might be my bias, but Taehyung is my favorite. Tete or Tae, as I usually call him when chatting with friends, loves his dog (a Pomeranian named Yeontan), eats a lot of noodles, and has type AB blood. Like others with his blood type, namely Kim Heechul of second-generation boy band Super Junior, Taehyung is delightfully *weird*. In season one of their travel show, *Bon Voyage*, he gets himself lost and stays lost. He can ramble senselessly and sometimes needs to be corralled on a red carpet or on a stage by the other members. He can often come across as spacey, distracted, and absent-minded, and he even seems to confuse himself at times, pausing mid-ramble to stare up at the sky.

I like weird. I'm weird. As a type B, I'm also considered an alien.

We know the type A stereotype in the West, and it's similar in Korea, though the personality scale based on blood types is perhaps less known here. The general stereotype goes that you shouldn't date a man who's type B because he's a flake, and types AB and B are considered to be aliens, a little out there and spontaneous and weird. I'm surprised when I find out that Jaejoong, one of the original members of TVXQ, is type O because he's so all over the place and hilariously 4D, another way Koreans like to describe people who are weird—we exist in the fourth dimension.

In the mid-2010s, when I donate blood, I finally get my blood tested to find out my blood type. If we're going by Korean personality types, I'm most definitely not an A, and, based on my limited knowledge of biology and genes, I can't be an O. O is a recessive gene. Given that my mom is an O and my dad an AB, I can only be either an A (with recessive O) or a B (also with recessive O).

I'm a B negative. My parents laugh when I tell them because that kind of tracks with my life—I have always been good but not good enough, a finalist but never a winner, close but never quite there. In Korean, I would say 운이 없다, which still gets me a brief scolding from my Christian mom who demands to know how I can say I have no luck or fortune because how can I believe in such a thing as *luck* when I should believe in God, even though I don't really believe in fortune—or do I? Maybe a part of me would like to because it would be nice to fall back on something that exists out of my control to explain what have often felt like short-comings in my life.

(Maybe that's what God is to a lot of people.)

━ ━ ━

For many years, I resented the idea of a chosen or found family because of the truth that some of us *have* to lean into chosen families if natal families have rejected us for whatever reason. Maybe they're anti-queer or they were young and accidentally pregnant and didn't have the resources or support to raise a child together, but, whatever the circumstance, some people have no choice *but* to sentimentalize chosen and found families. It's a common theme in K-dramas, too—if you watch them, you're familiar with the scene: An angsty young person sits at a dinner table with a family that isn't theirs. They aren't really eating because they're uncomfortable, but then the matriarch of the family reaches over to place a piece of meat or deboned fish or some choice banchan on their bowl of rice and tells them to eat up, eat a lot, they need to eat to be strong. It's a simple act of love but one that is so emotionally charged, the scene never fails to make me tear up. There's a reason that the phrase to ask how someone is in Korean is 밥 먹었니?—Have you eaten?

In November 2023, I drive up to Vegas for a friend's baby's 돌 (first birthday). She's the one who introduced me to Bangtan, to Yoongi, and we've spent the year jokingly fighting over him. I even have a purple T-shirt made that says 윤기내꺼 (literally "Yoongi mine") to wear around her. I spend the twenty-four hours I'm in town helping run errands, wash dishes, set up and break down, not because she puts me to work but because that's what I expected to do when I said I'd drive up—I wanted to be there, to show up, to help.

When I was in my twenties and lonely and angry, still processing the effects of body-shaming, I used to think of friendship from a more one-sided perspective. I wished I had people next to me but didn't think much of how it would feel to be the one standing by someone else. At the time, I couldn't think beyond what I needed because I needed to heal first. Over the last few years, though, I've come to realize just how vital it is for us to have people we want to show up for and celebrate, people we stand beside and pour love into and build up, and my resentment regarding chosen families has softened at the same time. Yes, I still think it's sad and angering that some of us have no choice but to lean into chosen families because of rejection from natal families for a myriad of reasons, but I've also come to experience how special it is to have people in your life who show up and take up space. As someone who grew up lonely, who spent so many years isolated from people because of body-shaming, it means a tremendous amount to me to have people in my life.

And this makes me think of Taehyung. Taehyung might be known for his good-looking face and husky baritone voice, but, as a human, he can come across as very awkward, often in his own world. When he does media appearances for his 2023 solo mini-album, *Layover*, he isn't the most charismatic or well spoken, lacking the interpersonal social ease of RM or the extroverted outgoingness of J-Hope.

When he's with Bangtan, though, or others close to him, Taehyung is funny, charming, and comfortable, and, the more I watch him, the more I think how powerful it is to find people who accept you as you are—and the more I think that there is no such thing as normal, that we've *all* got our weirdnesses and quirks and flaws, and how much healthier we would be as a society if we would wrap ourselves around our individuality instead of trying to conform to a model of human that frankly doesn't exist. I'm glad Taehyung found his way to that audition in Daegu that led him to BigHit. I'm glad he became a member of Bangtan. And I'm also glad that he's found people outside of the group who bring out the gentleness and warmth I so love in him.

In 2022, Taehyung appears in 서진이네 (*Jinny's Kitchen*) (tvN), a reality TV show produced by veteran producer Na PD, in which actor Lee Seo-jin sets up a restaurant serving Korean street food in Mexico. Lee is the CEO and boss, while actress Jung Yumi is second-in-command and the kimbap roller. Actor Park Seojun is the manager, and Taehyung and actor Choi Woosik are the interns who wash the dishes and take out the trash and generally perform the grunt work. Park, Choi, and Taehyung have been close friends for years, but this is a rare program where Taehyung appears on his own, not with the other Bangtan members, and not on a BigHit-produced show.

As with any show, there's promotional activity involved, and I wonder how Taehyung will do. He can be awkward when alone, when his 4D-ness can make him appear out of place, but he's just so at ease with the cast of *Jinny's Kitchen*. His interactions with the cast are natural, and he's still his weird, 4D self—but it's how he engages with Jung Yumi that stands out to me most. She's the nuna, older than he is by twelve years, and Bangtan doesn't have much by way of interactions with women, K-pop and its fandom being what they are. Taehyung looks out so thoughtfully for her, though, making sure she doesn't get hurt during a jump rope game and bantering easily with her as they sit around, just like she's his nuna, in a way that's natural and really heartwarming and speaks to the ease she also extends to him. It squeezes my own nuna heart.

THE POP STAR: 전정국 JEON JUNGKOOK

◇◇◇◇◇◇

Stage Name: 정국 Jungkook

Birthday: 1997 September 1

Hometown: 부산 Busan

When Jungkook's solo album, *Golden*, is released on November 3, 2023, the settler state of Israel is almost a month into its open genocide of Palestinians. It has dropped more than twenty-five tons of explosives on the Gaza Strip, killing roughly ten thousand, at least four thousand of whom are children, with the support of the United States and other Western powers. Hundreds of thousands around the world, from the US to Europe to India, have been taking to the streets to protest and call for ceasefire, the protesters including many Jews, even those in Israel who face an even greater threat of violence and retribution for standing up against the Israeli government. Meanwhile, Israel continues its ethnic cleansing and settlement of both Gaza and the West Bank and doesn't stop its harassment campaign of forcibly removing Palestinian families from their homes, burning olive groves, and physically assaulting and torturing Palestinians.

There are too many parallels between Israel's ethnic cleansing of Palestinians and what Japan tried to do to Korea in the early twentieth century. Japan didn't mercilessly bomb Korea or slaughter Koreans at the scale that Israel has Palestinians (though the US carpet-bombed Korea during the Korean War), but Japan did try to subsume and erase Koreanness, illegalizing the language, breeding out Korean strains of rice by bringing in Japanese strains for Japanese consumption, and more. The definition of genocide isn't only the eradication of physical people but also the erasure of their culture. It isn't just carpet-bombing entire neighborhoods, targeting hospitals, and devastating the environment to make land inhospitable for years to come—it's killing journalists, destroying buildings of cultural significance, erasing history and culture and any evidence that this people lived, that this is how they told their stories and this is what they ate. It's forcing them to have names in another language and making them eat more bread and taking their women to be sex slaves for their military.

The United States plays an active role in the genocide of Palestinians, as it does in the active war status of the Korean peninsula— the Korean War never officially ended and was just paused when an armistice agreement was signed between North Korea, China, and the United Nations on July 27, 1953. (The South, under the presidency of Syngman Rhee, declined to sign.) Because the peninsula is still technically at war, all Korean males have to serve roughly two years in the military, which is why Bangtan went on group hiatus in 2023. The US military industrial complex is a profitable machine, after all, and the Korean War being active is a fitting excuse for the US to build and maintain a significant military presence in East Asia, conveniently right next door to "bad" Communist China.

But how does this tie into K-pop? Americanness-as-aspirational has been woven into Korea since the immediate postwar period, when Korea was a poor, famine-stricken country with nothing. The peninsula had been destroyed by the war, and, as a way of rallying, the Korean government looked toward American prosperity for inspiration. Korea, too, political leaders said, could become like America. Korea, too, could have might and power. Korea, too, could follow in American footsteps and become an economic force. Former President Park Chung-hee, in particular, was instrumental in pushing Korea far along that path, which is why older generations remember him kindly.

Even as the Korean government has gained power via its economy, it has also been aware of the necessity of developing soft power, establishing cultural policies and programs since the late 1990s that would help pump money into cultural industries ranging from dramas to video games to, obviously, pop music. This is in line with what the Korean government perceived to be their asset—the southern half of the Korean peninsula lacks the natural resources that the northern half has, but what they lacked in minerals and steel and whatever else, South Korea could make up with labor, with people. By the end of the twentieth century, the government was investing in the export of Korea's cultural products, and the Hallyu Wave wasn't an accident so much as a planned development supported by money, resources, and government incentives.

(This doesn't mean the Korean government necessarily *values* its culture stars, though. If it did, Bangtan would have received a military exemption; instead, the government decided that they would be more valuable as propaganda for military enlistment.)

Of all the Bangtan members, Jungkook, to me, is the consummate pop star. He is a dancer and a smooth vocalist, and he has a look that appeals the most to the West, an ideal blend of masculine with his muscles (without crossing into aggressive sex appeal) and feminine with his softness. He has a full arm of tattoos, a lip piercing, and attitude, but he's also cute in that soonhan way, with plenty of natural charm and sweetness. He is, without a doubt, a prime example of the kind of soft power Korea has been investing in for decades.

With Jungkook's solo effort, HYBE is blatant about wanting to develop a Western pop star, playing not by BigHit's style or rules but by the West's. "Seven" and "3D," two of Jungkook's lead singles, both sound like old Western pop, hitting notes some might call nostalgic, but I call recycled. He sings lyrics that are overtly sexual, not in a way that seems cool or natural but in a way that makes me cringe because of how contrived it is. Both songs take on Western misogyny and female objectification, as if Korea doesn't have its own misogyny, and both have lyrics that make no sense and are dumbed down, simplified, and repetitive. The music video for "Seven" continues in the hallmark tradition of romanticizing stalker behavior, with Jungkook following the object of his desire (played by actress Han Sohee) around for seven days, even as she constantly rejects him, until she finally gives in.

BoA and Se7en followed a similar model when trying to break into the US over ten years ago; both discarded the qualities and strengths that made them K-pop stars in order to mold themselves to Western pop. BoA took on songs that were reminiscent of old Britney and Rihanna, while Se7en collaborated with Lil' Kim and tried to be like Usher. Both sang clumsily in English, though that actually was more understandable in the early 2010s, when it definitely wasn't okay to sing in Korean or appear on American talk shows and speak in Korean. Bangtan *did* help change that, speaking Korean on American TV and refusing to release music in English until COVID-19 shut the world down and they wanted to offer something of comfort to English-speaking fans. Still, it's disappointing to see Americanness-as-aspirational written into even the biggest boy band in the world.

For the most part, in their career trajectory until 2023, Bangtan has refused to pander to Westernness, sticking to who they are by speaking Korean, singing in Korean, and being Korean. They have carried their identity unapologetically with pride, and, as a Korean American, I have found it immensely gratifying and hilarious to witness their refusal to engage. From declining to sing in English to refusing to become fluent in English, even though they've been in the global spotlight for over five years now, to dyeing their hair the same color and wearing the same suit to the White House in June 2022, Bangtan has played by their own rules on the global stage. I hope that this deviation, exemplified by *Golden*, then carried into Taehyung's "FRI(END)S" (2024) and Jimin's *Muse* (2024), has been an experiment during this in-between period, as the members have been on hiatus as a group, taking the time to release solo projects that explore other aspects of their own personal tastes, because it has been fun to see how each member approaches his solo music, giving us a range of solo work that has shown us a different side of each member.

In general, though, I look forward to the latter half of 2025, as Bangtan starts to come back (slowly, I hope, taking their time) into the public eye as a group with RM and Suga back at the helm, steering the group back to who they are as Bangtan, playing by their rules, not those of the West.

I may have avoided Bangtan for years because I knew who I was—a bbasooni who would fall for one member and become obsessed with him—and, sure, that is *exactly* what happened, but it has also been a whole lot of fun coming back to this part of me.

10

동방신기 TVXQ

- - - - - - - - -

시작은 달콤하게 *At the Start, Sweetly,*
평범하게 *In an Ordinary Way,*
나에게 끌려 *You're Pulled Toward Me*
TVXQ, "Mirotic"
***Mirotic*, 2008**

don't call it queerphobia, just like I don't call it transphobia or
Islamophobia. To call anti-queer bigotry or anti-trans hatred
or anti-Muslim racism a phobia is to grant that kind of ugliness some measure of validity by implying that there is something to be afraid of. A phobia is a phobia because there is an
irrational degree of fear behind it, which presupposes that there
is something *to fear*, and, therefore, the person with the phobia
deserves a degree of compassion and understanding.

I don't stand for that.

Call it what it is: hate. Hate that leads to and calls for violence. Hate that has consequences for people, for real human beings and their lives.

— — —

When I'm barely twenty years old, I go to a friend's house for an impromptu church reunion. I haven't kept in touch with most of the people from my high school youth group, so I wander around the house looking for someone I know. Eventually, I end up in the kitchen, seating myself in a free chair as someone mentions in a hushed voice, *Did you hear about him? He's gay now.*

I miss his name, so I wonder who it might be, running through the different youth group boys in my head. I never figure out who it is, but the moment stays with me: the lowered voice, the quiet that falls over the group, the way my stomach churns with a discomfort I can't name.

In the conservative Korean church I grew up in, homosexuality—queerness, however you want to label it—wasn't something I really ever thought about. Heterosexuality was the norm, what was expected of and modeled for me and everyone I knew, and I don't know exactly if or to what extent I was even aware that people could be gay or trans or asexual. Even though I had friends at my public high school, my primary social group was at church, where no one ever questioned the trajectory expected of us—we would all go on to college, where we would continue to be active in the church, meet our spouses, get married young, and have children. If we were girls, we would stay home and homeschool our kids.

If we were boys, we would support our families and lead them as Christlike heads of our households.

It was weird enough that I didn't want kids. I didn't think much about getting married, either; I was told no one would even want to marry me unless I lost weight, anyway. Instead, I suppose I assumed the second-best thing for my future was that I would be celibate. I would serve God in that way, even though I was failing to fulfill my ultimate purpose of procreating.

I'm sure that, had I stayed in the church, I would have somehow come across other ways to live, other ways to have families, other ways to be. At least, I hope I would have.

■ ■ ■

TVXQ debuted in 2004, a five-member boy band from SM Entertainment. Implicitly, they were meant to continue on and advance the legacy of H.O.T., which had launched the pop industry in Korea. With "Tri-Angle" from their first studio album, *Tri-Angle* (2004), TVXQ even took inspiration from H.O.T.'s style, both satorially and musically, in the song "I Yah!" With their looks, powerful choreography, and vocals (TVXQ was also known for singing a cappella), they rapidly rose in popularity, debuting in Japan in 2006 and also achieving success there, much like BoA before them.

At the height of my TVXQ fandom, 2005 to 2010, I was still deep in the church. I never would have described myself as being "anti-gay"—I didn't *hate* gay people. I loved them in the Christian way of hating the sin and loving the sinner, and I would never condemn them—I just wanted to save their souls. I also believed they deserved equal rights, but my twenty-year-old self couldn't explain what I meant by that, as I rambled about civil unions and other ideas picked up in my conservative church, the only social circle I knew. Like many Christians, I did mental gymnastics to try to appear loving, kind, and open-minded. Besides, it wasn't like I actually *knew* anyone who was openly queer. "Homosexuals" were entirely theoretical, making it all too easy to discuss anything related to LGBTQ+ identity in a casual way, with no personal stakes.

Given how anti-LGBTQ+ some Koreans can be, it's ironic that K-pop fandom is where I first actively encountered queerness via shipping. While it isn't exclusive to K-pop fandom, there's a homoerotic intensity to K-pop shipping that I find curious but unsurprising—idols aren't allowed to date because romantic relationships would fracture the idol/fan fantasy.

Shipping often made me uncomfortable when I was younger, and I never sought it out in fan communities, though it felt unavoidable because most of the good fan fiction writers I found within TVXQ fandom were all about shipping, writing very gay stories featuring pairings like YunJae (Yunho and Jaejoong) or YooSu (Yoochun and Junsu). I admit that I found it distasteful to read about same-sex desire and sexual acts, even if some of the writing was beautiful and erotic, and I could only read up to a certain level of intimacy—yearning, touching, kissing, never anything beyond that. I'd scroll past the more explicit sex scenes, never stopping to let myself consider *why* depictions of men being attracted to men made me feel so bad or to question the anti-LGBTQ+ messaging I had been taught.

Once, during college, I sat with my best friend in my car in the parking lot of a Jack in the Box. It was late, and we were discussing gay marriage, and she wasn't a Christian. She kept asking how I could rationalize this idea of "hate the sin, love the sinner." What did that even *mean*? How could you separate a person's identity from the person? Could I make it make sense to her? Eventually, the conversation ended with me pleading for her to understand that this was my faith. I didn't have all the answers, and I couldn't summarize everything neatly for her because I didn't know everything, but I believed—I *had* to believe. That's why it was called faith. I knew my replies weren't satisfactory, that they were empty and confusing, but I needed her to accept that this was all I could give her.

Even then, I knew how feeble I sounded, and I hated my inability to defend myself, to make a case for my faith and provide concrete rebuttals to her questions and scenarios. I didn't like to sit and think about these gaps in my knowledge, though—and I wouldn't, not for another ten years. My personal inability to reconcile the notion of a loving God with how viciously anti-queer Christians can be, to the point that they don't care that queer kids die by suicide because of anti-queer bigotry, came to a head when Trump won the election in 2016. His hate-filled, racist, misogynistic, violent campaign had received the support of so many so-called Christians, and I realized I could no longer find comfort or peace in the unforgiving spaces of organized religion by closing my eyes and pretending the bigotry didn't exist.

Leaving the church, leaving faith, is the most difficult, painful thing I have ever done, but, eventually, I did. In the mid-2010s, as I went through a period of questioning my own sexuality, I came face-to-face with the knee-jerk viciousness toward and sheer hatred of LGBTQ+ people in the Christian community I'd grown up in. Even the *idea* that I could be gay caused people's eyes to go immediately cold, their voices to turn frosty and tense—and these were people who had known me since I was a child. I became a monster just for questioning the heteronormative expectations placed on me, and it was immediately clear how swift and absolute the consequences would be if I *were* queer, not only for me, but also for my family. Korean culture is collective, not individual, and my parents would also lose their friendships, their social standing, and their respect in the church they had served for decades.

Since then, I haven't been able to reconcile the church's rejection of homosexuality with the gospel's message of love. I am aware of what the Bible says about marriage being between a man and a woman, and I don't actually expect conservative Korean churches to start appointing openly queer deacons and elders, ordaining gay ministers, or performing marriage rites for queer couples within their churches. I do support the right of these churchgoers to practice their religion, insofar as that religion keeps its fingers out of government and stops trying to impose its morality upon the law of the land and harm people, but I do question the merit of Christians' faith and humanity by virtue of how they regard and treat LGBTQ+ people. Are they able to approach queer people with love and respect, to break bread with them without judgment, as Christ did with tax collectors, or does the very thought make them red-faced and angry? Are they keen to throw the first stone as the Sadducees were with a prostitute in John 8:1–11, or are they able to recognize that no one is in a place to judge? Does their faith open them up to the world, or does it make them narrow-minded, rigid, and hateful?

■ ■ ■

aejoong has woven himself into my identity. My online ID, jjoongie, is a play on his name, shorthand for what you might affectionately call him in Korean. He's beautiful, though he looked maybe a little alien when he wore circle lenses that made his immense eyes look even wider and glassier. My favorite phase of his was during TVXQ's second album, his hair dyed jet-black and cut in a shag around his face. His lips are full, his skin pale: his is the ideal kind of male beauty on which to project queerness and femininity.

In 2006, the public learned that Jaejoong was adopted. He was actually born Han Jaejun; his natal parents divorced when he was young, and his mother placed him for adoption.

After TVXQ debuted, his birth father filed a lawsuit against Jaejoong's adoptive parents for parental rights. He dropped the suit a few months later, but Jaejoong had to release a public explanation—yes, it was true, he had been adopted, he had learned of this a few years prior when his adoptive parents had told him, and he had been in contact with his biological mother. He said that he preferred to continue living as Kim Jaejoong as he had for most of his life.

From what I remember, this was a scandal when it came out, mostly because it was a surprise. Jaejoong's birth father bore a lot of criticism because the lawsuit seemed clearly a play to profit off his now-famous son's success, even though he, of course, publicly claimed otherwise. The news eventually blew over, and Jaejoong, with TVXQ, continued to rise.

The narrative of adoption, though, is written into Christianity, more strongly in certain branches and sects than others. I grew up in a nondenominational English ministry that was an offshoot of Master's Seminary, which was formed by Grace Community

Church under John MacArthur. Master's theology tends to be more conservative, and the lifestyle it espouses is fairly rigid—men are meant to be the heads of the household, women are to submit to their husbands, and children should be homeschooled. Adoption is a virtuous act supported by James 1:27, which reads, "Religion that God our Father accepts as pure and faultless is this: to look after orphans and widows in their distress and to keep oneself from being polluted by the world" (NIV). The verse is commonly interpreted as an exhortation to adopt.

When my Sunday schoolmates and I would talk about how many kids we wanted, we would always break it down into two parts—we wanted X number of kids biologically and wanted to adopt X number. Girls who said they wanted to adopt more children than carry and deliver physically had a slight edge over those who didn't, so we learned from an early age that there was a tinge of holiness around adoption, that it was a means somehow of being Christlike and sanctifying ourselves, and, much like attitudes toward homosexuality and queerness, we never questioned it.

I don't remember how I started to undo the evangelical perspective on transnational adoption in my brain. I had some kind of turning point in the mid-2000s, though, and I think I came into it first via a gender-based perspective, as it's women who get pregnant. I stick to the gender binary here intentionally because Korean society exists within the gender binary, and Korea's patriarchal society is what enforces the gender-based shame that once made Korea the largest exporter of babies to the Western world.

There is little to no support for single mothers in Korean society, even today. It is difficult for them to get apartments or jobs because they're considered shameful and, therefore, of bad fortune, and they receive basically no financial support from the government. This isn't restricted to age, either—teenage girls are, of course, shamed, but so are adult women, even when they are single because of divorce or widowhood.

Transnational adoption first took root in Korea in the post-war period, when American GIs stationed in Korea started getting Korean sex workers pregnant. The Korean government basically encouraged Korean sex workers to service American GIs as a way of bringing American dollars into Korea's poverty-stricken post-war economy, but the government's response to the mixed children born from some of these relations was to shun them. Part of president Syngman Rhee's policies then was the idea of "one blood," and this clinging to "pure" Koreanness is darkly hilarious when you consider that he was a Korean American man married to a white woman. Mixed-race children, especially those born to Black American men and Korean women, had no place in Korean society, and the easiest solution was to remove them.

This was conveniently implemented by white American missionaries who happily took on the plight of these mixed-race children. Agencies were set up, and the transnational adoption business—essentially the sale of human children across borders—was established. White evangelicals in the United States, where the birth rate was falling, seized upon the ability to (1) get access to babies and (2) do something good and holy by "saving" them.

As Korea became more prosperous and there were fewer mixed-race babies, the government essentially turned to the babies born of single girls and women. Homes were set up where families could send their pregnant daughters, homes where they were physically cared for while being shamed and pressured to give up their babies for adoption. Baby boxes were set up where families could leave babies without the mothers' consent. Babies couldn't be adopted out without being orphans, so agencies like Holt International essentially created (and continues to create) orphans, removing babies from their family records—which also means that, when grown adoptees return to Korea years later looking for their natal families, there are often no records, no history, no way to learn where they came from.

Domestic Koreans can often still be weird about lineage and blood—if you've watched a Korean melodrama, you've likely seen an adult crying about their 핏줄—literally, their bloodline. That makes domestic adoption a challenge, to put it lightly.

This made Jaejoong's situation unique. His parents divorced when he was very young, and his father didn't want custody, leaving him to his mother. Even though she had been married when she had him, she would have borne tremendous stigma for being a single mother, and that, combined with the difficulty of supporting her child, pushed her to give him up for adoption. The family he was adopted into didn't have a son, just six daughters, which hearkens back to the role of adoption during the early Joseon dynasty, when a male heir was often brought into a family that lacked one.

From what I remember, at least in international fandom, Jaejoong's news was received with shock, but it wasn't seen as scandalous or terrible.

■ ■ ■

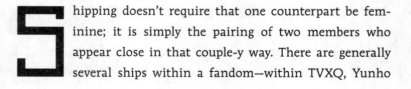

hipping doesn't require that one counterpart be feminine; it is simply the pairing of two members who appear close in that couple-y way. There are generally several ships within a fandom—within TVXQ, Yunho and Jaejoong (YunJae) were the biggest ship, but Jaejoong and Yoochun (JaeChun) were also one, as were Yoochun and Junsu (YooSu). In any fandom, there could be multiple combinations with various members, and fans can get *super* intense about their ships, which can even pit certain corners of fandoms against each other (remember the hate Jimin gets from TaeKook shippers when he's around Jungkook). Within TVXQ, YunJae was the most popular because Yunho, as the leader, was depicted as the appa of the group, while Jaejoong was the umma, and, physically, they also made for a striking pair, with Yunho's more masculine appearance. "YunJae is real" became the tagline as fans devoted to the ship created websites, blogs, and forums dedicated to providing proof that YunJae wasn't just a fictional ship but existed in real life. YunJae fans went wild over fan service that Yunho and Jaejoong threw at them during concerts or signings, playing at affection to please fans, but I always wondered—what *would* happen if Yunho and Jaejoong were a "real" couple? How would people *actually* react in Korea?

■ ■ ■

Korean culture today is synonymous to me with anti-queer bigotry, and I wonder if, historically, this was always the case. I assume so, at least as far as Joseon Korea is concerned, given how gendered and heteronormative that society was and how much goodness was ascribed to fitting proper gendered norms.

I've long wondered if Korea's anti-LGBTQ+ bigotry is mostly the result of religious belief or if it's also built into Korea's patriarchal culture. Korea, as far as religion goes, is a plurality—roughly 30 percent of the population identifies as Christian (whether Protestant or Catholic), roughly 25 percent as Buddhist, and roughly 45 percent as without religion. Christianity has a long, complicated history in Korea, and the most vocal objections to queer people in Korea come from within its Christian communities.

Homosexuality isn't illegal in Korea, but there are no anti-discrimination laws to protect LGBTQ+ people, and anti-LGBTQ+ sentiment runs strong. Being openly queer in Korea means risking so much loss—loss of your family, your career, your social standing. In a communal culture like Korea's, where the social unit (on a micro level, your family; on a macro level, your country) overrides the individual, your personal actions reverberate through all your social ties. This is why parents will take the babies of their single daughters and abandon them; why the fear of shame will make people conform and remain in toxic, abusive marriages; and why it's remarkable and powerful that a movement like #MeToo has gained traction in Korea, spurring investigations in the offices of prominent male politicians. A photographer in Korea who shoots portraits of gay couples blurs out their faces when sharing on social media, captioning the photos with the hope that one day, it will be safe for them to openly share their love and joy.

All this risk means that I don't do much speculating about any Korean public figure's sexuality; that's their business. As much as I understand the desire to see more queer representation in Korean media, that doesn't mean any of us is entitled to knowledge of any idol's sexuality. Our collective need for representation never overrides a person's right to privacy and safety, and we've seen this actually harm queer people in the publishing space, as the #OwnVoices movement quickly became distorted to force queer authors to out themselves in order to avoid doxing by online vigilantes. This prejudice and consequent risk spill into the diaspora, too, and many of my fellow second-generation Korean Americans, whether within or outside the constraints of Christianity, are never allowed the space to examine our sexuality or identity. We are assumed to be straight. Queerness is acceptable only within the hazy realm of shipping.

K-pop idols are well aware of shipping, and they'll often cater to their fans, playing it up at concerts, on variety shows, and during fan meetings. In 2006, TVXQ appeared for several episodes on a variety show called *Banjun Drama* (SBS, 2004–2006). In one of the episodes, "Dangerous Love," Jaejoong comes out to their van to see Yunho hiding out alone, clearly concealing something he's been looking at. When pressed, Yunho holds up a sheaf of papers and asks eagerly, "Hey, have you seen this? It's fanfic about us—and, in it, we're *that way*." The rest of the episode is filled with fan service as the two enact romantic, sexually tinged scenarios that play up the YunJae ship. There's laughter when Yunho leans in to whisper, "We're *that way*," into Jaejoong's ear, more laughter as Jaejoong reads lines from the fan fiction portraying YunJae in a romantic act. It's meant to be funny, all of this homoerotic tension acceptable because it exists within the realm of fiction, of shipping. The thing is, though, turning homosexuality into something so outrageous it can only be laughed at is actually anti-gay.

This is why I can't get fully behind shipping in K-pop—because so much of it is grounded in anti-queerness, in the desire and imperative of fans to control their idols and refuse them agency. If Yunho and Jaejoong *had* come out as a gay couple, they might have been pilloried, their careers ruined. Playing into shipping, however, is okay, even encouraged, because it's a part of fandom. As idols age, they're allowed to date, because even idols ought to get married and have children, but these relationships are expected to fall within heteronormative expectations. Thus, shipping is also acceptable because of its impermanence. As far as I know, the members of TVXQ have all grown up and started dating their rumored girlfriends; Junsu, the most flamboyant of the five, has been public about his relationship with EXID's Hani.

— — —

That isn't to say there aren't openly queer people in Korean media. When I was growing up, actor and comedian Hong Seokcheon was a pretty popular figure in Korean media, appearing in the popular sitcom 남자셋, 여자셋 (*Three Men, Three Women*) that aired on MBC from 1996 to 1999, until he came out publicly in 2000 and was shunned by media. The singer Harisu is an openly transgender woman who went through gender reassignment surgery and, in 2002, became only the second person in Korea to change her gender legally. She had a fairly successful career until she got married in 2007 and retired from entertainment. I'm sure both received plenty of hate throughout their careers, but they were also widely known and open, clearly receiving enough support from the general public to have active careers.

In 2018, Holland debuted as the first openly gay K-pop idol. Born 고태섭 (Go Tae-seob), he took his stage name from the first country to legalize same-sex marriage, and, because he was openly gay, he was unable to find a company that would take him on, so, instead, he worked two jobs to self-fund his debut single, "Neverland," released in 2018. The music video for the song quickly went viral, even though it depicts two men kissing, and Holland amassed a sizable following, crowdfunding his first album.

In recent years, other artists have come out as queer—Jo Kwon of second-generation boy band 2AM confirmed in 2020 that he identifies as genderless, and Korean American R&B singer MRSHLL is an openly gay vocalist active in Korea. They are still very much in the minority, though, with no major, mainstream idol publicly out, though speculations about idols' sexualities run rampant constantly. Kim Heechul of Super Junior has had rumors that he is gay chasing him his whole career because he has a 4D, flamboyant personality, often leaning into his more femme appearance and not seeming to care what anyone says about his sexuality. In 2020, though, he finally clarified that, no, he is not gay, he is indeed straight. When asked why he never spoke up against the rumors during his long career, a Soompi article reports that he said, in his usual blunt but thoughtful manner, "At first, I wanted to deny it and say that I'm not homosexual. However, I felt that if I did, I could be disrespecting sexual minorities. . . . Whether it's abroad or in Korea, there could be a gay person among the male fans at our concerts, and I think I'd feel really sorry towards them."

— — —

In 2010, three of the members of TVXQ—Jaejoong, Yoochun, and Junsu—broke away from SM and formed their own group, JYJ. The trio released a few albums but never reached the success of TVXQ, which continued on as a duo. Junsu has crafted himself a strong career in musical theater, releasing a few solo albums. Yoochun built a solid acting career before he was accused of sexual assault in 2016, though he was acquitted for lack of evidence, and, in 2019, he was arrested on suspicion of purchasing and using meth. Unsurprisingly, it was the meth charges that caused his company to terminate his contract and force him into retirement, which lasted all of a year. As far as I know, he is still active and has an active fanbase, but I don't think he will ever attain the degree of fame he had as part of TVXQ. Jaejoong released some solo music, also went into acting, and was caught on video verbally abusing and physically striking sasaeng fans who had followed him home yet again.

Sometimes I wonder what happened to the YunJae shippers. I'm sure there was plenty of fan dramatization of how Yunho felt betrayed by Jaejoong in 2010, but Yunho and Jaejoong have moved on, and so maybe the shippers have, too. Whoever they were, wherever they are now, they changed my life by introducing my sheltered young Christian self to queerness almost fifteen years ago, allowing me to eventually take my first steps away from the world I'd grown up in. Sometimes, I miss the old comfort of faith, of being able to fall back on *but this is what I believe* as an excuse, but I am more grateful to have escaped the built-in bigotry of the churches I attended.

— — —

When I walk away from the church, it is ultimately because of rage.

It takes me a year of holding on, of wanting desperately to keep the faith that has shaped my worldview since birth. Near the end of that year, in the summer of 2016, in a last-ditch attempt to find my way back to faith, I attend a women's book club at my church. During one of the sessions, a woman shares that, yes, we're taught that God only takes us to the edge of suffering that we can endure, but the thing is that he takes us just beyond that edge because that's when we fall to our knees. The other women nod along and seem to find comfort in this supposed wisdom, but I sit there and recognize that this, here, marks the end of my faith. I refuse to believe in the existence of a God who is an abuser.

I understand that there is a kind of poetry to the idea of being put through fire to be tested and shaped, and I do agree that trials and tribulations can teach us to be better people. I don't, however, agree with the self-flagellating perspective I've encountered in many churches, this idea that if you aren't suffering, you aren't growing spiritually (meaning, being sanctified), so, therefore, you must suffer, even if you must generate that suffering for yourself.

When my mother gets sick in 2023, she reminds me that life is not in our control, that there is a God whose will be done, that she finds comfort and peace in that. I don't have much heart for religious debate, but I mention briefly that, no, the thought of there being a God in control of this cancer in her does not give me peace—it makes me rage. She has spent her life in faithful service to God and her church, so it makes me phenomenally angry that God would allow her to get sick. Even as I admittedly miss faith, the communal aspects of church, the liturgy, even as I occasionally wonder if I might not one day go back, I do not currently let myself think about faith or God or Christianity. I feel furious every time I think about the world—about the genocide in Gaza and the exploitation and displacement in the Congo, about the girls and women around the United States who cannot get the abortions they need, about the proliferation of deepfakes and the rape and assault of women around the world, so often by men they know who either participate in the violence or enable it by remaining silent—every time I think about the world, I feel overwhelmed with an incandescent rage at the idea of a God who tolerates and arguably metes out so much cruel violence and hurt against the children he purports to love. What kind of will is this?

What kind of will is that of a God whose name is invoked to support and justify the hate against queer and trans kids? To drive them to their deaths? To hold them as barely human second-class citizens around the world? Why create people who are queer or trans if the goal is for them to be criminals or dead because of the way they have been created? How can I reckon with this unsurmountable problem of pain and return to faith?

Ultimately, I know that God can't necessarily be held responsible for the actions of his believers because believers are humans and humans can be phenomenally narrow-minded, cruel, and selfish. Anti-queer and anti-trans bigotry, ultimately, are about power, about the patriarchy maintaining a heteronormative grip on society that keeps the powerful in their positions. The fight against abortion isn't actually about saving lives but about controlling women; if people were actually pro-life, they would also be fighting for a society that invests in maternal health care, education, and community spaces instead of militarizing the police, defunding libraries, and dismantling public education. If the pro-life movement were actually pro-life, its proponents would care about the actual lives of the mother and the child, both in the womb and out, and the United States would not have one of the highest maternal mortality rates in the developed world.

In Luke 15:4–6, Christ tells the parable of the lost sheep: "Suppose one of you has a hundred sheep and loses one of them. Doesn't he leave the ninety-nine in the open country and go after the lost sheep until he finds it? And when he finds it, he joyfully puts it on his shoulders and goes home. Then he calls his friends and neighbors together and says, 'Rejoice with me; I have found my lost sheep'" (NIV). If Christians would actually read and practice their gospel, they would not be responsible for the deaths of so many innocents—they could not carry even a single lost life so lightly.

▬ ▬ ▬

Maybe, ultimately, faith makes me cranky because I find it to be naive—or maybe naive isn't exactly the word I'm looking for either. Sometimes I think faith acts as blinders for people, and, sure, Marx is famous for dismissing religion as a crutch. Sometimes, I think there's such an arrogance to the religious.

I do, however, often miss the church. I miss the solidness of faith, and I miss the warmth of my church communities. I miss the liturgies of service, the worship, the sense of belonging. I miss hope.

Occasionally, my parents like to challenge me as I am right now, almost as though to lure me back to faith, but I do not have the arrogance to claim I have any answers for their questions. I cannot claim to have any hope rooted in anything, and I do not claim to be able to stand for any kind of absolute truth. I cannot even fully argue that I do not believe God exists—all I can say is that I acknowledge that my choice *not* to believe in God is exactly that—my choice. My lack of belief in God, I know, is also faith. It is an empty faith I cannot substantiate or support.

I am not someone who would turn to another form of spirituality or another religion to fill the void Christianity has left in my life. I don't believe in "the universe," and I don't need another faith system.

In June 2016, as my personal struggle with faith came to its breaking point, the Korea Queer Culture Festival held its pride parade in Seoul. There was plenty of turmoil leading up to it, with a court denying a petition by a gay couple seeking legal status for their marriage. Anti-LGBTQ+ protesters showed up, unsurprisingly, with signs condemning homosexuality as a sin. They prayed and collected signatures for a petition to outlaw homosexuality outright.

Along the route, though, there was also a tent with a group of middle-aged women gloriously decked out in full ajumma gear—perms, matching T-shirts, accessories—all of them dancing together, holding their arms out to the youth marching by in the parade. They were mothers of LGBTQ+ children, there to show their support and offer encouragement to young queer people, many of whom continue to face rejection and familial loss in Korea.

Many of the young people sobbed in the arms of these ajummas, and it was heartbreaking but incredible to see, especially as someone who still witnesses anti-LGBTQ+ hatred and disgust in the Korean Christian community I grew up in. These ajummas looked like ajummas I know, bounced around like I've seen ajummas do, dwarfed by the young people who crouched down to find comfort in their arms—and, in the face of all that familiarity, as the faith-based foundation of the world I'd known crumbled away under my feet, I thought, *Goddamn, maybe there is hope for us all.*

김종완 KIM JONGWAN

This feels like such a heavy thing to lay at someone's feet, but I wouldn't be alive today had it not been for Nell.

Nell isn't a K-pop idol boy band but a four-member rock band that debuted in 2001 in the indie scene and eventually broke into the mainstream, a rare occurrence in the Korean music industry. Nell consists of vocalist, songwriter, and rhythm guitarist 김종완 (Kim Jongwan), lead guitarist 이재경 (Lee Jaekyung), bassist 이정훈 (Lee Junghoon), and drummer 정재원 (Jung Jaewon), though Jaewon left the band in 2023. I don't even remember how I first learned of them, but Nell is the band I describe as my whole heart, the band that got me through multiple suicidal episodes and still carries me today.

I love pop music, but guitars are my forever soft spot. I was classically trained in music from the age of four, starting with the piano before moving to the flute around third grade, and I was part of an orchestra in middle and high school. I performed in recitals regularly, participated in competitions here and there, and, when I was applying for college, I started prepping a demo tape to apply to conservatories in flute performance at the same time. I ended up dropping that pretty quickly, though, because, while I thought I was good at flute, I knew I didn't have the skill or discipline to pursue it professionally.

My musical background is one reason I'm chuffed by SM's regular collaborations with the Seoul Philharmonic Orchestra or its own in-house orchestra, SM Classics TOWN Orchestra, to arrange hit songs by SM artists into orchestral pieces. The project started in 2020, and SM releases new songs (with music videos) every few months—and I *love* them. Every time SM does one of these arrangements, I feel something in my belly swell and surge. I appreciate the arrangements because they aren't simple renderings of pop songs in orchestral form, but pieces that have been thoughtfully reformed and shaped for the orchestra, which is an organism of many parts. When all those parts move together to create that rich, full orchestral sound, it's the closest I come to believing in the existence of God.

This is similar to how I feel when it comes to guitars.

Like I said, Nell is my whole heart. They're a band often described as having a "cold healing sound," and that seeming contradiction is what makes them so special—their music might have cold, minor tones, but it's also so full of warmth and comfort, Jongwan's throaty voice wrapping itself around you. His lyrics often reflect loneliness and sadness, evoking the weighted feeling of wading through a world that feels blue and chilly, but there is a warmth and fundamental hope to Nell's overall sound that feels like an embrace. It's been almost twenty years since I was first drawn to them and first learned to lean heavily on them for comfort, and I still do so today.

December 2009 was the first time I made an actual attempt to take my life. It was a Sunday morning, and I was still living with my parents, and they were gone at church. Without going into much detail, I set everything up, and I sat there, on the cold tiled floor in the silence and cried. The California sun cast everything in its annoyingly beautiful light (there's a reason photographers love the light), but I felt like I was locked in suffocating darkness with no way out, no hope to hold onto, no reason to stay alive, except for this one thought—if I died then, I'd have died never having seen Nell live. At the time, Nell was on hiatus for the members to serve their mandatory military service, and I was a few years into my first lie about finishing college when I'd failed out, at the end of being able to maintain it yet unable to find a way out, but I had to stay alive. I had to see Nell.

The second time I feared for my life, it was 2013, and I was in my second semester of my first (and only) year of law school. I'd spent six months becoming increasingly depressed and more and more suicidal, and, by June, I was terrified for myself, even more than I'd been that Sunday in December 2009. In an effort to save myself, I formally withdrew from school. I found a tattoo artist nearby and got my second and third tattoos—a line map of the cities I visited in Japan in summer 2012 on my left wrist, and Nell's logo, a lowercase *n* inside an uppercase *N*, on my right.

The third time stretched from 2016 well into 2017, even into 2018, and this episode was bad enough that my parents noticed and flew across the country to move me back to Los Angeles, where I finally got professional medical help in the form of a psychiatrist, medication, and therapy. Underneath all that, though, there was Nell's "습관적 아이러니" (Habitual Irony, *C*, 2016), which I played over and over and over again, the one constant and comfort I could find. The song is about a breakup, but the second verse resonated with me, as Jongwan sings:

아무렇지 않게 다 지난 *That this will pass like it was nothing,*
일인 듯 그러는 게, 그게 난 싫다 *I don't like that.*

Even though I wanted to get through that suicidal episode, I still found something profoundly sad about knowing that this moment, too, would end, like it was nothing. I was in so much pain then, but time would dull that, maybe even to the point of erasing it, so it would become just a smudge in my memory.

Or maybe I remember how I felt then, the hopelessness and despair, with these tiny pinpricks of light that Nell managed to slip into the darkness of my depressed, suicidal brain through this song. In such ways, Nell has been my anchor—they are the band I carry with me, their logo tattooed onto my inner right wrist, a visual reminder that I have gone through this before, I have survived this before, and I will likely continue cycling through depressive, suicidal episodes for the rest of my life because this is the brain I have, but I also have this band that held me close on that quiet Sunday morning in December 2009 and has continued to keep me here.

It's also Nell who first brought me to Bangtan. The first song by a Bangtan member I ever listened to was RM's "everythingoes" (*Mono*, 2018) because it featured Nell; I didn't actually know who RM even was then. The first of Suga's solo work (under his moniker Agust D) I listened to was "어땠을까 (Dear My Friend)" (*D-2*, 2020), which featured Jongwan—not only his vocals but also on guitar and keyboard and as a songwriter. It remains one of my favorite songs because Jongwan's fingerprints are all over it, beautifully bringing in the rich electric guitar sounds I love, as well as the cold-but-warm tone that is Nell's signature. Incorporate into that Suga's rapping, his raspy voice pulsing with emotion as he reflects on a lost friendship, and here is a song that I feel represents me today. I feel wonderment at what my life would look like had I made different decisions, at my love for K-pop that has been a steady constant, and at Nell, my whole goddamn heart, the reason I am still alive today.

11
태연 TAEYEON

펄럭이는 귀 *Your Fluttering Ears,*
삐진 입꼬리 *The Pout at the Corner of Your Mouth,*
너와 함께라면 새로워 다 *When I'm with You, Everything Is New*
Taeyeon, "To the Moon"
What Do I Call You, 2020

2017

August 20, 2017: Zero is born.
December 18, 2017: Jonghyun of SHINee dies by suicide.

2018

March 10, 2018: Gom is born.
August 15, 2018: Som is born.

2019

October 14, 2019: Sulli, formerly of girl group f(x), dies by suicide.

November 24, 2019: Goo Hara, formerly of girl group Kara, dies by suicide.

2020

March 8, 2020: Taeyeon's father passes away from a sudden cardiac arrest.

March 15, 2020: The US starts to go into lockdown, state by state, due to COVID-19.

But let's go back to the beginning.

— — —

Taeyeon is the leader and lead vocalist of Girls' Generation, the nine-member girl group that debuted from SM Entertainment in 2007. Girls' Generation was one of the biggest, most influential girl groups in second-generation K-pop, though maybe it's not appropriate to refer to them in the past tense because Girls' Generation is still active, but with fewer members. In 2014, SM unceremoniously and abruptly kicked Jessica Jung out of the group. In 2017, when their contracts were up for renewal, members Sooyoung, Seohyun, and Tiffany chose not to renew and parted ways with the company, though they would return for Girls' Generation activities occasionally. Girls' Generation released one single in 2018 as Oh!GG, a smaller unit, and, since her solo debut in 2015, Taeyeon has become one of Korea's top-selling solo artists and most successful OST (original soundtrack) singers.

Taeyeon has weathered a lot of shit throughout her career. Girls' Generation endured a fair amount collectively during their early years, disliked for their supposed closeness to TVXQ and Super Junior, both also from SM. In 2008, when they were still fairly new and hadn't yet skyrocketed to fame, they were black oceaned during Dream Concert, an annual production featuring the biggest K-pop acts. Often, at group concerts and music shows, fans are seated in sections, the sizes of which are determined by the idol group's popularity and fandom size, so each section lights up a different color in honor of its group. That year, Girls' Generation had somehow gained the reputation of being rude to their seniors, which added to the grumbling from other fandoms over the girls being too close to these oppas. When it was Girls' Generation's turn to perform, all the other fandoms turned their glow sticks off and turned around, essentially creating a silent black ocean with random sections of pink, Girls' Generation's fan color.

Girls' Generation wouldn't be the last idol group to be black oceaned (Bangtan has been black oceaned twice over their career), but I can't imagine what a blow that might have been to the members' confidence, especially given that the group was only one year old at that point. It's an unflattering example of how Korean fans commit. Sometimes, fan commitment can be inspiring, like when fans unite to do community service or raise money for good causes in their idols' names. Often, though, it's simply terrifying how much power netizens wield. Their online bullying has ruined lives; it has *taken* lives.

To be a woman in any public sphere is to be vulnerable to abusive behavior from the public, and it's no different for K-pop stars. Female K-pop stars, in particular, are expected to toe an impossible line—to be both youthfully cute and sexy—and aren't allowed much autonomy. Like all K-pop idols, their images are micromanaged, their public personas chosen for them; they're expected to perform all the time, to be bubbly and effusive and full of aegyo, a constellation of behaviors I can't even begin to try to translate. K-pop idols, in general, aren't supposed to date—that would ruin the fantasy relationship between idol and fan—but it's always worse for women.

In 2014, Taeyeon was exposed as dating a younger man from the massive third-generation boy band EXO, also under SM. She was intensely shamed for it, accused of faking her depression when she was running around with her boyfriend, of showing off her relationship, of trying to get caught. She was slut-shamed because she was his senior in both age (by three years!) and hierarchy, as she had debuted five years before he did. When she tried to apologize to her fans—crying at Incheon International Airport, where fans had gathered to see her off, and apologizing personally— she was accused of faking her tears, of being manipulative and shameless.

She lost massive amounts of weight, when she was already a waif to begin with, and retreated from the public eye. When she and Baekhyun broke up a few months later, it was assumed to be her fault.

As all this unfolded, I watched from across the Pacific, worried because we already knew she lived with depression. In a 2009 Cyworld post by Leeteuk, leader of Super Junior, Taeyeon had been listed as "Court Lady Taeng" of the Milk Club (the unofficial group of SM members who live with depression and gather to bond over it). With this knowledge in mind and my own intimate familiarity with how many people in Korea still stigmatize mental illness, I've worried whenever Taeyeon has lost a significant amount of weight, gone through hard times, or lost friends or loved ones—like Jonghyun and Sulli, whom she was close to, and her father. I worry constantly. And I'm glad she has Zero.

— — —

n November 2017, Zero makes his debut on Instagram. He's a silver toy poodle, a tiny floof of curly fur, named after the dog in *The Nightmare Before Christmas*. We watch him grow up on Instagram as Taeyeon shares photos and videos of him, and his fur lightens to a silvery gray as he becomes her shadow, accompanying her to dance practices, photo shoots, fan meetings. He's the perfect size for her to cradle and carry in her arms.

When Zero was first introduced, the idea of an emotional support animal was still an abstract one to me, but I was glad Taeyeon had Zero because I could see how much comfort he brought her. Over the late 2010s, Taeyeon had become more open about discussing her depression publicly, admitting to seeking treatment and taking medication during one of her Q&A sessions on Instagram Stories. She'd spoken about spending too much time alone, wanting to work constantly and stay busy, valuing certain friendships because they helped pull her out of her dark places. Much of this was hopeful to me—that she was willing and able to put words to it, to say, *This is what I am going through*, and to ask people to be understanding of others who live with depression.

I could see how much better she seemed with Zero, but, even with my own personal history of depression and suicidal thinking, I wouldn't exactly get *why* until GomSom.

I toggle my life between Brooklyn (where I live) and Los Angeles (where my parents live), and, when I'm in Los Angeles, the day goes like this: at 7:00 a.m., my dogs, Gom and Som (known collectively as GomSom), wake up and go outside to pee. At 8:00, they eat breakfast, then they go outside to roam before they spend the bulk of the morning napping inside. Noon is snack time (they each get a dental stick), followed by a little playtime before they nap again. Around 4:30 p.m. during the winter months and after dinner during the summer months, they go on their daily walk around the neighborhood, a route that Gom sets according to his mood that day. They come home, have their feet washed and teeth brushed, then eat dinner at 5:30. After their humans eat, they get "dessert"—a piece of freeze-dried liver—and have more playtime and naptime until it's time for "night-night pee pee" at 10 p.m., then bedtime shortly thereafter.

I didn't grow up with dogs, though my parents made a few attempts when I was in elementary school. We didn't really know what to do with dogs then; the Korean way (as we knew it) was to keep dogs outdoors and kind of just let them be there. Our last dog in my childhood was a jindo named Teddy, and we *really* didn't know what to do with him—jindos, as we learned much later, are notoriously smart and active and require very intentional socialization. Teddy would escape from our yard, get into fights with coyotes and other dogs, and cause so much trouble that my parents gave him away and swore off dogs.

Then, around 2014, my youngest aunt got two bichon frises. On visits to Baltimore, I was surprised to see how my dad warmed up to them, how even my mom seemed to enjoy them, happily letting them sit on her lap. As they lived alone in Los Angeles, I decided that my parents should have a dog. I spent a few years looking, off and on, for a young dog for them, scrolling through websites and visiting local shelters in hopes of finding the right one (small, young, and non-shedding). Finally, on a late Friday afternoon in May 2018, as I was wasting time until I could leave work, I was scrolling through shelter pages and Craigslist when I saw him: a little bichon puppy, eight weeks old, recently weaned. There wasn't much more information, but I sent my parents the photo and texted the number. I said I would drive down to Riverside the next day to meet the puppy.

My mother, though, insisted we drive down that night, even though Riverside is a two-hour drive—someone else could take the puppy, she feared. We stopped by Petco and bought a crate, a soft bed, some food, pee pads, one toy. My mom had cash tucked away. I already had a name—Gom, Korean for *bear*, my dad's childhood nickname.

When we first met Gom, he was a tiny ball of the softest fur that shook in my arms as I cradled him. His high-pitched whimpers went straight to my heart as he tried to lick my face, sniff me, figure out who the hell I was. My mom handed over the cash as I took him to the car, giving him gentle scratches to let him know he was safe, he was okay, he was coming home with us. As my dad drove, Gom stopped shaking and started trying to look out the window, crawl all over me, give me more curious licks, and, by the time we got home, he was chasing at my heels, doing a little sploot by my feet as I brushed my teeth and washed up.

My parents brought this puppy to their home, but he really became mine. What I didn't know then, even as I could feel myself sliding into another suicidal, depressive episode, was that Gom would keep me alive.

— — —

I didn't start off thinking much of Taeyeon. When Girls' Generation debuted, she was their leader, sure, and I liked her voice enough, but I was so repelled by Girls' Generation's cutesy image that I wouldn't admit how much I enjoyed her voice. Taeyeon's voice, like other SM vocalists', is on the thinner side, but she has a tone that's unique in the realm of K-pop, a warmth and twang that adds a dimension to her vocal clarity. In recent years, she's gotten more nasal, but her voice is still pleasant and steady, and I appreciate that she's very much a singer. She didn't get into idoldom to use it as a way into another career or field.

When I learned that Taeyeon lives with depression, that changed how I saw her, especially given that she was talking about it openly. As a fellow Korean woman, albeit one from the diaspora, I understand that there are stakes when it comes to being public about mental illness, even something that feels more acceptable like depression. To this day, my mother doesn't understand why I'm on Prozac, attaches shame to it, and is uncomfortable with the fact that I openly talk about it.

It is undeniable that I do tend to be pulled toward idols and artists who live with depression. The sentimental part of me wants to say that I recognize something intrinsically in these specific artists, as if we carry ourselves in the world differently because of this shit in our brains. In the real world, there's something deeply comforting to me about the idea of being able to recognize "my own," people to whom I don't need to explain myself. I don't have to worry about them freaking out when I so much as mention depression or suicidal thinking—I don't have to reassure them while I try to seek comfort and understanding.

When Taeyeon talks about depression, I believe her, just like when Suga raps in "So Far Away" (*Agust D*, 2016), "나 죽지 못해 살어" (*I live because I can't die*), I feel the sucker punch of recognition in my gut. When I finally listen to Bangtan's "Blue & Grey" (*BE*, 2020) and Suga raps, "어디서부터 잘못됐는지 잘 모르겠어 / 나 어려서부터 머릿속엔 파란색 물음표" (*I don't really know where I went wrong / I've had a blue question mark in my head since I was young*), I start crying on the train I'm riding back home to New York City from Boston.

Living with a suicidal brain is an isolating experience. It wasn't until I was in my thirties that I learned that "normal" people don't move about their day-to-day constantly thinking about death and dying. It's just so normal for me, even when I'm not actively in a depressive, suicidal episode—like, whenever I cross a bridge, I wonder if it's high enough for me to die if I jumped. That thought might scandalize "normal" people. If you live with depression, though, you might recognize it, just like I recognize something familiar in these idols and their music, and that counts for something. When you live with this darkness in your brain, that recognition often counts for a lot.

■ ■ ■

Zero, the silver toy poodle, is six-ish months older than Gom and a year minus five days older than Som. Zero still pops up everywhere with Taeyeon, on her vlogs and social media, at rehearsals, on photoshoots, and I feel relief whenever I see her with him.

In those first few months, when I'd see her with Zero, I assumed that emotional support animals were considered so because they made their human feel better. How, I didn't exactly understand, until we brought Gom home, and suddenly here was this two-month-old floof who needed to be fed and played with and potty trained. He was still so small that he needed to be taken out to potty during the night—it's said that a puppy should hold his pee for the number of months he's been alive plus one hour—so, at two months old, Gom could go three hours between bathroom breaks. I was responsible for training him, so I would wake up and take him out to pee, then we would fall asleep on the sofa in the living room because we were trying to set boundaries then and crate train him, but I was too soft for that. I couldn't put him back in his crate when he cried because he didn't want to be separated from me, so he would fall back asleep on my chest, a little bundle of warmth on my heart.

As my therapist at the time explained, animals aren't emotional support animals just because they make us feel good—they're emotional support animals because they need to be cared for. And, in taking care of them, we end up taking care of ourselves.

Gom fell into my lap at the right time, as I was spiraling down into that familiar darkness, unsure if this would be the episode that finally took me, but, as I learned that summer, a puppy is *a lot* of work. A puppy is a fantastic, constant distraction because a puppy demands attention and care. Even in my depressed state, I still had to get out of bed to take Gom outside and do the work to potty train him, feed him, play with him, give him the love he demanded and knew he deserved. I had to take him to puppy classes, where I had to interact with the trainer and other dog parents. I had to exist, even if existing sometimes meant hugging a wriggling puppy and crying, and I was so caught up in that existing that I was able to get through those days without having the time or energy, frankly, to think about dying.

In October, five months after we brought Gom home, we went back and picked up his younger brother. Som (which means cotton in Korean) was born to the same parents in a separate litter, and he was smaller than Gom, three pounds with a kind of smushed face. I drove us back to Los Angeles from Riverside; my mother cradled Som in the back seat, my father holding Gom in the passenger seat. Gom spent the entire two-hour drive staring pointedly at the ball of floof in the back, whining occasionally as though to ask, *Well?!? When are we dropping him off?! Wait, you can't be serious—is he coming home with us?!*

For the first few days, we wondered if Som's back legs worked correctly because he couldn't seem to sit up, his legs sliding into a sploot immediately once he put his butt on the floor. He was brazen and fearless in his new home, nipping at hyung and taking everything Gom had—toys, snacks, affection—though we learned very quickly that Som was actually scared of everything outside his home and couldn't really exist without hyung. Gom, from the beginning, was gentle and patient and confused. The two never did bond in the close, affectionate way we had hoped when we decided to get a little brother for Gom, but they're brothers (I call them the 사이가 좋지 않은 형제 [the brothers with a bad relationship]), and it's hilarious to me how much they, too, have their own personalities and act like any human sibling pair.

Most importantly, I understand *why* I was so relieved to see Taeyeon with her dog. I get it. It's comforting to have a dog, to be able to cuddle that warm softness when you need it, and it's also kind of dumb how soothing it is to give a dog scratchies—like, you would think the dog would feel good because the dog is the one getting the scratchies, but there's a comfort to you, the human, as well. I think it has to do with the act releasing oxytocin in your brain, but, whatever it is, I'm glad when I'm in Los Angeles and can go whining to my dog whenever I want a hug.

▬ ▬ ▬

When Jonghyun dies by suicide in December 2017, I think about Taeyeon.

What I want is never to have to wake up again to see an idol's name trending on social media, to know without even checking the news that what I feared has happened. I firmly believe that every single life we lose to suicide is one we could have saved if we could get our heads out of our collective asses and stop cloaking mental health issues under so much stigma, if we could stop putting cruel, exorbitant amounts of pressure on people, if we could truly act like it really is okay for people not to be okay instead of simply spouting the words as a nice catchphrase.

I surmise that one reason people find openness about mental health off-putting is that there is no simple cure. There is no easy fix. It's easier to prescribe certain things (Go to therapy! Get on medication!) than to consider the considerable barriers to accessing them, and it's so much simpler to dismiss the mental health crisis as grounded in privilege—like, we are so much more depressed and anxious as a society because we have so much.

We're too comfortable. We aren't waking up with the sun to till the fields to physically feed ourselves, so we have too much time on our hands.

There is a place for theory and research, but, in my day-to-day, I find it largely irrelevant to obsess over the why, especially when it's used as a diminishing factor.

Because what *do* we need when we're in a mental health crisis? We need support of all kinds—financial, emotional, physical—and we need access to health care. Finding the right psychiatrist or therapist isn't a simple feat—on a purely practical level, it feels almost impossible to find one who is affordable or covered by insurance. Once you do find someone within your affordable range, the next challenge is finding the mental health professional who's right for you, whose approach to your mental health fits with your needs, who isn't, well, an asshole. For instance, as a second-generation Korean American woman with a history of trauma from body-shaming, I would want a mental health professional who is also a woman of color and who has training in disordered eating. In order to find the correct mental health professional, you have to have the time and energy to make appointments and show up for them, hoping you find the right fit sooner than later.

Then there's medication—it takes roughly three to four weeks to figure out if and how an antidepressant is working for you. That means time. It often means trying one medication and realizing it doesn't work, then having to switch to another and waiting out those three to four weeks again. It's having to play with dosages and waiting out those three to four weeks. It's a long process, not as simple as just "going on meds," and medication has side effects. For me, antidepressants tend to hit my stomach, so I'm constantly battling terrible nausea. I can only take a low dosage of Adderall for my ADHD because I also have an anxiety disorder and Adderall can often make me feel like I'm going to die from a panic attack.

I personally don't actually *enjoy* sharing any of this publicly, but I've never been the type to journal, so I've always overshared in my public writing instead, first on Xanga, then on LiveJournal, Tumblr, my own blog, and now, mainly, on Instagram and in essays. I'd love, one day, to stop talking about my stupid broken brain, but what keeps me word-vomiting is that I want more conversations about mental health. I want more honesty, *real* honesty. I want to get rid of this idea that it's okay to talk about something like suicidal depression only when we have come through to the other side and we're somehow "safe." Maybe that is some people's experience—to go through a suicidal episode once, "survive" it, and then move on with the rest of their lives—but it certainly isn't mine. I cycle through depression, which means I have periods when my depression is severe and potentially debilitating, when I am actively suicidal, and thus far, I have been able to fight through those episodes, be stable and "okay" for some time, until I'm back at that cusp, sliding back down into a depressive episode.

— — —

As much as I need my dog, I spend most of my year away from him.

In December 2018, when Gom was nine months old, I moved back to New York City. I'd been wanting to move back as soon as I could, and I was excited to be back but absolutely heartbroken to be away from Gom. I was actually surprised by how sad I was; I spent one night crying so much my eyes would barely open in the morning.

For a month, I cried in the peanut butter aisle in the market. I cried when I saw a basket of hard-boiled eggs for sale at my bagel place. I cried when I walked by the cheese section and saw Kraft singles. I couldn't eat any of these foods for weeks, not until I got to fly back to Los Angeles for the holidays and hug my dogs again.

Gom currently lives in Los Angeles with my parents and his younger brother while I live and work across the country in Brooklyn. I've thought of bringing him to live with me, but I imagine it would be difficult for him to transition from living in the suburbs with a spacious house and yard to a tiny apartment in a loud city that is mostly concrete. My parents are also more financially stable than I am, so they don't have to worry as much about pet medical emergencies. And, even though both my parents work, my dad comes home for lunch, so GomSom never have to be alone for more than four hours a day.

Also, Som is so emotionally dependent on Gom that I am certain Som will wither away if I take his hyung.

It's a particular challenge being away from my dog, especially during depressive episodes. It's comforting, yes, to be able to hug my dog, bury my face in his soft fur, and let his warmth melt into me, but what I miss most acutely is the routine of caring for him. Gom makes his needs and wants known, and, no matter how shitty I'm feeling, his routine must be respected and maintained. My ADHD-addled brain makes it difficult for me to keep a routine away from him and the external structure his schedule provides, so it's a struggle to keep my life from falling into chaos and erratic sleep and eating schedules without him.

This has been one beneficial effect of COVID-19. Because the pandemic shut everything down, in late 2020, I was able to get a job that let me work remotely. I got to spend longer stretches of time in Los Angeles with my parents and GomSom, and that continued even as the US started to open up because my team was spread across the country and my company *couldn't* bring us all into the office because none of us would relocate and they would have had to hire a whole new legal team.

When I'm in Brooklyn, though, I text my parents 곰솜뭐해 (What are GomSom doing?) almost every day. We FaceTime often so I can make sure my parents are well but also so I can see GomSom and whine at my dog to look at me, I know he can't see me, but, hello, has he already forgotten me, can he *please* love me back? I joke that I'm in a 짝사랑 (one-sided love) relationship with my dog, which makes me sad—but then I go back to LA, and there he is again, glued to my side.

— — —

wonder constantly where the responsibility for mental health falls. It's fair, I think, to call out companies like SM for failing to support their artists or to fulfill the basic task (in my opinion) of keeping them alive. Companies like SM take so much from their idols—their youth, their talent, their privacy—that it feels fair to expect them to invest in their mental health.

Sometimes, I think that one of the most unfair things about mental illness is that we have to be our own best advocates. In general, this applies to all health, of course, more so when you're a woman, even more so when you're a woman of color, and your pain is regularly disregarded or diminished—but, with mental health issues, there is often no clearly visible symptom. There are no clots, no hematomas, no bruises to mark the points of injury. There is nowhere to point to other than your head, and, often, to be believed, you have to scream, to exist on extremities that people with neurotypical brains cannot comprehend.

It took me decades to learn how to speak up for myself, to get the professional help I needed. It helped that my parents also took me seriously by this point, getting me on insurance via Medi-Cal and setting up appointments with a primary care doctor and a psychiatrist at Kaiser Permanente. They were supportive when I started seeing a therapist, treated me with tenderness at home, and provided practical day-to-day support by cooking for me, not expecting me to clean or do laundry, and just letting me be. I didn't have to worry about maintaining a car or paying utility bills on time, and it is largely because of their support that I was able to make it through that year.

I am *glad* most people don't know what it's like to think about dying every day. I'm glad most people don't live with such high baselines of anxiety that they're always panicking. I'm glad most people don't struggle to focus on basic tasks and don't have to exert double the effort during a conversation because they're constantly having to pull their attention back to the person sitting across from them. I'm glad most people don't wonder if they'll die if they jumped every time they cross a bridge. I just wish people would learn to extend more sympathy to those of us who do.

■ ■ ■

From late 2022 through 2023, I found myself increasingly worried about Taeyeon because she'd dropped so much weight, and her eyes, to me, showed the pull of sadness. Mental health isn't something that only exists in our brains—it can have physical manifestations, too—and, as a fan who observes from a distance, all I can do is worry and hope I'm misreading things.

Someone's weight isn't something I like to comment on; I know very well what it feels like to have people fixate on your weight, to deliver unkind opinions of it. I wonder if I'm just being one of those assholes, if I'm also not simply masking behind concerns of her well-being, but, given her history with depression and the amount of personal loss she has suffered in the last few years, I worry. We also have a phrase for this in Korean: 얼굴이 반쪽이 됐다. Literally, it translates to *your face has become half*, and we use it to describe someone who seems to be stressed or going through a difficult time.

It always annoys me to hear someone, especially a woman, described as strong. It feels like an excuse not to extend kindness or care to vulnerable, hurting women, women who need tenderness and love in some given moment. *You're so strong* is meant to imply that you can tolerate pain, that you are able to withstand anything you come across, that you can be left alone to hold yourself up because you're capable of taking on more hurt, you're not weak or sensitive or fragile.

You're so strong. It also sounds to me like a justification for abuse that's masked in care. *You're so strong, so I'll say shit to you I wouldn't say to someone else. You're so strong, so I know you can take this criticism. You're so strong, so I don't have to filter myself; you can handle this ranting and raging*—and I think I don't want to live in a world where we have to be strong. I want to live in a world that lets us be soft.

As I have learned, though, it's a lot to expect from people. That's what makes it so easy to love a dog.

— — —

t's a strange thing to worry so much about a stranger, about a K-pop star, but I hope that Taeyeon is well. When she's not promoting, I hope she's keeping busy. I hope she has people in her life who recognize when she's sliding into another depressive episode and know how to keep her safe, pull her outside, physically and mentally, listen and care and offer the support she needs. I hope she continues to get treatment, and I am thankful to her for speaking up about life with this Thing in her brain. I know it is not easy to do as a woman in Korea, even more so as a hugely successful female K-pop star.

There is no great secret to living with depression; for me, it's waking up every day and making tiny decisions to fight against it. It's getting out of bed, taking a shower, eating a bowl of cereal. It's the constant upkeep of the boundaries that help fend off depression. Sometimes, it's saying out loud, *I need help*. It's taking medication, going to therapy, seeing a psychiatrist. Living with depression is a lot of things, most of them banal as shit. And it's also worrying about a K-pop star and hoping hard for her, even though I feel foolish doing so.

It is so much easier to extend sympathy for Taeyeon and hope she is being kind to herself instead of pushing herself all the time. It is easier for me to see that she deserves that kind of grace, whereas I sometimes feel like I am useless, unworthy of saving.

In caring for and worrying about Taeyeon, maybe that's one way I care for myself, too. I often wonder how we can become so attached to certain public figures we'll never meet, never know— and I think, again, that maybe it comes down to recognition.

My soft spot for Taeyeon is rooted deep in my heart because

I know what she lives with, how insidious and terrifying depression is, how much we are shamed for it. I know what it's like to lean on a dog for comfort and companionship. I don't think her massive fame and millions of Instagram followers make us all that different in the ways we struggle daily with our brains and try to stay alive.

In the end, she and I are both just human, and we both struggle to be okay.

If there is something having dogs has taught me about myself, it's that I have a deeper capacity for love than I thought. For so long, especially as a woman who doesn't particularly like babies and has never wanted children of her own, I thought of myself as selfish, emotionally damaged, and cold, not super prone to affection, but getting Gom shattered all of that. Even my mother has expressed her surprise over how I've taken responsibility for him and generally just become more open with my expressions of love. Having Gom gave me practice in how to play with and engage with my niece when she was born during the pandemic, as she grew out of babyhood and started talking and walking and displaying her vivacious personality.

Gom has also taught me that I have a greater need *for* love.

As someone who lives with depression and suicidal thinking and panic disorder and ADHD, I feel like I'm broken. Even basic existence on a daily level is exhausting. I struggle every day at my day job, which requires a greater level of executive function than I possess, and then we have to layer all the trauma of body-shaming on that. It wasn't until I was in my early thirties that I started to be able to function properly as a social human being in the world, having gone through my twenties barely interacting with people. There were times in that decade when I would go days without talking to anyone, except for, maybe, a barista for brief small talk, and I live with the awareness that I will be alive until I'm not, hyperaware that every depressive episode could bring me closer and closer to the one that will kill me.

For now, though, I am still alive. When I'm in Los Angeles, my dog sleeps next to me. This is another little routine of ours. I like to sleep curled up on my right, but he sleeps on my left. In the early morning, he'll growl and let out a little bark, and, when I turn over onto my left side, he'll come and curl up against me, shoving his butt into my armpit. I bury my face in his back, in his warm softness, and go back to sleep—until 6:30 a.m., when we wake up and go through another day together.

12
신화 SHINHWA

Yo, 너 뭐 될래?   Yo, What Are You Going to Be?
신화, "Yo!"
T.O.P., 1998

서울 SEOUL

I t's April 3, 2023, around 10 a.m. I'm sitting on a set of steps leading down to the water at 청계천 (Cheonggyecheon), a stream and walkway running through central Seoul. It's a cool, gray morning, my first in Seoul in eleven years, and, as I sit by the stream and sip my iced latte, I feel surprisingly calm and at peace. The lead-up to this trip has been a tangled mess of anxiety and fear, and I didn't expect the sense of calm that settled over me and stopped the uneasy roiling in my stomach as the plane's wheels touched down on the tarmac at Incheon International Airport yesterday. Here I am again, in the country I fled eleven years ago in fear and shame.

Startled to realize that this feels like home, I think I would like to live in Seoul. I could see a version of myself here, writing in coffee shops and traveling around to learn more about Korean food, soju, and history, which feels odd—I didn't expect to feel so comfortable, so at ease, especially not after my disastrous trip in 2012. I grew up with my culture, toggling between two languages and consuming Korean media, but I was also severed from Korean-ness for over a decade because of body-shaming.

I've wanted to come back to Seoul for a while, but I didn't expect to feel like just another person in the crowd, walking around in my cropped sweater and wide-legged jeans. When I was in middle school, I wanted a pair of white wide-legged jeans so badly because the members of Shinhwa wore them in their music video for "T.O.P. (Twinkling of Paradise)" (*T.O.P.*, 1999), and baggy jeans were all the rage then. I was never allowed, though, because the style wasn't considered flattering on my chubby body, so it's a bit funny to me that, as I was shopping for this trip to Korea, I bought four pairs of wide-legged jeans, which are trendy again, finally hitting the US after months of Korean celebrities running around in them.

Shinhwa is the longest-running boy band in K-pop. They debuted in 1997 from SM Entertainment, a six-member group led by Eric Mun, and they followed H.O.T. and S.E.S. In 2004, all six members opted not to renew their contracts with SM, leaving the company for Good Entertainment. Because SM owned their group name and music, they had to go to court to win the rights to use the name Shinhwa and perform their old music, and I remember it not being smooth, per se, but also not being as contentious as one would have expected from SM. Eventually, Shinhwa opened their own company, Shinhwa Company, from which to manage their group activities, while the individual members signed with other companies to manage their solo careers. This has become a more common thing nowadays. Girls' Generation operates similarly, with Sooyoung, Tiffany, and Seohyeon having left SM in 2014 but SM continuing to manage their occasional group activities. In 2021, Mamamoo also went this way, as Wheein signed a solo contract with another company, and, in December 2023, after months of speculation, YG announced that all four members of girl group BLACKPINK had decided not to renew their solo contracts with the company. YG would continue to manage them as a group, but the girls would individually go their own ways.

As I walk around 경복궁 (Gyeongbokgoong), gaping at the architecture of this old palace, I feel a sense of possessiveness swell in me. This is mine. As I travel more around Korea, the feeling increases: this is mine. This culture, this heritage, this history—mine. This food and language—mine. I might be a Korean American who was born and raised in the United States, but I come from this people who refused to be broken by Japanese occupiers, who survived the cruel division of their country, who stood up against military dictatorships and struggled through economic failure and rose up to become the twelfth-largest economy in the world. This fierceness runs through my blood, and these people are mine.

K-pop, too, is mine. I've loved this industry basically since its beginning, long before it was cool even among the Korean diaspora. I have followed it for almost three decades and can mark significant moments of my life with K-pop.

Korea is mine, and, despite having been fiercely proud to be Korean my whole life, this feeling of possessiveness is new to me, and it feels good.

전주 JEONJU

Suga releases "사람 Pt. 2" (People, Pt. 2) (featuring IU), the prerelease track to his solo album, *D-DAY*, under his moniker Agust D, when I'm driving down to Jeonju. This is my first time driving in Korea, and it's my first time driving a Kia, and I'm slightly nervous (which has nothing to do with the Kia)—the two times I have previously been certain I was going to die have been in Korean cabs.

I didn't grow up traveling to Korea; both sets of grandparents and all my aunts and uncles, excluding two aunts, had already immigrated to the US by the time I was born. The first time I visited Korea was for two weeks over Christmas break when I was in the eighth grade, then I came back for a week in December 2001 when my paternal grandfather abruptly passed away. It was eleven years between that trip and the disastrous one in July 2012, when I cut my twenty-one-day trip short after ten days because I couldn't take the open judgments of my body anymore.

I'm horribly anxious in the lead-up to this trip. I'm supposed to be in Korea for a month, and I've never been outside of Seoul before. I'm going to be solo for the first two weeks, while working my day job, until my parents fly in for the second two weeks, when I'll be taking time off. It will have been twenty-two years since my parents were in Korea.

So much has changed in the eleven years since I've been here. I moved across the country from Los Angeles to Brooklyn to go to law school. I did one year and then withdrew. I struggled to freelance for a few years while working on a novel-in-stories, but then I had to move back to LA with my tail between my legs because I was suicidal and depressed and couldn't financially support myself, having been unable to find a full-time job. In LA, I worked in an accounting office as a bookkeeper for almost two years before getting a job as a copywriter for a company in New York and moving back to Brooklyn. After working long hours and performing multiple roles there for almost a year, I left to freelance, and then the pandemic hit. In the years since, I've flown back and forth between Brooklyn and Los Angeles and started a job with a legal team at a software company, and I wrote a column about K-pop that grew into this book.

Eleven years ago, when I started down this period of my life marked by healing and growth, I had Shinhwa. Before Bangtan had 달려라 방탄! (*Run BTS!*), Shinhwa had 신화방송 (*Shinhwa Broadcast*), a variety show that aired on cable channel JTBC from 2012 to 2013. At the time, it was the first variety show hosted by a boy band, and Shinhwa was already a veteran of the industry, a group of six men now in their thirties who had mostly long shed the self-consciousness of idoldom and were willing and able to run with jokes, even at their own expense.

Today, as I drive around Korea for the first time, blasting K-pop on my car speakers and stopping at rest stops to eat 닭꼬지 and tiny whole potatoes and 콰배기, I have Bangtan.

광주 GWANGJU

n Gwangju, I stay at the Holiday Inn, considered a more upscale hotel in Korea (this is common to a lot of American brands—they get a makeover in Asia), and I get coffee with a friend from my youth group years. She happens to be in Gwangju at the same time for an art conference, so we make plans to meet up. We were never close while at church, and it isn't like we've stayed in touch over the years, but we got back in contact during COVID-19 thanks to Instagram.

Sometimes, I'm surprised by the people still in my life. Not everyone is super deep in it, but, over the years, I've stopped thinking that all friendships need to be deeply close, ride-or-die relationships to have value. There are people in my life who are superficial acquaintances, people I see and touch base with once in a while, and there are those who are actually *in* my life, for whom I will make birthday soup and hang out with their babies and run errands. All types of friendships, in my opinion, are necessary and vital.

Idol groups being like family is a part of K-pop lore. It doesn't matter who the group is; they must play at being like family to each other. It was a big deal when Brian Joo, of duo Fly to the Sky (SM, 1999), admitted that he and Hwanhee had hated each other in the beginning, so much that they were on the brink of splitting up many times. When three members of TVXQ sued SM and left both the band and the company, that shook up the industry, not only because of the scandal of idols suing their company but also because it shattered the illusion that the five members were like family. The fact that Shinhwa is still together and intact seems to support their reputation for truly being close—like, they must mean a lot to each other because all six members left SM and fought to keep their group name and came together periodically to release new music, hold concerts, and host a variety show after gundae.

If there's something I truly envy of K-pop idols and want to be true, it's this sense of family. BoA has also spoken of the loneliness of being a soloist and how she envied labelmates in groups because of the camaraderie they shared, the comfort of having other people there who are in it, whatever "it" is, with you, and I wonder if that sentiment isn't why we, as fans, so insistently hold onto the illusion that idol groups are like family. It's a very human desire to want to belong, to look at a group of people and think, *If you can have this, maybe I can, too.*

여수 YEOSU

When I think of Yeosu, I think of Busker Busker, an indie band active from 2011 to 2013, which surprises me to learn because Busker Busker was so big for a while, it feels like they must have been around longer. Busker Busker became famous after being the runner-up on the music audition program *Superstar K3* on Mnet, and one of the songs on their self-titled debut album (2012) was "여수 밤바다" (Yeosu Night Sea). I can't not hear that chorus every time I see the word *Yeosu*, and I've had Yeosu on my travel list ever since, despite knowing nothing about it.

Korean geography isn't really something I knew much about before going to Korea in 2023. I had never traveled outside of Seoul before, and I had certainly never driven. I don't know that I'd ever really even looked at a map of Korea before—I didn't know Busan was on the southeastern tip of the peninsula and had no idea where Jejudo was situated relative to the mainland.

Driving in Korea is fun. Koreans generally drive like Californians—*fast*, even though the speed limits are slightly lower—and Korea's response to its high accident rate was to install speeding cameras everywhere. I have three voices in my navigation, two women and one man, who honestly seem more concerned with telling me *there is a box camera five hundred kilometers ahead; there's a box camera three hundred kilometers ahead; there's a box camera one hundred kilometers ahead; you are now in a box camera zone* than with giving me directions—but the thing is that they don't even have time to finish one announcement before having to say the next. In school zones, the speed limit is thirty kilometers per hour, which is apparently enforced even on weekends when there are clearly no students around, and Kakao Maps gets aggressive with these school zones, my phone screen flashing red until I slow down to thirty kilometers per hour. I'm from Los Angeles; it physically pains me to drive this slowly when the streets are empty.

It's nice, though. There are no cops roaming the roads trying to catch people in an infraction, rapidly escalate a non-situation, and murder a person of color; the cameras record your license plate and mail you (or the owner of the car) speeding tickets. There's generally no fear of cops in Korea because, here, they fulfill a different, more community-based role, and they aren't militarized so you don't have to be afraid that they'll assault or murder you—most police officers in Korea don't even have guns, just Tasers.

But, anyway, in Yeosu, I do a lot of driving. I listen to a lot of K-pop as I zip along bridges and hop along the many tiny islands dotting the South Sea, and I wonder where I'd be today if it hadn't been for K-pop. Would I be so interested in my culture? Would I have this connection to the language, the food, the land? Or would I have been severed from all Koreanness because it was my Korean community who shamed me, rejected me, and disconnected me from my Korean identity? Who would I be today if it hadn't been for these idol groups, these boy bands, from H.O.T. to Shinhwa all the way here, twenty years later, to Bangtan? Would I even be alive?

대구 DAEGU

I eat Subway three times in Daegu. I've been continuing to work these first two weeks in Korea, working LA hours, which means working from 1 a.m. to roughly 9 a.m. Seoul time. The first week in Seoul wasn't so bad; I took things super easy during the day, staying in a pretty small radius in central Seoul, and often skipped dinner to sleep from roughly 7 p.m. to 1 a.m. This second week, though, I did a lot of driving during the day around Yeosu, then it was a day of driving to get to Daegu, so, by the time I arrive, I'm too tired to want to do much. I've luckily booked an officetel by the trendy downtown area, so I can walk around and get a glimpse of the city before going back to the officetel to nap.

Daegu is the fourth-largest city in Korea, and, when I drive in, I'm surprised at its size. There's still a sense that Seoul is The City and everywhere else, even Busan, the second-largest city and a major port city, is the 촌 (countryside). One of the things fans love to point out about Bangtan is that none of the seven members is technically from Seoul, though some might say that it's stretching it for RM and Jin because they're from Ilsan and Anyang respectively, both in Kyeongki-do, where Seoul is.

Each region in Korea has its own dialect, which we call 사투리 (satoori). The standard Korean accent is 서울말, literally "Seoul words," and it's expected that Koreans "fix" their speech when they move to Seoul. I like to sit and listen to locals talk because I love satoori and I particularly really like Kyongsang-do satoori—it's cute with a musical lilt, and cursing is a lot more fun in the dialect. (Jimin, in particular, slips into his Busan accent easily, and I love it.)

Daegu is in Kyongsang-do, which has had a contentious relationship with neighboring Jeolla-do (home to Jeonju and Gwangju) for, like, ever. Koreans joke that people from the two regions shouldn't be allowed to get married because they'll fight all the time since the two regions are *so* different—Kyongsang-do represents the more conservative region, while Jeolla-do is more liberal. Jeolla-do is also the agricultural region in Korea and boasts the best food. Kyongsang-do holds Busan and Gyeongju, the former capital of the Silla dynasty.

Daegu is Suga—Yoongi's hometown, and a friend texts me constantly, *You won't see Yoongi there.*

But, to go back to language: a few years ago, somewhere in the mid-2010s, I got on an elevator with a friend in LA's Little Tokyo. I was holding a paper tray of 붕어빵 in my hands, little fish-shaped cakes stuffed with 단팥, sweet red bean paste. There were two Korean Koreans in the car with us, and, as we ascended the parking garage, they snickered quietly as one asked the other in Korean, "Do you think they even know what that is?"

I promptly turned to my friend and loudly started talking about 붕어빵 and how nice it is to find them here. They are one of my favorite pastries, a popular street food in Korea that was rare in Los Angeles when I was growing up, and I didn't know there was a cart selling them here. I did genuinely hope that we would start seeing more Korean pastries, like 호떡 (glutinous pancakes stuffed with a cinnamon and brown sugar filling) and 호두과자 (walnut-shaped pastries filled with sweet red bean paste), in the US, both because they were delicious and because they were so much a part of Koreanness to me. To know these foods, to recognize and crave them, was a way to claim this identity for myself, as I pointedly tried to get across to these Korean Koreans on the elevator: okay, I know my Korean foods, I can speak the language, don't try to condescend to me because I don't look Korean enough for you. They were silent the rest of the way.

I honestly expect more of this bullshit in Korea because I feel like it is so obvious when you look at me that I am not Korean Korean but Korean American. I anticipate more of how I felt in Japan in 2012, when I had to learn to be alone with myself because I didn't speak any Japanese, though that makes no sense—I speak and understand Korean. I guess the thing is that I don't really expect Koreans to recognize me as one of their own and, I don't know, talk to me.

Korea in 2023, though, isn't silent; it's filled with small talk and laughter exchanged with strangers on the daily, and it's kind. I came to Korea expecting people to be rude to me, to dismiss me, to treat me unkindly for not being thin enough or not wearing trendy enough clothes or not putting makeup on. I expected more of the same open judgment I received in Seoul in 2012, but Korea is so markedly different this time, so much that I wonder if everything was just in my head eleven years ago. Did I make up the cold looks, the up-and-down assessments as I went up escalators, the stares on the subway? Was that all just my own insecurity interfering? Was I projecting the behavior of my Korean community back in LA on all Koreans?

Instead, the ajusshi in the tiny parking lot across from the officetel I've rented in Daegu kindly helps me park butt-first into a tiny spot, and he generously offers to move my car into another spot on Friday before he leaves work so I can pull out easily on Saturday when the lot will be unattended. The next morning, a cab driver chats with me as he drives me across town to a bakery, laughs kindly at my frazzled self when I try to exit before paying. I communicate with my officetel owner via chat in my clumsily written Korean, and they are nothing but polite, apologizing for failing to clean out a trash can.

The whole month I'm in Korea, I'm surprised when Koreans speak to me in Korean. Koreans in the US don't really, assuming either that I'm Chinese or that I don't speak Korean, and I assumed that my gyopo appearance would make people in Korea treat me like a foreigner, an outsider. I'm so used to being treated as one in Korean communities in the US—not Korean enough for Korean Koreans, not American enough for Korean Americans—my default spoken language primarily English, yes, but heavily reliant upon the ability to scatter it with Korean. I've internalized the idea that Korean Koreans look down on gyopos, and, sure, I think, in many ways, that is still true, but it's also true that Koreans marvel over fluent English and covet that fluency.

Since H.O.T., every K-pop group, whether male or female, has had The One Who Speaks English. In the earlier generations, we would more commonly see The One from America (Or Maybe Canada, But Do Koreans Know the Difference?), like Tony in H.O.T., Eugene in S.E.S. (who was from Guam), Brian in Fly to the Sky. Shinhwa had two—leader Eric and maknae Andy (who was actually supposed to debut in H.O.T. instead of Tony, but his parents thought he was too young). I don't think this had anything to do with wanting to appeal to an English-speaking audience, especially on SM's end because SM focused more on China and Japan for international expansion; it was simply an extension of Americanness-as-aspirational and, thus, English-speaking as desirable.

As for the judgment, though, I think that both Korea and I have changed. In the last ten years, Korea has become even more global, with the wider proliferation of Korean entertainment and correlating Korean geopolitical presence. More Koreans are, also, becoming exposed to the West, to different ways of looking and being, especially as more Koreans travel and study abroad. As for myself, I have learned to be more comfortable in my skin.

양평 YANGPYEONG

Here, too, is another thing that has changed in the last eleven years: from Daegu, I drive up to Yangpyeong to meet a friend and her friends. They've rented a pension that's famous for its pork belly and duck barbecue, and it's my first time at a pension, and I'm nervous because I get nervous when meeting new people, especially when an overnight stay is involved because I know I snore.

As we grill our meat, I make ggooljoo of nine parts soju and one part beer in a shot glass, and I drink Chilsung Cider, Korea's much superior equivalent of Sprite, because Korea doesn't have Diet Coke, just Coke Zero, which is far inferior to Diet Coke. We grill pork belly and duck and get our own refills of banchan, rice, and soup. After dinner, we pile into a car and drive through the darkness to the nearest 7-Eleven to try a new coffee ice cream cone, and my friend buys a deck of hwatu cards. They've already brought snacks from Seoul, so we gather in our room, turn off the ondol floor, and lay down a blanket. I've unofficially designated myself the person who teaches all her Korean American friends how to play hwatu, and we play for hours, listen to the family in the room above us get into a screaming match, and, eventually, we go to sleep, scattered around the room on blankets.

In the morning, we stir awake one by one and slip into the bathroom. We tidy up, separate our trash, and pack, then go back down to the dining area for breakfast. It's a simple meal—bap, soup, banchan—and there are two burners set up in one corner, trays of eggs and a jug of oil next to it. We wait for our turn to fry eggs, oiling a pan and filling it with egg after egg until it's full, and we slide the mass of fried eggs onto a plate and carry it back to our table and eat quickly to make room for other parties.

We load up our cars with our luggage. *Coffee?* we ask, looking at each other. *There's a huge Starbucks nearby. I'll Ka-talk you the address*—then we're off in our cars on the tiny, winding roads, before we convene at a Starbucks on a small river. We get our drinks and desserts and sit on the third floor and watch as other cars arrive and park, questioning drivers' choices in parking spots: *Wow, that guy parked really close to that car; if Hyundai brought the Casper to the US, I would want to get it even though I don't need or want a car in Brooklyn.*

This feels so normal, just a thing one does with friends, but I think how, eleven years ago, Korea was such a lonely, hostile place that I fled—I was so afraid and felt so isolated because I didn't have the right body or wear the right clothes or put on the right makeup—but here I am now, still not skinny enough or in the right clothes or wearing any makeup at all, but how different this country is, how warm and welcoming, how familiar.

서울 SEOUL

When I go back to Seoul, I do my one K-pop pilgrimage of the trip: I go to SM Entertainment's headquarters in Seongsudong by Seoul Forest.

I just stand there and look at the building. There are giant LED screens in the lobby flashing photos of various SM artists, and I see a few other scattered fans taking photos and softly squeeing when their bias's photo shows up. I think there's a spot around the corner meant for photo taking, but I take a cursory look before walking up to a restaurant nearby that I've bookmarked for lunch.

This is the company that, for better or for worse, has shaped me. H.O.T. introduced me to a world outside of my conservative Christian one. S.E.S. showed me from the very beginning that this world wasn't just for men. Shinhwa taught me not to take things too seriously. BoA came alongside me, figuratively, as we grew up together, struggled with loneliness together. Fly to the Sky taught me how to fall in love with a voice, and TVXQ helped me put words and action to things inside me. Girls' Generation taught me how to work through my internalized misogyny. After a while, I stopped following SM so obsessively, and many of the groups from the third generation, like EXO, NCT, to their newest fourth-generation boy band, RIIZE, are largely unknown to me, but it is still SM artists, from Taeyeon to Red Velvet to aespa, I continue to watch and root for. SM is, after all, the only one of K-pop's Big Four to hold four generations of female idols and have a range of gender expression, from f(x)'s Amber to SHINee's Taemin, and I still wish constantly that SM would do better by its women, but this is K-pop—we take what we can get, and we hope for better as the industry changes at snail's pace.

Shinhwa is no longer with SM but is currently the longest-running boy band in K-pop history, and the group is technically still active, though it's unclear if or when they'll do anything new as a group of six members. In late 2022, lead vocalist Hyesung was arrested for driving under the influence, and he was convicted and fined in early 2023. If there are three things the Korean public truly can't forgive, they are (1) driving under the influence; (2) doing drugs, even weed, even abroad; and (3) avoiding mandatory military enlistment.

Which is why Bangtan is off to fulfill their service. In the year leading up to Bangtan going off one by one, I'm thrown by how unnerved people seem, from the fandom to HYBE to the members themselves—though, to correct myself immediately, I suppose I'm most surprised by the energy Bang Sihyuk, the chair of HYBE, spends assuring the public that Bangtan will be together again in 2025, that Bangtan isn't broken up, that this hiatus is temporary as the members serve. A friend reminds me, though, that I have grown up with K-pop; I know how this works. I have seen all my favorite idols and actors disappear for two years to fulfill their service, and I laugh every time an actor has his post-discharge comeback drama, including the obligatory shower scene (while wrapped in a towel) to show off his post-military physique.

And, so, I know: as Shinhwa came back together after gundae, so, too, will Bangtan. And, of all the boy bands since Shinhwa, I tend to think that Bangtan have the best chance to be the next longest-running boy band in K-pop.

제주도 JEJU ISLAND

Halfway into my month in Korea, my parents fly in from Los Angeles, and I finally go on vacation. Three days after they arrive, we fly down to Jejudo, where we buy 귤 (oranges) every day (which makes me think of Yoongi the whole time because he, too, loves 귤), spend a lot of time driving, and eat so much fish, from braised beltfish to grilled mackerel to hwe.

We've come a long way from preadolescent me. Maybe K-pop *was* the source of our woes because it showed me a world so different from the church-based, studious life I was living, or maybe it was the body-shaming, or maybe it was both. My parents and I went through years when we barely spoke, when I would avoid their texts and calls for weeks, when I would shut down when I was being scolded and just let them talk at me until we were all exhausted. Over the years, once I finally started talking and processing my brokenness from the body-shaming, we fought a lot, getting into screaming matches in the car, in the kitchen, around the dining table, and maybe we still don't *really* understand each other (my mom thinks I'm an alien), but, in the end, we do deeply love each other.

When we're in Korea, my mom has been dealing with acute abdominal pain for a few months. It's still very sporadic and seems to come and go, and it's a mysterious pain that seems to be triggered by eating but doesn't have a clear source. In Korea, she's mostly fine, but, a year later, we'll learn that she had a tumor growing in her as we were driving around Jejudo, stopping to walk through the Osulloc green tea fields and marvel at the architecture of a church and visit the Snoopy Garden.

I'll snipe with my mom because she won't let me buy an orange hat because she says I'm not a child even though I make my own damn money, and we'll bicker as my parents want to go hiking *before* we eat breakfast, but I'll still come down the mountain first, hurry to the closest pyeonejeom, and backtrack up the trail to bring them barley tea and the Korean equivalent of Gatorade because none of us has learned to estimate the difficulty of a hike correctly or to prep for it properly. That's a trait my parents and I seem to share—a lack of ability to plan and a tendency just to go, though that impulsiveness and connected fearlessness have been passed down to me (along with stubbornness) in much more potent form. My father has told me multiple times that that part of me sometimes scares him.

남해 NAMHAE

My fifth gomo tells me that each of the three seas surrounding Korea has a different temperament, but the South Sea is the only one I get to visit, and it is now one of my favorite places. I had already spent three days driving along Namhae when I was in Yeosu, but I'm glad to be back—there's a tranquility to the water that puts me at ease.

In Namhae, we meet up with my fourth and fifth gomos and gomobus and one cousin, and we start by glamping for a night then stay at an upscale Japanese-style inn. We arrive at both locations in the late afternoon when the tide is out and leave in the morning and never actually see either bay filled with water.

My parents joke that I'm the niece my aunts seem to care the most about, and I laugh. Other than four cousins who were born and lived significant portions of their life in Korea, I'm the one who speaks the most fluent Korean and who lives her life between two cultures. I watch the dramas they watch, know the yeonaein and drama writers they talk about, and have some sense of the political goings-on in Korea. I'm also the one who caused the most trouble—I was a bbasooni in high school, dropped out of school twice and lied about it both times, and exposed my lie when at least two aunts were around to witness it. My aunts and cousins were around during the body-shaming, and, unlike all my other cousins who went to Ivy Leagues or other elite institutions, didn't get into trouble, and got married and had kids (for the most part), I struggled to become financially independent, publicly talked about my life with depression, anxiety, and suicidal thinking, and left the church. I am the liberal who supports abortion and LGBTQ+ rights and stands against transnational adoption, and I believe churches should be taxed, and I think the US military industrial complex is a global scourge.

I am the one who still doesn't have the "right" body and still, even in my late thirties, am a bbasooni, this time for some dude eight years my junior. Sometimes, I wonder what they might think of that, what they even remember of my youth when they think of me. Maybe I'm giving myself too much credit; we did live across the country from one another, and they all had their own lives and jobs and families to worry about. They likely never thought about me at all.

Still, I wonder how different my life would have turned out

had my father gotten a job in the tristate area after graduating from his doctoral program. What if our family had never moved to California and I had grown up in close proximity to my cousins? If I had had a chance to get to know them, to grow up with them, would they have been the figures who shaped my life instead of H.O.T.? As it was, H.O.T. felt more real and knowable and familiar to me than my own extended family, and my favorite K-pop idols over the years were the guiding figures in my life. I couldn't talk to them or seek advice from them directly, obviously, but K-pop was the filter through which I learned how to be, and it gave me the words, both literal and cultural, to close some of the barriers between me and my parents. My fellow second-generation Korean American friends struggled to communicate with their immigrant parents, but I was fortunate not to experience that distance—first, because my father had insisted my first language be Korean and, second, because I fell deep into an industry that connected me to my heritage—so, when I finally started breaking the silence between me and my family, brought on by years of pain, trauma, and shame, I, at least, had the words and the voice to fill the spaces between us and pull us closer.

경주 GYEONGJU

I try to listen to Suga's *D-DAY* while taking an early morning walk in Gyeongju. By this point, the album has been out for over a week, and, while I purchased it on iTunes immediately, I haven't listened to it yet. It's a combination of things. I get a little nervous before consuming new content by an artist or writer I deeply admire because what if it disappoints? The deeper, more complicated part of my hesitation, though, is that I have been struggling with writing, with being a writer, for the better part of a year, and that has exhibited partly in resentment over how Suga has achieved his dreams—and more—at such a young age.

In 2023, Suga is thirty years old. He's one of the biggest K-pop stars in the world. He's about to embark on a solo world tour. I didn't know who I was at age thirty, and I still feel like I am flailing now at thirty-seven, no capital-C Career, no partner or spouse or even potential significant other, no family of my own. I am tired of being alone and having to do life solo, and I'm feeling particularly worn down emotionally and discouraged and exhausted.

I start listening to the first track, "D-Day," as I take my morning walk around the royal graves. The grassy mounds of the tombs of Silla dynasty royalty are roped off, so I can view them only from a distance, unsure who even lies underneath these mini-hills. At the time, I don't know enough about Korean history to know really what the Silla dynasty was or what role Gyeongju played as that dynasty's capital city, but I do know that I am curious, that this trip to Korea has made me want to learn more about this heritage and country that is mine.

It's a weird contrast, though—seeing this history around me as I blast Suga in my ears. *Future's gonna be okay*, he starts out saying in "D-Day," and the song is meant to be declarative, with electric guitars, a heavy bass, and a full sound. I like anthemic songs, but, on that chilly spring morning, as I walk around in the sunlight alone, taking some time away from my family, I feel sad.

Each K-pop idol group has its own narrative, and Bangtan's is that of the underdog. They debuted from a small company, Big Hit Entertainment, without the financial or political backing enjoyed by their counterparts EXO (SM) or Winner (YG), though it isn't that they had nothing—Big Hit was founded by Bang Sihyuk, a songwriter and producer who had cut his teeth at JYP, writing some of K-pop's hit songs in the late nineties and early aughts. Bang had a positive reputation in the industry, he wasn't a nobody, and he was going to launch a boy band.

(Also, it isn't like you have to debut from the Big Three, now Big Four, to achieve success. Idols and groups like IU, T-ara, Kara, Infinite, and Mamamoo are proof of that.)

Bangtan started hitting their stride fame-wise around 2016, but success didn't necessarily mean their problems went away. They still had to deal with antifans, hate trains, and criticism, and, as they became more popular internationally, the weight on their shoulders seemed to grow heavier, too, with this burden of representing Korea on a global stage at a scale that was a first for a K-pop group. Suddenly, they were being scrutinized at a level they hadn't been before, and they felt adrift, having accomplished everything they had wanted when they'd debuted—and more.

In 2018, Bangtan released their third studio album in Korea, *Love Yourself: Tear.* The final track, "Outro: Tear," is written and performed by the rap line (RM, Suga, and J-Hope), and it's an emotionally intense track about the dissolution of dreams. Later, at the end of 2018, the public learned that Bangtan had considered disbanding that year, that RM, Suga, and J-Hope had written this song in the midst of that turmoil. The other members had broken down crying when the rap line first played this song for them.

I had mixed feelings when I first learned of this, but, in 2023, I'm also dealing with burnout and discouragement, and it's admittedly hard to feel sympathetic. Most creatives don't get to the place Bangtan has. Most of us don't hit any measure of success. Most of us work day jobs and second jobs to do the creative work, and many of us burn out and quit.

In the end, I make it halfway through "D-Day" and switch to another artist. It'll be a few more weeks and I'll be back in the States, DMing with a friend who metaphorically holds my hand, when I finally listen to the album. I ultimately find D-DAY to be overproduced, many of the tracks sounding too similar tonally, with a few standouts like "Amygdala" and "Snooze," and D-DAY lacks the knife edge of anger that sliced through both Agust D (2016) and D-2 (2020). The album lacks the blazing confidence that electrified Suga's first two mixtapes and, instead, feels heavy, weighed down by the burden of being the final work of this trilogy, an insecurity that means that all the effort of creating a Great Piece of Art has not been trimmed away but has unfortunately been left for the listener to witness. I do commend Yoongi for taking risks and trying, though, for bringing all of himself into his solo work instead of sitting back and resting on his fame as "Suga of BTS," and I will always appreciate his willingness to be vulnerable, open, and raw in ways we still don't see too often in K-pop.

서울 SEOUL

I leave Korea wanting to come back to Korea, to move here temporarily. I want to dig into the artisanal soju scene and write about it, and I want to travel more, get a more intimate sense of Korea's various regions. I want to become more fluent in Korean, fall into the literary scene, see if I can build a community, a home for myself here, even at this age when making friends is a challenge now that I am out of school, work a remote job, and don't go to church.

As my uncle and I hang out at Incheon before our respective flights, his and my aunt's to Baltimore, my cousin's and mine to Los Angeles, we share our anticipation for Diet Coke once we get back to the States. It's one of my primary grievances against Korea, and I think about how I'll need a plan if I do move here for a year or so—which I'm tempted to do, asking myself how long I might be able to do the working-from-1-a.m.-to-9-a.m.-Seoul-time thing. Still, I want to learn more about soju, and I want to experience more K-pop firsthand, not from across the ocean, and I want to immerse myself more in the history of this relatively young industry.

I like to stress that Bangtan didn't come out of nowhere—their music throws back to Seo Taiji and the Boys, H.O.T., and Epik High. *Run BTS!* is modeled off other variety programs and has a predecessor in *Shinhwa Broadcast*, and to contextualize Bangtan within a larger history isn't a diminishing act but one that I would argue actually strengthens the group by placing it in dialogue with the larger industry. There are influences Bangtan took and improved upon—their active involvement in their songwriting is a testament to that—and there are massive accomplishments Bangtan achieved that have turned K-pop into a mainstream, global phenomenon—but they didn't get there on their own.

As I watch Bangtan and dive into their mountain of content, I find myself drawn to the members and their shenanigans; there's something about them that stirs up the nostalgia in me, as they remind of how much joy, comfort, and happiness I found in K-pop so many years ago. I scroll through my explore page on Instagram, which quickly becomes full of Suga, and, every day for half a year, I post something to Stories, calling it "Daily Suga Content." I'm in my late thirties, maybe too old to be stanning another boy band, but I don't particularly care—K-pop has been a foundational part of my life since middle school when I fell into H.O.T. and they changed the course of my life by taking me outside my conservative Christian upbringing for the first time. K-pop helped me develop and maintain a hold on my Koreanness as I grew up in suburban Los Angeles; it gave me a connection to Korean culture and language when my connection through food was severed because of body-shaming.

Beyond that, music has saved my life.

When I get into Bangtan, it's the end of October, basically November. December is notoriously the hardest month of the year for me, the end of the year bringing all my anxiety and depression crashing down on me. I go into every December afraid of another suicidal episode, but, in 2022, there is Suga. I don't know him, and he'll never know me, but he's somewhere out there, going for what's real and authentic in the best way he can, even within the confines of fame and its expectations—and, as I finally fall into Bangtan after having witnessed their meteoric rise from a distance for years, I think, what a joy it is to be here. What a joy it is to have borne witness to the growth of an industry, as it went from something clumsy and uncool to this shiny behemoth known around the globe. What a joy it is to be Korean.

슈가 SUGA

And so, Suga.

In Esther Yi's fantastic novel, *Y/N* (2023), the unnamed narrator falls for Moon, a member of a fictional K-pop idol group, when her flatmate drags her to their concert in Berlin. Immediately, she is transfixed by Moon and only Moon, even though there are four other members on the stage and one of the rules of K-pop is to love the group, not to stan just one member. The narrator has keyed onto this as she listens to the fan chants, but she doesn't care, stating, "But I was no egalitarian."

I laugh out loud and immediately mark the line with a star because I am a bad bbasooni in that I also am not an egalitarian. I'm not someone who's particularly OT7 or OT5 or however many members a given idol group may have—I like the members I like, take a group as it is, but have no particular allegiance to a group as a group since H.O.T.—so it isn't surprising to me that I would fall for Suga and have my particular favorites in the group. Bangtan means a lot to me mostly because the members clearly mean a lot to Yoongi.

In May 2023, I go to see Suga in Los Angeles on his solo tour. This is my first time seeing him live, and I only manage to get a ticket to his solo concert via a friend's friend because the concert ticketing system in the US is a shit show thanks to the Ticketmaster monopoly (the legality of which is *so* questionable). I go alone and spend too much on merch, hugging my sweatshirt and T-shirt to me as I stand throughout the concert, grateful a friend reminded me to bring earplugs. Suga is incredible, a ball of energy as he raps through his solo work and carries the stage on his own, jumping around and yelling at the crowd to scream, and, when he pulls out a guitar for an acoustic rendition of "사람" (People) I swoon inside. I think he sounds a little congested, like he's come down with a cold, but that wouldn't surprise me given how much goes into preparing for a tour and that he's been bouncing from Seoul to New York City to Chicago to Los Angeles.

As I drive out of the parking lot of the Kia Forum, my right ear ringing lightly because I hadn't put my earplug in properly, I think how much I just want him to be happy and healthy, loved for who he is as a real-life person, not as an idol or a musician or a celebrity. I think about how much I would hate to be famous but how great it can be to be a person of influence, able to provide hope and encouragement to people around the world by sharing who you are through your art. Maybe that's what initially drew me to writing, this idea that stories can provide hope and insight into another way of being, though that feels horribly naive to me now. In the ten years since Bangtan debuted, Suga has given so much of himself, and I hope he has people in his life who give him the comfort, encouragement, and hope he has given so many people around the world.

I have spent so much of my life hoping for these idols, loving them, and letting them pull me through life, and I think with wonderment that I have somehow made it here, around the corner from my forties. For most of my life, I didn't think that I would live past thirty; I believed I would die by suicide before then; but here I am, buoyed for almost three decades by the idols, the musicians I have loved, because, since I was four years old and started taking piano lessons, I have always had music. All through the body-shaming, the loneliness, the suicidal depression, the pain of healing, the anger, I have had K-pop.

I suspect that Bangtan will be my last boy band, that Yoongi will be the last idol I fawn and obsess over. The age differences between me and the idols debuting today are in the double digits now, which makes me squeamish, and idols today look so young—or maybe it's that I am now middle-aged and have a longer perspective on life. Since I first fell into H.O.T. in 1997, I have gone through the trauma of body-shaming and come out, more or less intact, on the other side. I've moved across the country three times and in and out of seven apartments, and I dropped out of school twice and applied to law school twice. My parents and I fought our way through keeping our relationship intact. I have made it through four major suicidal episodes.

K-pop isn't perfect, and, in many ways, it fills me with so much rage because of how misogynistic and toxic it can be, but it also provides me with so much joy and hope. There is something to admire about these young idols who sacrifice so much just for a shot to stand onstage, to sing and dance and perform, to be people who have some kind of influence and impact on their fans' lives. This flawed, shiny, complicated world is mine—and, as I jokingly text a friend to rile her up, so is Yoongi.

윤기내꺼. Thank you for being here.

BIBLIOGRAPHY

BOOKS

Buswell, Robert E., and Timothy S. Lee, eds. *Christianity in Korea.* Honolulu: University of Hawai'i Press, 2005.

Cha, Victor, and Ramon Pacheco Pardo. *Korea: A New History of South and North.* New Haven: Yale University Press, 2023.

Deuchler, Martina. *The Confucian Transformation of Korea: A Study of Society and Ideology.* Cambridge: Harvard University Press, 1992.

Jung, Hawon. *Flowers of Fire: The Inside Story of South Korea's Feminist Movement and What It Means for Women's Rights Worldwide.* Dallas: BenBella, 2023.

Kang, Myeongseok, and BTS. *Beyond the Story: 10-Year Record of BTS.* Translated by Anton Hur, Slin Jung, and Clare Richards. New York: Flatiron, 2023.

Kim, Eleana J. *Adopted Territory: Transnational Korean Adoptees and the Politics of Belonging*. Durham: Duke University Press, 2010.

Kim, Kyung Hyun, and Youngmin Choe, eds. *The Korean Popular Culture Reader*. Durham: Duke University Press, 2014.

Kim, Sonja M. *Imperatives of Care: Women and Medicine in Colonial Korea*. Honolulu: University of Hawai'i Press, 2019.

Kim, Suk-Young, ed. *The Cambridge Companion to K-Pop*. Cambridge: Cambridge University Press, 2023.

Lee, Heijin S., Monika Metha, and Robert Ji-Song Ku, eds. *Pop Empires: Transnational and Diasporic Flows of India and Korea*. Honolulu: University of Hawai'i Press, 2019.

Lee, Namhee. *The Making of Minjung: Democracy and the Politics of Representation in South Korea*. Ithaca: Cornell University Press, 2009.

Lie, John. *K-Pop: Popular Music, Cultural Amnesia, and Economic Innovation in South Korea*. Oakland: University of California Press, 2014.

ARTICLES

Baik, Kyuhee. "The Roots of Modern K-pop: The Influence of the US Military and Underground Clubs." Maekan. Accessed December 1, 2023. https://maekan.com/story/the-roots-of-modern-k-pop-the-influence-of-the-us-military-and-underground-clubs/.

Chong, Kelly H. "Negotiating Patriarchy: South Korean Evangelical Women and the Politics of Gender." *Gender & Society* 20, no. 6 (December 2006): 697–724.

Kim, Andrew E. "Korean Religious Culture and its Affinity to Christianity: The Rise of Protestant Christianity in South Korea." *Sociology of Religion* 61, no. 2 (2000): 117–33.

Kim, Sandra So Hee Chi. "Korean Han and the Postcolonial Afterlives of 'The Beauty of Sorrow.'" *Korean Studies* 41 (2017): 253–79.

Lie, John. "The Transformation of Sexual Work in 20th-Century Korea." *Gender & Society* 9, no. 3 (June 1995): 310–27.

McKee, Kimberly D. "Monetary Flows and the Movements of Children: The Transnational Adoption Industrial Complex." *The Journal of Korean Studies* 21, no. 1 (2016): 137–78.

Min, Pyong Gap. "Korean 'Comfort Women': The Intersection of Colonial Power, Gender, and Class." *Gender & Society* 17, no. 6 (December 2003): 938–57.

Oh, Arissa. "A New Kind of Missionary Work: Christians, Christian Americanists, and the Adoption of Korean GI Babies, 1955–1961." *Women's Studies Quarterly* 33, no. 3/4 (2005): 161–88.

Ryu, Dae Young. "The Origin and Characteristics of Evangelical Protestantism in Korea at the Turn of the Twentieth Century." *Church History* 77, no. 2 (June 2008): 371–98.

Strawn, Lee-Ellen. "Korean Bible Women's Success: Using the *Anbang* Network and the Religious Authority of the *Mudang*." *Journal of Korean Religions* 3, no. 1 (April 2012): 117–49.

ACKNOWLEDGMENTS

All writers say this, but publishing truly is a team effort, and the writing is only one part of getting a book out into the world. Thank you, Ayesha Pande (my agent) and Retha Powers (my editor), for believing in this project, and thank you to my entire team for all the work you've put in to make these words into a book and put it out into the world—Hannah Campbell, Amber Cherichetti, Sonja Flancher, Leela Gebo, Gabriel Guma, Jane Haxby, Slin Jung, Clarissa Long, Emily Mahar, Caitlin Mulrooney-Lyski, Elisa M. Rivlin, and the many others who have touched this book, thank you so much. I'm still in disbelief that a book about K-pop, which was so niche and uncool when I was young, could be received so enthusiastically, and thank you, Ruby Rose Lee, for your initial excitement for this!

Nicole Chung! You accepted my column pitch for *Catapult* back in 2021, which is why this book exists at all! Allisen Lichtenstein, thank you for picking up the column halfway through and being such a thoughtful editor.

I'm privileged to know such warm, generous people and have to extend gratitude to so many: Jess, for being the first person ever to support my writing over a decade ago, for helping create our little fictional world based on TVXQ, and for driving down to Buena Park at least once a week to eat fried chicken and hang out in the parking lot; Helen 언니, for reading a draft of this book even though you're busy with work and kids; and Kelly, for being wildly supportive from all the way across the Pacific even though we have yet to meet in person; thank you for reading the book and providing feedback! 혜린아, 너 때문에 내가 이 나이에 또 빠순이가 됐네. 내 친구여서 고마운데 윤기는 그래도 내꺼다.

My NYC fam—Amy 김선혜, Amy K., Becky, Laura, Lisa, Mimi, Rachel—I love you more than I can ever say. [#Famous]Dan, Mamamoo's Number One Fan, thanks for being such a supportive, generous human and giving me kimbap. Sseugi Circle—Amy 김선혜, Archana, Julia—my lovely writing group! I cannot wait for your books to be out, and I will always be ready to send over raccoon memes as inspiration if need be.

To the Asian American writers who have been so encouraging, whether directly or by example, especially at times when my own faith in my writing has failed—your writing buoys me along and gives me something wonderful to be in community with. Christine H. Lee, your frank guidance has been a shining light, and I'm so extraordinarily grateful for your advice, the hangouts (and tomatoes and honey), and all your support.

To the K-pop fans who spent time chatting with me over summer 2022—Maia K., Kim Y., David K., Ji Hye K., Vicky N., Cody B.,

Archana M., Mindi, Leidy, Anna H., Tea, Tiphaine—thank you for your time and perspectives!

그리고 우리 식구: John, Fan, Evie—I wish I'd been a better 누나; I'm sorry, and I appreciate everything you've done and continue to do! 수지니, you're basically my little sister; 널 생각하면 내가 자랑스럽다. 고모 고모부들, 사촌 오빠 언니 동생들, 옆에 있어서 감사해요. 할머니 돌아가신지 13년이 됐지만 항상 생각하고 보고싶어요, 특히 여름에 매미가 울때.

내 새끼 곰곰이! 너가 세상에서 제일 귀여워! 솜이는 형아 한테 자꾸 싸가지 없게 하지 말고.

엄마빠! 우린 참 먼 길 왔지. 내가 몇 번 놀랍게 하고 실망시키고 오랫동안 힘들게 했지만 날 항상 사랑해주고 날 위해 기도해줘서 고마워. 엄마 한테는 난 아직 외계인 같겠지만 그래도 틀림없이 엄마빠 딸이야. 그리고 엄마빠 딸로 태어나서 너무 감사하고.

말론 가끔 표현하지 않지만 아주아주 많이 사랑해요.

ABOUT THE AUTHOR

Giaae Kwon (권지애) is a food and culture writer whose work has appeared in *Whetstone*, *Electric Literature*, and *Taste*, among other publications. She wrote a column about K-pop for *Catapult* and attended the Tin House Summer Workshop in 2022. She divides her time between Los Angeles and Brooklyn, where she's working on her next project, which explores Korean food through the lens of the diaspora.